Ritual Imports

Ritual Imports

Performing Medieval Drama in America

Claire Sponsler

CORNELL UNIVERSITY PRESS | *Ithaca and London*

First published 2004 by Cornell University Press

Printed in the United States of America

Library of Congress Cataloging-in-Publication Data

Sponsler, Claire
    Ritual imports : performing medieval drama in America / Claire Sponsler
        p.   cm.
    Includes bibliographical references and index.
    ISBN 0-8014-4295-8 (cloth : alk. paper)
    1. Drama, Medieval—History and criticism.   2. Performing arts—United States.   I. Title.
    PN1751.S66   2004
    792.1'6'0973—dc22   2004017453

Cornell University Press strives to use environmentally responsible suppliers and materials to the fullest extent possible in the publishing of its books. Such materials include vegetable-based, low-VOC inks and acid-free papers that are recycled, totally chlorine-free, or partly composed of nonwood fibers. For further information, visit our website at www.cornellpress.cornell.edu.

Cloth printing   10 9 8 7 6 5 4 3 2 1

Contents

Acknowledgments

This book owes its existence to the generous assistance of many individuals and institutions. Thanks are due first and foremost to the people who welcomed me into their homes and communities, gave me access to private photographs and recollections, and shared their memories and experiences with me. I am especially grateful to Dee Dee Galasso, Charlie Marrone, Msgr. David Cassato, Vera Badamo, Joe Peluso, and Larry Laurenzano, all of whom willingly submitted to filmed interviews and with wit and candor shared their experiences of the Brooklyn play. The company of Dan Marano, Carol Peeples, Jason Silverman, Christian Leahy, and Bruce Smith enriched my visits to Jémez and Santa Fe, as did the hospitality of Pauline and Gerry Romero and their family, who kindly invited me to lunch at their house in Jémez. Jack Cohen, director of the Philadelphia Mummers' Museum, went well beyond his curatorial duties in sharing information and providing contacts, and the members of the Woodland String Band kindly allowed me to watch their rehearsals and conduct interviews. Pam Clements's hospitality made research trips to Albany much more pleasurable than they would otherwise have been, and, along with Kate Forhan and Mary Meany, Pam offered a knowledgeable local perspective on Albany's Tulip Fest.

My debt to dozens of librarians and archivists will be obvious from my notes. Research for this book took me to the Free Library of Philadelphia, the Balch Institute for Ethnic Studies, The John Carter Brown Library, the New York Public Library, the Schomburg Center for Research in Black Culture, the New York State Library in Albany, the Albany Institute of History and Art, The Museum of New Mexico, the Special Collections Department of the University of Iowa Libraries, the Library of Congress, and the Folger Shakespeare Library. At all of these places, the staff was unfailingly helpful.

Generous support from the University of Iowa enabled me to conduct research, attend performances, and have the time to write this book. By offering me the chance to teach on the New Mexico campus of the Bread Loaf School of English during the summers of 1999–2001, Jim Maddox unsuspectingly paved the way for chapter 1.

I could not imagine having had more astute and supportive readers and listeners. Chapter 6 began as a paper delivered at the American Society for Theatre Research Conference in 1994 and later appeared in *Theatre Annual* under the title "Producing the Past: Modern Reconstructions of Medieval Drama," and I gratefully acknowledge the permission to reprint portions of my article granted by the College of William and Mary. The Simpson Center for the Humanities at the University of Washington invited me to present an early version of chapter 5 on American passion plays; that chapter benefited from the comments of Barbara Fuchs, Ben Schmidt, John Coldewey, and Barry Witham. A version of chapter 4, on Brooklyn's saint's play, appeared as "Brooklyn's *Giglio* and the Negotiation of Ethnicity" in *Essays in Theatre* in 1997 and profited from the comments of readers and editors for the journal. I also want to thank Kathleen Ashley and Véronique Plesch for inviting me as a plenary speaker to the New England Medieval Conference in 1998 and subsequently including my revised paper, "In Transit: Theorizing Cultural Appropriation in Medieval Europe," in their special edition of the *Journal of Medieval and Renaissance Studies* in 2002. Thanks are due also to Sarah Beckwith, who solicited "Medieval America: Drama and Community in the English Colonies, 1580–1610," for another special issue of the same journal in 1998. Although neither of those two essays appears in *Ritual Imports*, the work I did on them gave me the opportunity to reflect on broader issues of cultural appropriation and transatlantic exchanges.

A number of colleagues offered advice and encouragement that have helped move this project along. Max Harris, Bob Potter, Theresa Coletti, Charlotte Stern, Larry Clopper, Sam Kinser, Kathleen Ashley, and Bob Clark all shared their work or provided support for this project at crucial stages, for which I am very grateful. I am also indebted to my colleagues and students at Iowa and the Bread Loaf School of English for advice and a good ear, particularly Kate Flint, Jon Wilcox, Huston Diehl, Miriam Gilbert, Teresa Mangum, and Kim Marra. Judith Pascoe and Jeff Porter read the entire manuscript and offered suggestions that have made this a much better book than it would otherwise have been, and Jeff's films of the Nola, Brooklyn, and Philadelphia performances have been an invaluable help in recalling stories and scenes that would otherwise have been forgotten. Finally, no author could wish for better or more astute critics than Jody Enders and the second, anonymous reader for Cornell University Press, or for more supportive editors than Bernie Kendler and the staff of Cornell Press.

I do not imagine that the chapters that follow will live up to the expectations of all these supporters, but I trust that they will find parts of them captivating and illuminating—and will from time to time catch glimpses of their own indispensable contributions.

C.S.

Ritual Imports

Performative Historiographies
Medieval Drama and the Making of America

In 1583, sir Humphrey Gilbert sailed from Plymouth, England to Newfoundland, taking with him, so he said in his subsequent report on the expedition, "Morris dancers, Hobby horsse, and Maylike conceits" for the "allurement of the Savages" and the "solace of our people."[1] To anyone schooled in the standard history of late medieval and early modern theater, this is surprising cargo, since according to that history the years between 1569 and 1580 saw a thorough dismantling of the ceremonial year in England and along with it the death of the communal dramas and entertainments that had been its centerpiece for at least two hundred years. The large-scale urban biblical plays associated with cities like York, Norwich, and Chester were systematically shut down and parish-based festivities like morris dancing, king games, and Robin Hood plays were suppressed, making way for the professional, commercial theater of London, whose dominance would bring about the final destruction of amateur, community-based festivities. What, then, are these remnants of a supposedly banished medieval tradition doing in the hold of a ship engaged in the quintessentially early modern acts of discovery and empire building? Why did Gilbert devote precious space to the props and paraphernalia of an outmoded cultural form? What made him imagine that May Games would be useful in winning over the "savages" he expected to meet and bucking up the spirits of his own men? And, most important for anyone interested in the history of transatlantic exchanges, what happened to those props and the performances they presumably were used in once they reached the New World?[2]

This book considers these—and other—questions about the importing of ritual performances from the Old World into the New, a phenomenon that occurred with some frequency, despite how odd Gilbert's boatload of entertainments might now seem. Consider the twelve Franciscan friars, for example, who arrived in New Spain in 1524 with a repertoire of miracle plays, religious processions, and other ritual performances that they immediately put to use in converting the indigenous people they encountered, while also no doubt consoling themselves with familiar rituals in a strange land, as Gilbert imagined his hobbyhorses would do. In other parts of the Americas as well, dramatic performances were a crucial, even if now not often noticed, part of the cultural cargo shipped out of Europe—in the sixteenth century and beyond—and imported into the Americas. In the years since, many of those dramas have surprisingly persisted, although seldom without substantial reshaping. The performances examined in this book—Puebloan matachines dances, Afro-Dutch Pinkster festivals, Philadelphia mummers, Brooklyn saints' rituals, German-American passion plays, and scholarly reenactments of medieval English plays—are all in some way, albeit often an indirect and slippery one, tied to the dramas of medieval Europe. To tease out the implications of those connections, particularly in terms of what they say about the uses of the premodern past in America, is the task of this book.

To make a claim for medieval drama's influence on American history is to fly in the face of common perceptions that drama has played little or no role in the settling of what would become the United States. It is true that drama appears to be almost entirely nonexistent in the early history of North America—if by drama we mean secular plays produced by known playwrights, performed by professional actors in playhouses for paying audiences. The first such play known to have been performed in the English colonies by a fully professional company was Shakespeare's *Merchant of Venice,* which was staged in Williamsburg, the capital of Virginia, on September 15, 1752. As Christopher Bigsby and Don Wilmeth observe in their introduction to the *Cambridge History of American Theater,* it is notable that this performance took place in a southern colony, since theater did not readily find a home in the northern part of the continent, where the Bible was the authorized text and "the frivolous, the sensual, the illicit were to be shunned." In the English settlements, theater was, in their words, "born into an immediately hostile environment—physically demanding, philosophically suspicious, and culturally uncertain. A communal art, it found itself in a society whose priorities had to do with subordinating the natural world and enforcing covenants that foregrounded spiritual or commercial imperatives."[3] Even in southern Williamsburg, the first formal playhouse was not built until more than a century after the original settlement there, and the first theater in Boston was not constructed until fifteen years after the revolution.

Outside the English settlements, there is evidence of earlier quasi-professional performances, but they also apparently did not take place in playhouses for paying audiences. Two *comedias* were performed at a Spanish mission in Tequesta, Florida, near present-day Miami, in 1567, and *comedias* and interludes were performed in Cuba in the 1590s.[4] *The Jesuit Relations,* which detail the activities of the French in the Great Lakes region, note a performance on December 31, 1645, referred to as the *sit* (probably Corneille's *Le Cid*); the *Relations* do not specify who the actors were, but do mention that the audience was made up of both the Jesuit fathers and local Indians. *Le Cid* was performed again in 1651, the same year in which Corneille's *Heraclius* was presented. Moliere's *Tartuffe* was staged in 1694.[5] This sparse record certainly makes the theatrical landscape of colonial North America seem a near waste-land.

Early theatrical activity appears more pervasive, however, if we expand our sights to take in the performances often described as paratheatrical—that is, those enactments that were religious, nonprofessional, and staged in impro-vised locations such as streets, homes, open fields, or hilltops for audiences of nonpaying community residents. It is true that sparse settlement, enormous spaces, and in some cases lack of institutional and community sponsorship hampered the transplanting of Old World performance practices, such as the fairs, seasonal festivities, games, and folk rituals that were the basis of popular theater in Europe. But in streets, markets, plantation yards, religious camp-grounds, summer gardens, and museums traces of a dramatic tradition can be found.[6] The Dutch in New York maintained their ritual traditions, as did the French in the Great Lakes region, the Spanish in Louisiana and the Southwest, and even the English along the east coast.

Accounts from New France offer an unusually full record of these perfor-mances, with frequent mention of processions, plays, and other ritual cere-monies. *The Jesuit Relations* of 1640 describe processions and public prayers to drive out a plague of insects in Quebec, as well as bonfires, processions, and a tragicomedy performed in honor of the Dauphin's birth. The play for the Dauphin was staged by Sieur Martial Piraubé, who also acted the chief part. "In order that our Savages might derive some benefit from it" ("afin que nous Sauuages en peussent retirer quelque vtilité"), the governor asked the Jesuits to add something that might "strike their eyes and their ears"; accordingly, the Jesuits included the soul of an unbeliever pursued by two demons who hurled the soul into a hell that vomited flames. The account reports that the struggles and cries of the soul and demons (who spoke in Algonquin) made such an im-pression that "a savage" told the Jesuits two days later that he had dreamt that night about the demons pursuing him and a gulf belching flames ("vn gouffre horrible, d'où sortoient des flames & des demons"). In another instance of co-ercive symbolism, a procession was held in 1638 on the day of the Assumption of the Virgin. In the procession, Indians marched behind Frenchmen, in a spec-tacle that was reportedly a pleasure to behold, as the natives in their painted and decorated robes marched decorously along in pairs ("Il faisoit beau voir vne escouade de Sauuages marcher apres les François auec leurs robes peintes, & figurées, tous deux à deux, & fort modestement"); lines of soldiers saluted them with musket shots and cannons were fired on land and water to much joy. At the same time, three native jugglers or sorcerers brought the Jesuits five drums that they had used in their Sabbaths, thereby showing that they had abandoned the party of Belial for that of Christ—or so the writer of the ac-count chose to assume.[7]

A particularly elaborate and culturally complex performance took place in

1679, when a Three Kings pageant was staged at the Huron Mission of Tionontate at St. Ignace de Missilimakinac. The play was a collaborative effort between the French and Huron. The Huron helped construct a "grotto" inside the mission church for the "representation of the mystery" or Nativity. On the Feast of the Epiphany (January 6), the Hurons (Christian and non-Christian alike), in imitation of the three kings divided themselves into three companies according to the three nations that constituted their village, chose three chiefs, and provided them with wampum to give as gifts to the infant Jesus. The three chiefs carried scepters to which the offerings were fastened and wore head-dresses shaped like crowns. At the sound of a trumpet, the first company marched forward carrying a sky-blue banner with a star on it, led by their chief; the two other companies followed as they all marched into the church where the three chiefs prostrated themselves and laid their crowns and scepters at the foot of the cradle. They then made public proclamation of their submission and obedience.[8] As Martin Walsh has pointed out in a discussion of this performance, although the Jesuits erased themselves from this account, they must have orchestrated key parts of the pageant, such as the abasement and offering of crowns to the infant Jesus, which is an iconographic detail from art and drama that the Hurons probably did not invent. The play was followed by a request from the Hurons that the Jesuits carry the statue of Jesus (who perhaps recalled the Huron creator-figure Iouskeha) in a procession to the Huron village, where it was lodged in a house and where they offered thanksgiving and prayers. In this way, as Walsh notes, Jesus was brought from Jesuit to Huron space in a communal re-presentation "in which the [Huron] leadership could find appropriate roles within the personae of the foreign mythos." This re-presentation might have been particularly powerful, Walsh observes, given that the Huron in the Straits of Mackinac were essentially refugees (from the Iroquois), consolidating a new community. The Three Kings pageant might thus, in Walsh's perceptive reading, have helped forge a new Huron identity, one that allowed the Huron to align themselves with the French but also to re-create their own leadership roles in new, hybrid ways.[9]

Even in Puritan New England, which banished the old ritual calendar—on which so many medieval performances had depended—and wiped out most forms of public festivity, dramatic rituals continued to be enacted, even if in altered form. Especially common were those centering on "humiliation" days that featured public prayer, confession, and execution, all of which were highly theatrical spectacles involving costumes (rags worn by penitents), ritual actions (kneeling before those whom they had wronged), and speeches (recountings of sins). Theatricality at executions, youthful charivaris against inappropriate marriages, and the celebration of Pope's Day were all tolerated by authorities in New England, despite the presence of proscribed elements such as bonfires, gun shooting, and mumming.

There are a number of reasons why these imported performances have for the most part been overlooked. One is a privileging of writing over practice. Theater historians have tended to relegate unscripted performances to the limbo of the paratheatrical and have instead focused attention on plays that have scripts. Where play texts have not survived or never existed, the performance has often been ignored by professional scholars of the theater. In a similar fashion, studies of transatlantic encounters have tended to valorize written representations over performance as the key site of cultural contact and negotiation between Europeans and inhabitants of the New World. Tzvetan Todorov's influential *Conquest of America,* for example, rewrote the conquest as a contest between sign-systems, and like Stephen Greenblatt's *Marvelous Possessions* linked print literacy with European dominance: in this view, the battle for the New World was won thanks to the superior technology of writing possessed by the Europeans.[10] This bias toward writing, which is common to all historiography, is understandable. Since performances, especially unscripted ones of the sort represented by Gilbert's hobbyhorses, leave fainter traces in the historical record than written documents, it is perhaps inevitable that they often go unnoticed.

Two other reasons also help account for the widespread neglect of the role of performances in colonial America. The first has to do with the belief that medieval performances, particularly in England, had already died out by the time of colonization, leading to the assumption that the reformist sensibilities of many colonists left no space for drama, particularly religious drama linked to Catholicism, as much medieval drama was. As revisionist accounts are now suggesting, however, both the demise of medieval drama and reformists' aversion to it have been overstated, which ought to prompt a reconsideration of the cultural baggage that even reform-minded colonists brought with them to America. The second reason for inattention to the role of Old World performances in the New is the inclination on the part of many historians to emphasize processes of nation-building, while downplaying the pull of allegiance to a European homeland; the result has been to deflect interest from cultural forms that resist nationalism and assimilationism, as the following chapters will show that many imported performances do. It would seem that the study of medieval drama in America calls for a new approach that looks beyond writing and literate culture, beyond a dramatic history that focuses solely on the professional theater, and beyond narratives of triumphant nationalism. Only then can we begin to glimpse what part dramas imported from premodern Europe have played in the ongoing history of the United States.

That history, and especially the part of it that is grounded in relations with Europe, is inevitably complex given that America is both a new society and a successor culture to Europe. The earliest European settlements in America were arms of the home nation, designed to extract as much wealth as possible from the new territories and envisioned as extensions of the homeland. Despite this initial connectedness, all of the early settlements quickly developed into at least partially autonomous entities that evolved their own social, economic, and political structures in response to the new environment in which they found themselves. The creeping away of the colonies from the homeland was aided by the fact that their residents tended to be people—whether freelance adventurers or religious nonconformists of Catholic or Protestant persuasions—whose status at home had been in some way marginal or at odds with the authorities.

Although the extent to which these settlers distanced themselves from their home traditions is open to debate, cultural continuity might have meant more to them than we would expect. Writing about the New England colonists, Roger Thompson notes, for example, that while the typical pioneer is seen as having been a venturesome seeker of new challenges and freedoms, immigrants were in reality often reluctant refugees from poverty, persecution, and political absolutism who tried to conserve as much of the culture of the old country as possible rather than throw it off. Far from being born as new men in America, these settlers "could hardly move for all their cultural baggage," as Thompson puts it, and like the raj in India became "more English than the English."[11] Encroachment on tradition, not the desire for a new culture, drove them to America. Similarly, in the Spanish, French, and Dutch settlements—places less apt to reject the homeland's traditions, particularly its religious traditions—a strong sense of connection with the parent culture defined colonial life even in the face of local circumstances and sheer geographic distance that stretched the bonds linking the colonies to Europe.

While any study of the importing of ritual performances from the Old World to the New has to presume that the New remained connected in symbolic as well as real ways to the Old, it also has to acknowledge that change happened. Performances were refashioned when they were transplanted into new environments, particularly as they encountered already-resident people. Joseph Roach has described how, through a process he calls surrogation, New World cultures reproduced and re-created themselves by filling gaps in their cultural and social fabric and by reinventing themselves in the face of revolutionary circumstances.[12] Such refashioning was a distinctive part of the cultures being formed by intermingled groups of Europeans, indigenous people, and African slaves. New arrivals might have brought with them an impulse to preserve traditions, but those traditions were soon brushing up against and absorbing other cultural practices while also slipping away from the group that originally imported them. The other tricky thing about traditions, as Raymond Williams reminds us, is that they are always selective.[13] They do not and cannot encompass the entire range of a group's cultural experience, but instead capture only the especially useful bits of the past to maintain in the present. For that reason, resemblances between New and Old World performances are often masked, since the imported ritual is never an exact replica of the original.

If we think of early American settlements as subcultures—which to some degree they were, especially in relation to the country from which they came—engaged in formulating their own cultures in a new context, then we can better understand the active or covert reshaping that imported rituals underwent. As cultural theorists have argued, every subculture has a double allegiance, first to the parent or dominant culture and then to itself.[14] Subcultural productions—or productions sponsored by the dominant culture in which members of subcultures act—can disguise and repress as well as express or articulate the relations among these groups. As a subculture responds to shifts and fragmentations in social and economic relations, it develops a repertoire of strategies and rejoinders that offer ways of coping with and resisting any dominant cultural order. This at least partly adversarial relationship between sub- and dominant cultures often means that the two do not share precisely the same past and that local traditions do not always mesh with colonialist or nationalist ideologies.

Because of the light they shed on the unequal distribution of power and goods that shape social relations, concepts of cultural resistance and cultural imperialism have often been useful in the study of subcultures. But too great an emphasis on such concepts can hide the more complicated interplay at work in cultural transmission by overemphasizing what is lost in the process of cultural transmission or, alternately, what remains as traces of the original. Along the way, a sense of the hybridity, contextual specificity, and resilience of cultural forms can be obscured.

Fortunately, recent cultural theory has shown greater interest in hybrid forms and the processes that create them than in a search for origins or traces.[15] Such hybrids may be consensual as well as conflictual, may confound definitions of tradition and innovation, and may challenge expectations about development and progress. In terms of their relations with history, cultural hybrids do not merely recall the past as social cause or aesthetic precedent, but can also renew it. This means that for hybrid forms the past tends to function less as nostalgia than as part of ordinary life. In these instances, the past is not over and done with, but instead remains a force within the present. The performances in the following chapters, although not completely immune to a nostalgic view of the past, for the most part show the past as still present; this can make for some odd conflations of then and now that seem to fly in the face of historical accuracy, but it also helps account for the survival of these performances and their continued vitality within their communities.

Ritual Imports is primarily concerned with the appropriation of ritual performances imported into America from Europe from the sixteenth century up to the present. Although it sketches the routes that these performances took in coming to America, the book is focused less on origins than on outcomes. It is not at heart a study of sources, but rather of effects: while it asks, "Where did these performances come from?" it spends more time considering "What happened to these performances once they arrived in the New World and how have they functioned for the groups that enact them?" The underlying assumption of the book is that like written accounts, these dramas preserve a record of the past; they are performative historiographies that enact a set of relations with history.

With the partial exception of the academic reconstructions discussed in the final chapter, all of the performances in this book are rituals: that is to say, they are seasonal, not occasional; they are repeated on a regular, usually annual, basis; they are tied, often in an unarticulated way, to the belief systems and deepest values of their communities; and they survive in unwritten forms, passed on from performer to performer through practices, not documents.[16] Unlike the products of the professional theater, ritual performances encode a way of being in the world that is based on face-to-face exchange and a high degree of social interaction. As Richard Schechner notes, while in theater the domain of the spectator (the house) is larger than the domain of the performer (the stage), in ritual performances spectator and performer share the same space and the spectator is absorbed into the performance.[17] For that reason, rituals create their own world and, for the duration of the performance, draw all involved into that world. Ritual performances are also distinguished by their repeatability; they depend on regular—usually annual—repetition for their meanings, and those meanings are public, not private.

Social historians have shown how ritual theory can be usefully used to explore the role of culture as a mediator of social relationships and structures, and, particularly in the case of the rituals of lower-class or marginalized groups, to examine how rituals play a part in shaping a group's history and defining its own cultural identity.[18] Since ritual generally reorchestrates rather than reproduces or mirrors social reality, it should be taken not as an echo of a larger worldview or ideology but rather as a complex response to the surrounding cultural practices and ideas. In other words, rituals do not stand alone or create meaning all by themselves, but only in intersection with the whole culture of which they are a part. That means that the study of a ritual involves the daunting task of considering its position within the whole culture. I do not pretend to have fully accomplished this in the subsequent chapters, but I have tried to be attentive to the wider contexts for each performance. In particular, I have sought to maintain a dual perspective by considering the range of potential meanings the performance has for its participants (i.e., members of the sponsoring subculture) as well as for spectators who are outsiders to the sponsoring group, but who, given the nature of ritual performances, are also temporarily drawn into the universe of the performance. As Jack Goody has noted, participation may be all that is needed for rituals to work—belief is not a necessary condition for their efficacy.[19]

What rituals offer to the individuals who perform and watch them is the chance to participate in a shared experience that can lead to a sense of empowerment and even redemption. Ritual thus often serves as a way of dealing with problems of authority, the self, and society, even though its negotiations can never be absolute or deterministic. There is always a limit to what ritual can do. Moreover, unlike earlier ritual theory (such as that of Arnold Van Gennep, Victor Turner, or Mircea Eliade), which emphasized the integrative and harmonizing aspects of ritual practices, contemporary theory suggests that ritual articulates but does not necessarily resolve competing ideologies. Ritual simply is not that powerful or that uniform in its effects. And not only is ritual not always able to offer the salve of social integration, but it also seldom asks the hard questions. Rituals rarely test beliefs; they do, however, display beliefs and put them into circulation, where they can be amplified and ratified. For this reason, rituals generally promote social adherence and encourage individuals to hold fast to their particular understanding of the nature of the world and the people in it.

If this makes rituals sound conservative, well, to some degree they are. One way to view the ritual performances in this book is as a part of what Raymond Williams has termed residual culture, by which he means those remnants of once-dominant past cultures that still manage to keep a foothold in the present. Like other forms of residual culture, the performances in *Ritual Imports* contain experiences, meanings, and values that cannot readily be expressed or validated within the dominant culture, but that are nevertheless lived and practiced as remnants of previous social formations. Residual cultures cling to the past and in so doing are usually distanced from the dominant culture of the moment, although aspects of residual culture may be incorporated into the dominant culture in some way.[20] But while emergent or avant-garde cultures are often assumed to be the arena within which dominant cultural *mores* can be tested and rejected, we should not be too quick to dismiss the ability of residual cultures to accomplish the same critical and resistant feat. One argument of this book is that the residual nature of the performances, their insistence on clinging to the past, provides them with a means of dissent against the norms and values of modernity. Although rituals often are seen as merely the manifestation of an age-old practice, they are also dependent on present circumstances that they both respond to and shape; rituals thus have a distinctive historicity in which the interplay between past and present is of fundamental importance. In rituals, history is not merely what happened in the past, but what continues to be represented and communicated in the present moment through the performance. Although ritual is often seen as ahistorical, the examples in the following chapters suggest that it is more thoroughly embedded in specific histories than it is given credit for.

The histories that the performances in *Ritual Imports* embody and make available derive from the medieval past. But the relationship of these performances to the medieval past is complicated, not least because there is never an "original" for rituals, unlike scripted dramas that have a potentially knowable first script and first performance. Although many have tried, it is difficult to trace the originary moment of a ritual, in part because the performance of the ritual usually precedes any recording of it in other media, such as written or visual representation, that might offer a record of its existence. To the extent that this study is concerned with performances that in reality or in imagination derive from the medieval European past, it is also an investigation into the fascinating topic of modern medievalism. In an essay called "Dreaming of the Middle Ages," Umberto Eco pointed to what he saw as a wave of neomedievalism in America, found in everything from comic books to architecture (Trump Tower and Citicorp Center, "curious instances of a new feudalism, with their court open to peasants and merchants and the well-protected high-level apartments reserved for the lords," Hearst Castle, and the Cloisters), Barbara Tuchman's vastly popular medieval histories, crowd-pleasing museum exhibits of medieval art, and bookstores full of novels set in the Middle Ages.[21] Eco could easily have expanded his list to include phenomena like medievalesque role-playing of the Dungeons and Dragons type, Society for Creative Anachronism reenactments ("a great way to learn history," in the words of one participant),[22] frequent Hollywood recycling of medieval themes and stories (*Braveheart, The Princess Bride*), and of course, the enduring legacy of romantic medievalism in science fiction and fantasy writing. Even material culture participates in this enthusiasm for things medieval, as seen in the items for sale through *Past Times,* a British company that markets such reproductions as Celtic knot-work jewelry, illuminated notepaper, books of hours Christmas cards, tapestry pillows, and garden gargoyles, through a mail-order catalog that describes its items as "a collection of fine and unusual gifts and accessories inspired by Great Britain's historic heritage."

For Eco, this fascination with things medieval makes perfect sense given that America, like Europe, has inherited the legacy of the Middle Ages, including its vernacular languages, civic organization, economic systems, military complexes, class struggles, notions of romantic love, and conflicts between church and state, among others. "The Middle Ages," Eco says, "are the root of all our contemporary 'hot' problems, and it is not surprising that we go back to that period every time we ask ourselves about our origin."[23] In Eco's view the modern rediscovery of the medieval is simply another stage in the continuous return of all modern ages to the middle one, a kind of "permanent rediscovery" of the medieval past that has been occurring for centuries. The difference between the classical period and the medieval in this respect, according to Eco, is that we see the classical as an ideal and distant model, while the Middle Ages are always reconstructed as something we still inhabit.

A good deal of the story of medievalism in America has already been told as scholars have investigated the cultural history of things medieval and medievalist impulses within the United States.[24] Many of these studies suggest that while Eco is correct in claiming that the Middle Ages are a part of the historical past Americans still inhabit, it is also the case that medieval themes are invoked in order to provide a deliberate point of opposition to the present. Indeed, this has long been the case. Eugene Vance has noted that the very notion of a "middle age" (*media tempestas*) originated with fifteenth-century humanists as a negative contrast with their own culture. Successive centuries continued to reinvent an image of the years from 1100 to 1400 as, in Vance's words, "a diachronic prop in the drama of self-definition."[25] In the performances examined in this book, the medieval makes an appearance in both of these guises—as the past Americans still inhabit and as the deliberately chosen "other" that helps them define and defend their communities. In some cases, that medieval past is denied or forgotten, in others it is reinvented or enthusiastically embraced; but however it is incorporated, in each performance the past—and specifically the medieval past—matters. That alone is worth remark given America's generally amnesiac culture. Even more compelling, however, is the way that in many of these performances the medieval past becomes a way of evading a homogenizing dominant culture. Allegiance, real or imagined, to a premodern past gives the communities that perform these rituals leverage against the forces that threaten their survival. In that struggle, the medieval becomes a resource for resistance as New World communities invent themselves by, as Roach has put it, "performing their pasts in the presence of others."[26]

As a study in cultural appropriation, this book necessarily inherits the genealogy of that term. Appropriation was once understood as the study of influences transmitted from one more or less unitary source to another in a genetic or thematic lineage that reinforced canonicity and valorized the original. The search for origins has had particular force within medieval studies, which for most of its history has been a recuperative project preoccupied with beginnings, sources, and the recovery of lost originals.[27] Recent understandings of appropriation, and of its cousin expropriation, have in contrast focused on the work of appropriators acting as motivated agents. For much of the 1980s, the use of the word *appropriation* had negative connotations, given that it seemed to emphasize "taking over" as an act of power between unequal partners in which a dominant group (often seen as Western society) seized cultural material from a weaker (non-Western) one and took it over. The critique of appropriation launched by postcolonial theory has argued against this granting of near-complete power to Western hegemony and the silencing of the voices of those deemed unable to resist a dominating culture. Postcolonial theory has stressed the ways in which appropriation can be understood outside the dominance-subordination model by granting the subordinate culture a more active role in processes of appropriation.[28] Following that lead, *Ritual Imports* considers the strategies of resistance employed in these performances, strategies that range from mimicry to recycling to cultural hybridity, and that help us theorize appropriation without asserting an unassailable hierarchy of one culture being imposed wholesale on another.

The central concern of the chapters that follow is with the varied ways in which the medieval past in these imported rituals is used to shape communities and identities and to link a subculture to the larger culture—or, more often, to carve out a separate space where the subculture can survive in opposition to that larger culture and its assimilationist demands. While pursuing that central concern, I also consider an array of related questions about ethnicity, masculinity, regionalism, nationalism, the place of religion in American culture, the heritage industry, and cultural tourism. Many of the performances in *Ritual Imports* are tied to a specific ethnic group and most are enacted by men, with women usually relegated to supporting roles, if they participate at all. Most of the performances are local and are linked to distinct geographic regions or performance sites that play an important role in the rituals' existence and meanings. A number of the performances are explicitly tied to religious practices, and thus face charges of bigotry or excessively strong religious fervor. Nearly all of the performances are conscious of how they appear to outsiders and are aware of their position within the linked phenomena of the heritage industry and cultural tourism. All of this is to say that the performances examined in this book are not museum pieces but are fully engaged with the present they are part of.

Ritual Imports begins with a performance that was among the first to be brought to America and runs more or less chronologically up to the most recent imports, although a strict chronology is impossible to maintain with performances like these, which show history's zigs and zags more than its smooth continuities. The first chapter, "Performing Conquest: The Jémez Matachines Dances," investigates a ritual dance-drama that is performed throughout the Rio Grande Valley of New Mexico and whose history and meanings have not yet been settled. When the Spanish arrived in America, they came equipped with plays that they used as agents of conquest and conversion; among those plays were the *moros y cristianos* dramas that enacted Spanish struggles with the Moors, versions of which were performed on Spanish expeditions into what is now New Mexico, presumably with an eye to schooling the Puebloans in their expected role of submission. The Puebloans who perform the matachines dance today believe that it was brought to them from Mexico by Montezuma and view the dance as symbolic resistance to European conquest and forced conversion to Christianity. Mexicano/Hispano communities, in contrast, claim that the dance was introduced by the Spanish, and understand it to portray the Christianization of the Indians, represented by the expulsion or conversion of the Moors. At Jémez, uniquely, both of these divergent narratives of the past are enacted each year, when parallel "Spanish" and "Indian" versions are danced. The two versions of the matachines dance at Jémez Pueblo present a symbolically altered account of the conquest, a performative historiography in which the past, including the medieval European past, remains contested.

Approximately a century after the Spanish began staging their conquest dramas, Dutch settlers in New Netherland were celebrating Pentecost with house visits and other rituals that would soon be taken up by their slaves. The second chapter, "Selective Histories: Albany's Pinkster Festival," looks at one version of the African-American coronation festivals of colonial New England and New York that blended European and African traditions in a new context. These festivals, which took place annually in early summer and lasted for up to a week, typically began with the election of a king or governor who led an elaborate procession in which slaves wearing improvised uniforms and fancy dress paraded through the main streets accompanied by loud music punctuated by gunfire salutes. Speeches, sports, game playing, feasting, drinking, and dancing concluded the festivities. Such performances, which in many ways resemble the rituals of misrule practiced by the disenfranchised of medieval Europe, provided opportunities for welcome release from the daily routine of enforced labor while also licensing parodic and satiric attacks on white structures of rule; at the same time, they served as vehicles for the reproduction of African ritual tradition reformulated to meet new needs. The documentary history of these festivals, most of it in the form of recollections and secondhand accounts by white commentators and antiquarians, also shows how a particular image of black culture was fabricated to serve white needs. Pinkster Day in Albany, New York, is an especially striking example. Originally a Pentecost (*Pfingsten* in German) celebration of Dutch settlers, Pinkster was later given almost wholly over to African Americans and has since the 1950s been revived as a Dutch-heritage celebration known as the Tulip Festival—a festival that, ironically, preserves the coronation ritual now recast as the election of a debutante "tulip queen."

Chapter 3, "Philadelphia's Mummers and the Anglo-Saxon Revival," considers a more deliberate invocation of the medieval past, as late-nineteenth-century reformers sought to refashion Philadelphia's rowdy New Year's revelers into a more acceptable form. Boisterous holiday street theater had been a feature of Philadelphia's working-class neighborhoods at least since the early 1800s. On New Year's Eve, gangs of young men—often described as "shooters" or "callithumpians"—disguised themselves in "fantastic" costumes and blackface and paraded through the streets, stopping at taverns and demanding free drinks, firing guns, and violently celebrating the holiday. After the Civil War, Philadelphia's "shooters" began to be described as "mummers" and their riotous behavior was reshaped into a civic parade on New Year's Day. I argue that the restyling of "shooters" as "mummers" was linked to the Anglo-Saxon revival and its use of the medieval past as a tool of nationalism. The turn to an "Anglo-Saxon" performance tradition with roots in medieval England was a strategy aimed at reforming Philadelphia's revelers by giving the parade a new (Anglo-)American identity and transforming disruptive and impromptu street theater into the highly organized parade performed today.

If in Philadelphia at the end of the nineteenth century a nationalist-inspired vision of the medieval past was used to tame an unruly performance, in Brooklyn at the start of the twentieth century the medieval past was reinvented as an anchor for an immigrant community. The fourth chapter, "Reinventing Tradition: Brooklyn's Saint Play," explores the role of traditional religious festivals in preserving ethnic identities among Italian Americans. Each summer since the early 1900s an Italian-American community in Brooklyn, New York, holds a two-week celebration in early July on the feast of Saint Paulinus, which includes the performance known as the dancing of the *giglio*. In this performance, men lift and "dance" two huge structures—a tower (the *giglio*) and a boat—whose progress through the streets dramatizes the story of Paulinus's capture and release by "Turks." This performance, which participants claim dates back to the early Middle Ages, is in actuality a reinvented tradition that reshapes an Italian performance to meet the needs of early-twentieth-century immigrants in New York City. By imagining the *giglio* performance as part of a long tradition dating from medieval Italy, Brooklyn's Italian-American community works to preserve its identity in the face of growing cultural homogeneity and demographic changes.

The connection between religion and the medieval past, which plays a role in Brooklyn's saint's play, becomes more pressing in the case of performances that aim to re-create European passion plays in the United States. Chapter 5, "America's Passion Plays," examines a performance history that begins with the American fascination with Oberammergau, runs through the failed San Francisco Passion Play of 1879, and continues on to the Black Hills Passion Play. Brought to the United States by Josef Maier, an immigrant from Germany, the Black Hills Passion Play has been performed annually each summer in Spearfish, South Dakota, since 1939; it narrates the story of the crucifixion of Jesus and features a cast of some 250 players—community members as well as professionals. By cultivating clerical and community support, by using smaller-scale moral and educational venues rather than the commercial stage, and by aligning itself with a medieval performance tradition, the Black Hills Passion Play has found a successful formula for staging potentially volatile religious material and has managed to import passion plays when other attempts have failed.

The final chapter, "Medieval Plays and Medievalist Players," takes up another form of revivalism, this time by scholars of medieval theater who have increasingly turned to reconstructions of medieval performances as a form of scholarly inquiry. In recent years, university-based performance groups such as Toronto's Poculi Ludique Societas have become responsible for nearly all performances of medieval plays in the United States, dominating not only the production but also the teaching and study of medieval drama, with performances now routinely scheduled as part of academic conferences and symposia. These academic reconstructions, which play a formative role in shaping the direction of scholarship on medieval drama, harken back to the early-twentieth-century revival of medieval English plays—exemplified by William Poel's staging of *Everyman* in 1901—and respond to the specific history of medieval drama studies as a discipline. I examine the agendas of academic reconstructions, particularly their faith in performance as a source of knowledge about the past and their revivalist goal of appropriating for the present the values imagined to inhere in medieval plays, looking also at the way in which academic reconstructions shape how medieval drama—and more broadly the premodern past—is currently understood.

As will quickly become obvious, the performances in this book are culturally rich and interpretively complex. In each case, I have tried to strike a balance between a thick description of the performance at hand that seeks to do justice to its many features and a reading of the performance as an exemplary text for my investigation of the uses of the medieval past in America. Although this strategy runs the risk of diffuseness, it also retains the vitality and intricacy of the performances. My method of investigation likewise aims to mesh the archival research in which medievalists such as myself are trained with the tactics of ethnographic inquiry. To that end, I have supplemented library research with attendance at the performances I discuss and have conducted interviews with participants and spectators. This book is not, however, intended to be an anthropological study. Instead, I have used my experience of the performances and interviews with participants as a way of orienting the analysis and as a means of locating the performance's most important meanings for present-day participants.

As will also become clear, these performances are not easily interpreted as building blocks in a nationalist history; instead, they speak to the ways that traditions can be used to resist nationalist impulses and to signal a subculture's distinctive identity. Ernest Gellner has said that nationalism, as "the general imposition of a high culture on a society," is an ideology that benefits primarily elites while trampling on the folkways of common people.[29] Nationalism, in Gellner's view, encourages homogeneity for its economic and political usefulness, thus consigning regional and subcultural heterogeneity to the form of a stumbling block to maximum efficiency.

The performances in the following chapters tend to be just that sort of stumbling block. The identities of many of the communities whose rituals are examined in this book challenge definitions of "nation," since they are communities whose immigrant or ethnic origins (or whose cultural allegiances, in the case of the academics of chapter 6) frequently put them at odds with the imperial or national culture. While the past and tradition are commonly understood as aiding the development of nationalism, these performances are for the most part antinationalist in their most basic impulses. In them, local history resists the nationalist master narrative and proffers allegiance to European (or African or Mesoamerican) forebears as a sign of community distinctiveness. The invocation of a traditional past in these performances thus works against assimilation and the demands of nationalism. As performative historiographies, these rituals bear witness to cultures that have been produced, or that survive "otherwise than modernity."[30] That, as we shall see, is often the way of imported rituals.

CHAPTER 1

Performing Conquest
The Jémez Matachines Dances

The history of the matachines dance begins with the Spanish conquest of the Pueblo Indians in 1540 and the expedition of Francisco Vásquez de Coronado into New Mexico, although the fate of the Pueblos had arguably already been sealed—and many of the conditions for the implanting of the matachines dance already established—when Cortés vanquished the Aztecs some twenty years earlier. In the years that followed Coronado's expedition, the imposition of Franciscan clerical culture, along with Spanish-colonial administrative customs, brought about major changes in the lives of the Puebloans. Much of the early documentary record charting these historical events was destroyed during the 1680 Pueblo Revolt; what has survived are some journals, expedition itineraries, and records of jurisdictional feuds between the Franciscans and the provincial government over control of the Indians. But despite the lack of written records, other traces of the European invasion have persisted, among them the performances and ritual ceremonies that create an alternate testament of conquest and colonization. Like written records, these performances are legible—if often oblique and shadowy—texts that offer glimpses of past cultural encounters. Unlike written records, however, these performances—many of which are still performed today—have not been frozen in time but have changed along with shifting material and cultural circumstances. For this reason, in the performances that arose from and comment on the conquest of New Mexico, the historical past is not so much reflected as it is refracted—warped and bent in ways that both reveal and obscure cultural interactions and their historical outcomes. As refracted histories, conquest dramas present a contested view of the past, in which the nature and meanings of the conquest are fought over by its various inheritors. What is interesting about conquest dramas is how little of that struggle is immediately visible in them: rather than confront the conquest head on, they take a more winding route to historical resistance. If history, as Baudrillard has said, is "full of ruse and cunning," so too are these living enactments of it.[1]

Perhaps the most striking of the surviving conquest dramas is the matachines dance, a ritual dance-drama with religious overtones that is performed in

Pueblo Indian and Mexicano/Hispano communities along the upper Río Grande Valley of New Mexico and in other parts of the Southwest and central Mexico. Although there can be a good deal of variety among different versions, the dance typically consists of two rows of ten to twelve masked male dancers who wear miterlike hats with long, multicolored ribbons streaming down the back. These line dancers are accompanied by five other performers who dance among and around them. One of them is a young girl (La Malinche), who usually wears a white communion dress and is partnered with an adult male dancer, who is dressed like the line dancers but wears a floral crown (El Monarca). Another man or a boy costumed as a bull (El Toro) and one or two clowns (Los Abuelos, "the grandfathers") make up the remainder of the ensemble. Accompanied by music played on violin and guitar, the dancers move for approximately an hour through different sets of dances that are loosely structured around a dramatic narrative that in an indirect fashion restages Cortés's conquest of Mexico. Framed within processional and recessional *marchas* at beginning and end, the dance features crossings and interweavings between the two lines of dancers, an elaborate exchange of the *palma* (trident) and *guaje* (rattle) carried by La Malinche and El Monarca, and charges by El Toro, who in most versions is killed in the end. Throughout the performance the clowns orchestrate the actions and provide comic relief. Although in recent years the dance has become something of a tourist attraction and so has developed into a portable performance that can be taken to events like the summertime art fair in Santa Fe known as Spanish Market, the dance is traditionally performed in a specific location (usually the central plaza of a village or pueblo) on a set day of the year (usually a saint's day). While performers are still for the most part drawn from local communities, audiences today consist of mingled residents and outsiders, both invited guests and tourists.

The precise history of the matachines dance is uncertain. The dance either was or was not imported from Spain by the conquistadors. It either does or does not derive from European matachin dances or, alternately, from *moros y cristianos* performances. It either does or does not show the influence of the friars who ran missions in sixteenth-century New Mexico. It either is or is not the remnant of an indigenous (largely Nahua) dance-drama. It either was or was not brought to New Mexico by the early settlers who accompanied first Juan de Oñate and later Diego de Vargas. What we have in the New Mexican matachines dance, it seems, is a series of competing histories in which the contest is over not just whose, but what, past the matachines represents.

One consequence of these competing histories is that while the basic form of the dance is similar in all of the New Mexican communities in which it is performed, whether Indian or Mexicano/Hispano, the function and meaning of the dance is not the same for the two ethnic groups, as Sylvia Rodríguez has shown. Puebloans claim that the dance was brought to them from Mexico by Montezuma and thus usually view the dance as symbolic resistance to Euro-

© FRED HARVEY

Matachines Dancer. Painting by Gerald Cassidy on a postcard by
Fred Harvey for the 1922 Santa Fe Fiesta. Author's collection.

pean conquest and forced conversion to Christianity. Mexicano/Hispano communities, in contrast, believe that the dance was introduced by Juan de Oñate, the first colonizer of New Mexico, or by Diego de Vargas, the leader of the reconquest, or even by Cortés himself, and understand the dance to portray the Christianization of the Indians, represented by the expulsion or conversion of the Moors. As Rodríguez notes, the dance thus "has historical but differential meaning for Indian and Hispano groups because the advent of Christianity in the region does not have the same meaning for those who brought it as for those it subjugated."[2]

The matachines dance also has meaning for a third group: the outside spectators who each year make up a portion of the audience for the dance in its various venues. Unlike some Pueblo ceremonies, the matachines dance has never been regarded as a private or sacred affair and outside spectators have not generally been discouraged from attending it (although some communities, like Jémez, have tried to limit access, in part simply to avoid unmanageable crowds). As a result, the dance has long been on the cultural tourism circuit, albeit as a minor attraction. Whatever the dance means to these outsiders, their influence on it should not be discounted, since they also have an impact on its survival and meanings, as has been the case with other forms of "folk art" in the Southwest. The interest of outsiders has contributed to a heightened awareness of the value of the performance as a cultural tradition and in some cases has been a spur for revival or more attentive preservation of the dance. Although it is difficult to chart with any precision the extent of its impact, attention from outsiders has to be reckoned with as one influence on current performances of the dance.

This chapter focuses on one particular matachines dance performed at Jémez Pueblo, some fifty miles west of Santa Fe. What sets the Jémez performance apart from other matachines dances is that it exists in two versions, one "Spanish," the other "Indian," the latter introduced to the pueblo in the early twentieth century. Both dances are performed one following the other on the same day, December 12, the feast day of Our Lady of Guadalupe. In their differences and similarities, these two performances open a window onto conquest and resistance, tradition and change, and the hybridization of cultures. They also offer a glimpse of a past that is still being contested, as divergent versions of what happened four hundred years ago are enacted and, in turn, use that enactment of the past as a tool for living in the present. The Jémez matachines dances underscore the fact that historical consensus about any important event is hard to attain and is always open to challenge and revision.

Like all versions of the matachines dance, those performed at Jémez replay the conquest in symbolically altered fashion. Via incorporation of the key figures of that historical event, the Puebloans ritually return each year to what was one of the most significant moments in their cultural history and return in a way that offers a momentary rewriting of the terms of that conquest. Like the accounts of the Spanish colonizers and missionaries, the matachines dance provides a record—even if only a partial and blurred one—of actions that occurred more than four hundred years ago. Attending the dance today is like eavesdropping on a conversation about the deepest of cultural concerns being conveyed through innuendo, asides, and covert references. What the careful listener can hear are the resonances of a still unresolved historical conflict, one that gets reimagined on each annual performance of the dance. The parallel matachines dances of Jémez Pueblo offer a performative historiography of the conquest, in which gesture, movement, music, and costume combine in a mimesis that writes a local version of the past, one in which scores have not yet been settled and in which the medieval European past plays a contested role.

Conquest Drama

At the time of the Spanish entry into the upper Río Grande region, the Pueblo Indians resided in some 134 towns in the Southwest, most of them located along the Río Grande and with a combined population that may have reached 248,000. These towns varied in size from fifty to five hundred houses, which were typically arranged around a plaza holding several kivas. Ceremonial activity in Puebloan towns, which was under the purview of men, provided a unifying function that ritually erased fragmentation: gifting, feasting, and dancing were all important rituals.[3] Crucially for theater history, when the Spanish arrived, they found in the well-organized and ceremonially sophisticated Puebloan culture—as they had in Aztec culture some years earlier—fertile ground for the importing of European drama.

The story of the first European incursions into New Mexico has been told before, but deserves repeating, for two reasons in particular: first, it shows the fitful, stop-and-start quality of Spanish attempts to colonize New Mexico that makes any search for a continuous history of Spanish influence in the region—including influence on performance traditions—difficult; second, it reveals a persistent use of drama as part of the process of colonization that helps explain the logic behind the Puebloans' subsequent turn to performance as a technique of revisionary history. European movement into New Mexico began with the survivors of the 1528 Narváez expedition to colonize Florida, who landed near what is now Galveston, Texas, after failing to reach Cuba on a makeshift raft; they spent the next six years traveling west into Texas and up the Río Grande.[4] In 1536, Nuño de Guzmán encountered four survivors from the expedition—Alvar Núñez Cabeza de Vaca, Alonso de Castillo Maldonado, Andrés Dorantes, and his Moroccan slave Estevanico de Dorantes—who reported the existence of emeralds and great cities. Their report had the effect of inspiring Viceroy Antonio de Mendoza to send the Franciscan Fray Marcos de Niza to explore, taking Estevanico along as his guide. The small party made contact with the Pueblo Indians in 1539. Estevanico was killed just south of

Cíbola (the Zuñi village of Hawikuh), an event that is recalled in Pueblo performances that continue to be enacted today, including at Jémez Pueblo where on November 12 the two historical figures of Fray Marcos and Estevanico are impersonated by two actors, one in white face-paint wearing a long black coat with a knotted rope belt and a white skull cap, the other in blackface wearing a curly black sheep-pelt wig and carrying a snare drum.[5] That the earliest encounters of the Puebloans with Europeans was fodder for a ritual that still survives suggests the privileged role of performance in negotiating historical conflicts in the region. Impersonations like these turned dangerous interlopers into comic figures, whose actions could be contained and even mocked within the space of the performance. The result was a partially redressive and ameliorative retelling of historical events that worked to counter their actual outcome (Spanish dominance, Puebloan subjugation).

On his return to Mexico City, Fray Marcos engaged in a bit of fanciful retelling of his own when he reported having found a kingdom more beautiful than Mexico or Peru, a report that spurred Mendoza to send Francisco Vásquez de Coronado on January 6, 1540, to conquer Cíbola. A month later, Coronado's expedition—which included Fray Marcos, 292 soldiers, 800 Mexican Indian allies, and enough livestock to feed them all—reached Culiacán where Coronado divided his company into two groups, pushing ahead with Fray Marcos and fifty horsemen, while leaving the rest to follow. Coronado's company reached Cíbola on July 7, 1540, where Coronado discovered to his disappointment that Fray Marcos had lied about the city's riches. After two years of exploration, plunder, and slaughter, Coronado abandoned New Mexico in April 1542. For the next forty years, the boundary of New Spain was at the edge of the mining towns of the northern frontier—Durango, Guanajuato, Querétaro, and San Luis Potosí—and New Mexico remained beyond the reach of Europeans. Like Estevanico and Fray Marcos, Coronado is also commemorated in Pueblo feasts in which he is portrayed as a slightly comic figure (sometimes called "Santiago"), who rides on a dancing hobbyhorse and carries a sword. Max Harris has argued that the hobbyhorse points to the influence of medieval European performances, which would suggest that these "Santiago" performances revise conquest history by turning props from the Spaniards' own dramatic tradition against them.[6]

Other expeditions followed, culminating in a large-scale colonization attempt led by the wealthy miner Juan de Oñate, which was chronicled by Gaspar Pérez de Villagrá. In January of 1598, Oñate set out from Zacatecas with 129 young and single men described as being of "troublesome" character. Half of the soldiers were Spanish-born (coming primarily from Andalusia and Estremadura), fifty were from New Spain, and the remainder came from other European countries. Also included in the expedition were the wives, children, servants, and slaves of several of the officers, as well as Franciscan friars, hundreds of horses, and thousands of sheep, cattle, and goats.[7]

Oñate's expedition is of particular interest for theater history, given his deliberate use of performance as an instrument of conquest. As Oñate moved north from El Paso, he mounted ritual ceremonies of possession and submission at strategic spots along the way. These carefully staged political dramas were apparently intended to serve as theatricalized reminders of the Spanish version of the conquest of Mexico and were put on with an eye to showing the Puebloans what their expected part was to be in that ongoing drama: the anticipated Pueblo submission to the Spanish was scripted—presumably for the benefit of both the Spanish and the Puebloans—through a reenactment of various aspects of the Aztec subjugation in 1523. Oñate came prepared for the dramas he wished to mount, bringing along various props designed to echo Cortés's conquest of the Aztecs. These included a banner with the image of "Our Lady of the Remedies" similar to one Cortés carried in 1519; Tlascalan allies, who functioned as visible reminders of the power wielded by the Europeans; twelve Franciscans (apparently in imitation of the twelve Franciscans who initiated the conversion of the Aztecs in 1524); and a native woman called Doña Inés from near Galisteo, who had been captured in the unauthorized 1590 expedition by Gaspar Castaño de Sosa, and who was intended to act as translator and go-between for Oñate as La Malinche had done for Cortés.[8] While some of the echoes of Cortés's earlier conquest might have been lost on the Puebloans, the general impression of European might and Indian powerlessness would have been hard to miss.

Dramatic performances continued to punctuate Oñate's progress northward. On April 30, 1598, he "took possession of all the kingdoms and provinces of New Mexico, in the name of King Philip," an occasion marked by the performance of an allegorical *comedia* by Captain Marcos Farfán de los Godos that staged New Mexico's willing (and bloodless) conversion to Christianity. The Spanish continued up the Río Grande to where the Chama flows into it from the west and founded their first capital, which they called San Juan de los Caballeros, north of Santo Domingo Pueblo. There they built the first church in New Mexico, which was dedicated in September 1598 during a week of celebration.[9] Gaspar Pérez de Villagrá described the festivities as including battles with cane spears, bullfights, tilts at the ring, and a *moros y cristianos* play, which being accompanied by artillery fire was reported to have caused fear among the Puebloans who watched it.[10] This display of military strength on the part of the Spanish, only loosely concealed as festive performance, might well have been a factor in the decision of some Indian "chieftains" to render "voluntary" obeisance to Spain the next day, as Harris notes.[11] As Oñate continued his tour, some Puebloans fled, while others—especially at the larger, stronger pueblos—welcomed him ceremoniously. At Jémez, which Oñate described as a "great pueblo," the Spanish were greeted with gifts of water and bread.[12]

In launching his political dramas, Oñate was doing no more than imitating a tactic honed by the Spanish some eighty years earlier in Mexico. In August 1523, the first three Franciscans had arrived in Tenochtitlán (Mexico City) followed in May 1524 by the "twelve apostles," the friars who were sent in response to Cortés's request in order to convert and baptize the indigenous population. What followed was a period of intense and vibrant, if also coercive, dramatic activity as the Franciscans drew on traditions of medieval religious drama, which they blended with the rich local heritage of ritual, ceremony, and drama indigenous to Aztec (Nahua) culture.[13] As Robert Potter has shown, this culturally mixed evangelical theater thrived in the early decades of the sixteenth century as an integral part of the Franciscans' conversion project, despite condemnation in some quarters, less out of concern for the coerciveness of the plays than for preservation of the purity of the Christian rituals being used.[14] Fray Toribio de Benavente (Motolinía), for example, noted with dismay that indigenous and Christian practices—such as fasting, infant-bathing ceremonies, penitential rituals, and communal banquets (especially in the May celebrations of the god Huitzilopochtli, which resembled the rituals of the feast of Corpus Christi and included a procession and feast that culminated in the eating of a small idol made of maize and honey)—often overlapped so that pagan could not be distinguished from Christian, a situation that put Christian rituals at risk of being corrupted.[15]

The efforts of the Spanish to use theatricality to aid conquest and conversion, Potter notes, were made easier by the fact that, as Motolinía's complaint recognized, the Spanish had the luck to encounter a culture that was itself deeply theatrical. Sacrificial drama was a fixed part of the pre-Columbian Nahua ritual calendar, as were other dramatic performances, including mock combats, masked dancing, puppetry, and other dramas described by early commentators. One such drama was the flower dance performed in honor of Huitzilopochtli, described by the Dominican Diego Durán in his *Historia de las Indias*. The flower dance involved the building of a house of roses and a garden of trees, and featured boy-dancers costumed as birds and butterflies who climbed into the trees, while other actors dressed as gods shot blowguns at the boy-birds. A more elaborate ritual performance occurred during the annual festival for Quetzalcóatl, at which a slave was dressed like the idol of Quetzalcóatl and was worshipped for forty days (and caged at night so he would not run away) before being ritually killed on the feast day.[16]

Building on Aztec ceremonials like these, the Franciscans—and later the Dominicans and Jesuits—sponsored a didactic religious theater that used indigenous actors performing in the *lingua franca* of Náhuatl for an indigenous audience.[17] As early as 1526 the Spanish were celebrating the feast of Corpus Christi in Mexico, as we know from an act of the *cabildo* in 1529 describing the order in which the Corpus Christi procession should be organized. The earliest recorded missionary performance in Mexico was a play of 1530 on the conversion of St. Paul, which was performed in Náhuatl by an Aztec cast in

Tenochtitlán. A play on the final judgment, *El Juicio Final,* also in Náhuatl, was performed around 1533 in Mexico City, perhaps for installation of the new archbishop and first viceroy of Mexico, Don Antonio Mendoza; according to witnesses, the play was responsible for converting many spectators.

Didactic performances, many of them recorded in *cabildo* proceedings and in various firsthand accounts, continued throughout the century, forming a consistent part of Spanish colonization efforts. Festivals of Corpus Christi and St. John were celebrated in Tlaxcala in 1538. In Mexico City in 1539, *La Conquista de Rodas* was performed to celebrate the European alliance against encroaching Turks, and Tlaxcaltecans performed a related play, *La Conquista de Jerusalen,* on Corpus Christi of the same year.[18] The Tlaxcaltecan play, a version of a *moros y cristianos,* featured Turkish troops played by Aztecs who had been prepared for baptism; after the Turks/Aztecs were defeated, they were baptized on stage. Of particular interest for the Jémez matachines dances is the fact that already in these early plays there was evidence of Spanish inability to control the plays' meanings. In the Tlaxcaltecan *moros y cristianos,* for example, the Turkish sultan and aide were costumed as Cortés and his aide Pedro de Alvarado; at the play's climax, an Indian army thus defeated Cortés in a symbolic reshaping of the conquest that apparently escaped the notice of the Spaniards. Other early plays included *The Sacrifice of Abraham; St. Helena's Finding of the Cross,* which dramatized Emperor Constantine's conversion; and *Souls and Testamentary Executors,* all of which have been made available in English by Marilyn Ravicz.[19] This theater of conversion is exactly what the English Protestant writer John Rainolds exclaimed against in *The Overthrow of Stage Plays* as part of his critique of Catholics, who, he claimed, have "transformed the celebrating of the Sacrament of the *Lords supper* into a *Masse-game,* and all other partes of the *Ecclesiasticall service* into *theatrical sights;* so, in steed of *preaching the word,* they caused it to be played; a thing put in practise by their flowres, the *Jesuits,* among the poore *Indians.*"[20]

Despite their proven success as vehicles for conversion, popular festivities and ritual practices in New Spain had by the end of the sixteenth century come to be regarded with suspicion—not just by Protestant reformers like Rainolds, but by the Catholic church itself—in part because such festivities were seen as idolatrous and in part because of a deep distrust of Indian involvement in them.[21] It did not escape church authorities that these plays also sometimes flew in the face of official doctrines and practices, as was the case with the mass baptism that ended the *Conquista de Jerusalen* of 1539, a baptism that constituted an act of defiance on the part of the Franciscans in the face of ecclesiastical disapproval of their conversion practices. Perhaps not surprisingly, then, when the Inquisition was established in Mexico in 1571, one of its duties was to examine plays, performances, and dances.[22] Not long afterward, in 1577, performances were officially suppressed, when the church began to rein in the evangelical theater it had initially created and supported.[23] The official policy of discouraging religious drama continued in the seventeenth and eighteenth centuries: a royal decree by Philip IV in 1660 prohibited plays from being performed in churches or religious buildings in both Spain and Mexico. The ban was extended to outdoor performances in the early eighteenth century and in 1765 Carlos III prohibited even the *autos sacramentales* long associated with Corpus Christi day. But all these proscriptions came too late; religious drama was already firmly planted in New Spain.[24]

But what exactly had been implanted? Anthropologists and cultural historians agree that acculturation is generally a selective process, with the donor culture offering only certain parts of itself and the recipient culture accepting only some of those offerings. Part of the reason for this selectivity is that while we may use linguistic shorthand to refer to "the" donor culture and "the" recipient culture, neither of those entities is a complete or totalizable whole. The dominant culture of a society is never a homogeneous structure; instead it is, as Stuart Hall describes it, "layered, reflecting different interests within the dominant class (e.g. an aristocratic versus a bourgeois outlook), containing different traces from the past (e.g. religious ideas within a largely secular culture), as well as emergent elements in the present."[25] And the same layering can be found in any subordinate or recipient culture, such as that of the Puebloans. On the exporting side, the cultural material that came out of Spain with colonizers was a cultural hodgepodge—a blend of official Spanish culture and unofficial local customs deriving from the regions (primarily Andalusia and Estremadura) from which the earliest colonizers had come to New Spain.[26] In the sphere of religion, as well, the early friars transmitted not only, or even primarily, the official Christianity of intellectuals but rather the local religion of sixteenth-century Spain, which emphasized cults of local patron saints and local fiestas and which helps explain the church's turn against popular theatricality in the New World.[27] Thus only selected aspects of Spanish culture were transmitted while others never crossed over. On the importing side, some aspects of this selectively transmitted culture were absorbed and some were rejected, as new local customs were assimilated to what the Spanish had brought with them. So much selectivity of transmission makes it difficult to speak of a simple imposition of a unified Spanish culture onto a unified indigenous one or to trace the "origins" of any the hybrid cultural forms that resulted. Partial donation and partial acceptance of imported cultural forms inevitably blur the footprints that might let us track the routes by which performances like the matachines dance arrived within Puebloan ceremonial culture.

The tracking of routes of cultural influence is additionally complicated by the breaks in continuity of Spanish occupation of Pueblo territory in the subsequent decades. The history of colonization in New Mexico is one not of steady continuity of Spanish presence but rather of disruption, expulsion, and reinvasion. In the years immediately after Oñate's conquest, Spanish presence in New Mexico contracted, and the Spanish realigned their settlements. In December 1598, Spanish soldiers stopped at Acoma Pueblo for provisions and provoked an attack by the inhabitants. When he learned that thirteen soldiers had died, Oñate besieged the pueblo, eventually killing eight hundred of the residents and taking close to six hundred captive. All were condemned to twenty years of slavery among New Mexico's settlers, men over the age of twenty-five had one foot cut off, and children under twelve were distributed as household servants. This example of Spanish power had the intended effect of making the other pueblos realize they did not have the resources to resist.[28] Despite this squelching of resistance, however, by 1601, many of the Spanish colonists had withdrawn from the region, complaining of the lack of riches and the harshness of the land. The Franciscans, eager to limit settler activity in New Mexico, supported charges of excess violence leveled against Oñate by the remaining settlers, and he was found guilty by the viceroy and ordered to resign his governorship; in 1608, the king ordered exploration to cease.

Although Oñate's expedition had been launched because of a desire to secure the northern provinces against European rivals, religious factors in the end motivated the continued Spanish occupation of New Mexico. From 1609, New Mexico became largely a mission outpost of the Spanish Empire, with a skeleton government. During these years, the friars expanded their influence, running missions among the Pueblos and monopolizing church functions.[29] Cut off from the southern centers of Spanish colonial administration and from church officialdom, a distinctive folk religion, often organized around lay brotherhoods known as *cofradías* or *hermandades* (which in some cases are linked to matachines dances) came to flourish in New Mexico, brotherhoods that in some ways resembled the secret societies of the Pueblos, and that perhaps provided a crossing point for the trading of cultural materials between the Spanish and the Puebloans.[30]

Many of the Franciscans who arrived in New Mexico were radical ascetics, products of the Catholic Counter-Reformation, who envisioned a life of rejection of the flesh, sexuality, and materiality for the sake of union with a spiritual father.[31] Their religiosity was steeped in notions of personal sanctity and reverence for hierarchy, and was evangelical in its thrust. Their methods of conversion involved destroying visible forms of idolatry and weeding out all sexual activities that violated their codes of chastity, fidelity, and monogamy, often through such bodily punishments as public floggings or incarceration in stocks.[32] Since Christianity was an urban religion that flourished in towns and settlements, one task of the Franciscans was to concentrate dispersed Puebloan populations; during the seventeenth century, 130 or so villages were reduced to 43, as the Franciscans set up missions that subdued and consolidated the Puebloans.[33]

Under the Franciscans, Christian rituals were substituted for or in some cases meshed with Pueblo traditions in ways that resulted in hybridized performances:

the katsina cult, for example, was conflated with the European cult of saints, and prayer-sticks were merged with the cross.[34] A Christian ritual calendar was established, replacing Pueblo cosmology with events emphasizing Christ's life and using the didactic religious plays (*autos*) that were associated with the European ritual year.[35] Although we do not know the exact stages of these changes, at some point Pueblo dances gave way to Christianized celebrations, such as *Las Posadas,* which staged the story of Mary and Joseph's search for shelter, and *Los Pastores,* the enactment of the shepherds' travels to Bethlehem. On Christmas day in some pueblos, the matachines was danced, and on January 6, the Christmas cycle ended on the feast of Epiphany with the *Auto de los Reyes Magos,* the story of the three magi. Ramon Gutiérrez notes that the myths of the birth of Christ resemble the story of the Twin War Boys and that the nativity might thus have been taken as a war epic announcing the birth of a new warlord, which helps explain why at Santo Domingo Pueblo the Ahyana War Dance and at Jémez Pueblo the Bow War Dance are still performed on Christmas morning. Holy Week rituals in the spring followed a similar pattern of the substitution of Christian for Puebloan rituals, in this case incorporating Puebloan flagellant and penitential customs.[36]

But the imposition of Spanish and Franciscan ritual on the Puebloans was less smooth than this account suggests. In 1637–38, after waves of Apache raids that retaliated against Governor Luís de Rosas's slave raids on the Apaches and in opposition to Rosas's heavy extraction of tribute and labor, Puebloans revolted against the friars at Taos and Jémez and began celebrating their ceremonies again. Famine and drought hit in 1666–70, increasing discontent. Finally, on August 10, 1680, a San Juan medicine man named Popé organized a revolt. After successfully driving out the Spanish, the Indians destroyed all signs of Christianity: ritual objects, Christian names, the Spanish language, Spanish seeds, and other signs of the invaders were purged.[37] For a dozen years, the Spanish were kept out, until in 1692 Diego de Vargas led the *reconquista* of New Mexico, visiting all of the pueblos and, like Oñate before him, holding ceremonies of conquest. New Spain gained its independence from Spain in 1821, and the Franciscans were expelled in 1833. In 1846, Brigadier-General Stephen Watts Kearny led the United States Army of the West into Santa Fe and claimed New Mexico for the United States, paving the way for an influx of English-speaking and largely Protestant Anglo-Americans. The Gold Rush of 1849 sped Anglo-American immigration to California and the West and eroded much of Spanish, as well as Puebloan, culture.

The Matachines Dance

Somewhere and somehow in this complicated history, the matachines dance took shape. Although there is no consensus among scholars about its origins, the matachines dance appears to have connections with both pre-Conquest

Mesoamerican dances and medieval European folk dramas. While the name of the dance seems to link it to the sixteenth-century European entertainer known as the *matachin,* who often appeared as a masked grotesque figure who danced with a sword (watching Montezuma's dancers in Tenochtitlán in 1519, Bernal Díaz del Castillo commented that some danced like matachines), its closest affiliations are with the various "dances of the conquest," including *la danza de las plumas* (in Oaxaca) and *la danza de los santiagos* (in Central Mexico), which belong to the *moros y cristianos* tradition.[38] All of these dances feature performers on foot, who usually carry swords or lances and ride hobbyhorses. Dramatized battles of Moors and Christians were a common feature of late medieval European courtly revels and civic festivities, and were usually performed as part of royal visits or other ceremonial events. Their annual enactment, which often accompanied the procession of a town's saint, came later, in the sixteenth century, perhaps along with the formation of local militias that were responsible for guarding Spain against attacks from the Turkish navy and Berber pirates; large-scale *fiestas de moros y cristianos* continue to be popular in Spain.[39] With the conflict with the Moors still vividly in mind, the Spanish who arrived in Mexico in the sixteenth century apparently found the *moros y cristianos* play well-suited to legitimizing and ratifying the Spanish takeover of the Aztec Empire.[40] Since there were few doctrinaire limits imposed on the play (unlike with religious dramas), it quickly evolved, becoming an expression of a variety of New World points of cultural conflict.

The question of origins, which might in other contexts seem narrowly pedantic, matters quite a bit for the New Mexican matachines. Originary debates are in fact of great ideological importance for the Mexicano/Hispano and Puebloan communities that perform the dance and for whom its meanings cannot be disentangled from conquest history.[41] For the Mexicano/Hispano communities that believe it was brought to New Mexico by Oñate, de Vargas, or Cortés, the matachines dance is seen as a piece of cultural heritage that people can be proud of, a drama that stages the expulsion of the Moors and represents the conversion of the Indians to Christianity. For the Puebloans, who believe that the dance was brought to them by Montezuma, the matachines encodes the grimmer history of the subjugation of the Aztecs and thus represents resistance to conquest and conversion.[42] Interestingly, in neither case is the dance assumed to comment directly on the history of Spanish colonization in New Mexico itself. Instead, interpretations of the dance from both sides revisit local history obliquely, through a restaging of the earlier conquest of the Aztecs that, while obviously connected to the fate of the Pueblos, is nonetheless slightly displaced from it. The result is a performance that engages with local history from one or more removes rather than confronting it head on.

This historical sidestepping and the divergent readings that it gives rise to are in large part made possible by the elusiveness with which the New Mexican matachines dance incorporates historical persons and events. In the dance, conquest and conversion are represented only implicitly and covertly. The dance is anything but doctrinaire. This is particularly true of the major characters—El Monarca, El Toro, and La Malinche—who are all open to divergent readings that refuse to be limited to a definitive set of historical referents. That is, while El Monarca can be seen as Montezuma, the dance presents him as a generalized male authority figure who must be obeyed by the other dancers; El Toro, who might be a variant of the Cortés character from the *moros y cristianos,* functions in the dance as any kind of threat (or, more mildly, nuisance) that has to be banished; and La Malinche, the only character who bears a name directly associated with the conquest, in her communion dress appears as a figure of youthful purity and innocence, whose function in the dance is broadly conciliatory and beneficent.[43] The actions of the matachines dance are similarly multidirectional. There is no overt battle that directly refers to the conquest, except for the killing of the bull (and in some versions, the bull is not killed, but merely captured and led away) and the possible residual traces of two clashing armies manifested in the two lines of dances. About all that can be said definitively about the dance, based on its characters and danced actions, is that it dramatizes a basic battle between evil, represented by the bull, and innocence or goodness, represented by Malinche. No further clues as to intended meanings can be derived from a written script or from oral dialogues, since as it is performed today in New Mexico, the matachines is largely a pantomime, with no spoken parts, aside from the joking repartee of Los Abuelos with the audience and occasional chanted or shouted words and phrases. The matachines dance thus bears only indirect testimony to its origins in Spanish and Mesoamerican culture and to the clash between those two cultures, testimony that can be overlooked or interpreted in varying ways, depending on the cultural position of the person doing the interpreting.

The indeterminacy of the history encoded in the dance carries over from the characters to their dress as well. Although the visually striking costumes are uniform across most versions of the matachines, their meanings are unclear, to say the least. El Monarca ("the king") is the central figure in all of the New Mexican matachines dances. Like the other line dancers, Monarca usually wears dark trousers with a buttoned suit jacket, shoes or boots, and a cape; typically, he either wears gloves or has his hands painted a grayish white with a design that looks like stitching, to resemble gloves. In some versions, four of the dancers (the *capitanes*) and Monarca wear an elaborately decorated headdress known as the *corona* ("crown"). At Jémez, Monarca and the *capitanes* also wear white pillowcases over their trousers, giving the impression of a skirt. The other matachines dancers wear the *cupil* headdress—one of the most striking features of their costume—which consists of a headband that ties in back and a flat oval front-piece that stands upright; the headdress is decorated with long streaming ribbons and two feathers that stick up like ears and is worn with a cloth and fringe that hides the face. As Flavia Champe notes, the

Matachines dancers, Taos Pueblo, Taos, New Mexico, date unknown. By permission of the Western History Collection, Denver Public Library, Denver, Colorado.

possible cultural heritage of this headdress ranges from Moorish turban and face scarf to Spanish-Catholic bishop's miter to Aztec plumed headdress, once again suggesting cultural hybridity, the historical ambiguity of the matachines, and its openness to varied interpretations.[44] Each dancer masks his face behind a scarf and carries a trident or *palma* (resembling the Aztec feather-fan, but now decorated in any way the performer chooses) in the left hand and a ker-chief-covered gourd rattle in the right. (In a striking departure from this usual costuming, the costumes of the matachines in the "Indian" version of the dance at Jémez feature beaded moccasins and decorated trousers, and thus an-nounce a more overt cultural allegiance.)

The depiction of the other main characters is equally complex. Malinche is the only female character in the dance, and in all of the New Mexican versions (with the important exception of the "Indian" version at Jémez) she is played by a young girl. Malinche's name at first glance seems to signal her signifi-cance, since Malinche was the name of the Nahua woman who became

Cortés's interpreter and mistress and who was one of the earliest converts to Christianity.[45] But her name tells us less than we might wish to know about her meaning in the dance. In the matachines, Malinche is often identified not as Cortés's mistress but as Montezuma's daughter, in a move than realigns her sexuality as filial obedience; she is also usually costumed in a white dress, stockings, and veil, an outfit that associates her with purity and virginity as well as with Our Lady of Guadalupe (on whose feast day the matachines is danced at Jémez). El Abuelo ("the grandfather") is a clown figure who acts as master of ceremonies and whose costume is often a caricature of Franciscan dress: he usually wears a cassocklike coat with a knotted rope around the waist, hides his face behind a grotesque mask, and carries a whip. He is thus a somewhat frightening figure. Part of his role, however, usually involves drawing in the audience by joking with them at certain times in the performance. Like the clowns found in other Pueblo dances, El Abuelo perhaps symbolizes a topsy-turvy universe, marked by social factionalism and disorder, in which things are in disarray and need to be righted.[46] The last major character is El Toro, who is often played by a young boy wearing an animal costume and carrying two long canes on which he leans to simulate the bull's forelegs. He dances a comic bullfight, threatening Malinche, Monarca, and the *capitanes*. (In some versions, El Toro is killed in the end, but at Jémez he is more benignly roped and led away.)

A similar masking of historical origins and meanings marks the movements and music of the dance. In the course of the performance, which takes approximately an hour to perform, the line dancers, usually ten to twelve in number, stand in two parallel rows.[47] The performance typically opens with a dance of Monarca and the matachines, followed by Malinche's dance with Abuelo and the matachines. Next Monarca dances, followed by a pantomime of Toro's bullfight, at the end of which he is killed or captured. A series of dances by Malinche and Monarca with the matachines follow, including a "cross" dance and a bowing-stamping thanksgiving dance. The dances are accompanied by musicians, usually Spanish-Americans, who are sometimes hired to play at the performance (the Jémez "Indian" version once again proves an exception in its use of music). Champe suggests that the music for all of the New Mexican matachines dances is "partially of Indian origin" since it sounds different from the matachines music of Mexico. She hypothesizes that the early Franciscans in their mission schools encouraged the Pueblos to compose their own songs, resulting in a blending of Indian, Mexican, and Spanish elements.[48] Champe may well be right, but whatever historical connections the music of the dance contains lie hidden under a surface that seems determined to conceal as much as reveal.

Max Harris has persuasively argued that conquest dramas like the matachines dance contain a "hidden transcript," which acts as a masked protest against, and rewriting of, colonial history.[49] Beneath its surface, as Harris has

El Monarca and La Malinche, Taos Pueblo, Taos, New Mexico, date unknown. By permission of the Western History Collection, Denver Public Library, Denver, Colorado.

shown, the dance contains a concealed story that comments on and unsettles the dance's apparent meanings. What is striking about the matachines dance, however, is how open to competing readings even that hidden transcript is; at every level, it seems, the matachines dance refuses the imposition of a unilateral or definitive reading, remaining instead ambiguous and, we might even say, indecisive in its inscription of the past. In the two Jémez dances, that lack of a central and uncontested meaning is concretized in the twin versions of the dance, each of which focuses on one history, while glancing over its shoulder at the other.

Competing Pasts: Jémez's Two Matachines Dances

With a cartographic logic that suits the dualism of the two Jémez matachines dances, two routes lead from the tourist hub of Santa Fe to Jémez. A southern route via the Hispano/Mexicano town of Bernalillo veers first south toward the urban sprawl of Albuquerque and the heavy traffic of the nearby interstate, then west-northwest through hauntingly beautiful and dramatic high-desert landscape. A northern route loops through the Jémez Mountains, incongruously passing first the ancient cliff dwellings of Bandelier and then the modern technonuclear compound of Los Alamos before dropping down out of the mountains into the lower plains around Jémez. Whichever road they take, the relatively few outsiders who attend the Jémez matachines dances thus travel through selective reminders of New Mexico's pre- and postconquest history, as they drive along routes that seem to underscore Jémez's apartness as well as the two contrasting versions of the Jémez dance.

That apartness is visible even in the "Spanish" version of Jémez's matachines, which while remaining within the dominant tradition of the matachines dance shows a number of variations from the usual pattern and is perhaps the least typical of the New Mexican matachines dances. Jémez's "Spanish" version usually has two Abuelos, one who is dance director and one who is El Toro's companion. At Jémez the pantomime of foot and knee by Abuelo and Monarca is, in Champe's words, "an exciting dance episode that has no counterpart in other pueblos or Spanish communities."[50] At Jémez, the bull is not killed, but rather is roped and led away. In terms of the dancing itself, as Champe says, "The forward bend of the body [in the Monarca/Abuelo dance] and the flexed knees make this the most typically 'Indian' dancing of any of the matachines productions."[51]

While the Spanish version of the Jémez dance is unusual, the most distinctive feature of the matachines as it is danced at Jémez is that it exists in two versions: one "Spanish," the other "Indian," terms used by the Jémez themselves to differentiate the two dances. Although the two versions show the same basic structure, they differ in revealing ways, such as the costuming of the "Indian" Malinche in buckskins, the way that when the "Indian" dancers kneel they do so with their backs to the altar, or in the way that the dancers in the Indian version do not form a cross in one of the later parts of the dance, as in other versions, but instead circle each other.[52] According to Joe Sando's history of the Jémez Pueblo, the Jémez people say that in the years before the twentieth century, the pueblo's original matachines dance was a moveable ritual that could be performed on different occasions, especially on New Year's Day; this "Spanish" version was performed by the Turquoise group and was accompanied by music played on the fiddle and the guitar. Sometime in the early 1900s, two brothers from the Pumpkin group at Jémez Pueblo, Juan Baptisto Cajero and Santiago San Juan, saw at Santo Domingo an "Indian" version of the matachines danced to drums and Indian songs and introduced this version to Jémez.[53] The Spanish and Indian versions have been performed alternately since then by Jémez's two kivas (the Turquoise and the Pumpkin groups). Apparently through pressure from the Indian version, the Spanish version has been modified and is now danced in a distinctive, high-stepping, lively Jémez style that Champe described as "'Indian' dancing." Since World War II, the matachines dance has been performed at Jémez on December 12, the feast day of Our Lady of Guadalupe, on which day those named Lupe, Lupita, and Guadalupe invite guests to their homes to eat. The Indian version is thus a latecomer, which was deliberately adopted in imitation of the Santo Domingo dance. Like the earlier Spanish version, however, it has been assimilated to the Catholic ritual year, despite showing some covert gestures of resistance to Christianity.

Sando does not report what it was about the Indian version of the matachines that captivated the two men from Jémez when they saw it at Santo Domingo, nor does he offer an explanation for why the performance caught on and continued to be performed at Jémez, not in replacement of the Spanish version but parallel to it. We can perhaps assume that the chance to adopt a performance that was marked with the signs of "Indianness" was appealing to residents of Jémez as an assertion of a strain of community identity and history that had hitherto gone unrecorded in the dance. Perhaps one reason that the Indian version did not displace the Spanish one was because the latter was seen as "traditional" since it had a longer-standing performance history. Perhaps, too, the ethnic loyalties of the residents of Jémez were mixed enough to argue for retention of both dances. If these two conjectures are correct, then the continued performance of the two versions at Jémez can be seen as a compromise between innovation and tradition as well as between revisionist and received history. In any event, the juxtaposition of the two performances on the one feast day has the effect of vividly portraying the dual legacies of the dance and their competing histories in a way that would be impossible without the reduplication of the dance. Doubling and substitution function in the two Jémez dances to expose the hidden transcript of the matachines in a way that does not happen in other communities in which just one version of the dance is performed.

The effect of this doubling and substitution derives in large part from the temporal and spatial structures of the dance, particularly the way that the two versions are performed one right after the other in the same place. Although some spectators may wander away after the Spanish version is performed, those who remain get to see both versions in rapid succession; this sequencing of the dances turns both versions into parts of one larger performance that contains the two alternatives within one capacious whole. The logic of the Jémez matachines, it seems, is one not of replacement but of coexistence.

On matachines Sunday, the festivities at Jémez begin with a procession from the church following the morning mass.[54] This procession, which stages a kind of *entrada* that those so inclined might link to Oñate's invasion, includes Spanish-costumed dancers led by a priest and altar boys, who carry religious statues; spectators trail along behind the group. The procession crosses the large open plaza that lies in the center of the pueblo and proceeds toward a ramada that has been set up at the other end of the plaza. After the statues are arranged inside the ramada, people line up to be blessed by the priest. (This framing of the dance by Catholic ritual will be rejected in the Indian version of the dance, which takes place at the opposite end of the plaza from the ramada, which is assiduously ignored by the dancers in what can be read as a muted echo of Jémez's historical hostility toward the friars.)[55] After the entrada, the musicians take seats near the ramada and begin to play, and around 11:00 A.M., the Spanish matachines begin to dance on the end of the plaza near the ramada-shrine. Well-bundled against the December cold, spectators stand or, if they have brought chairs, sit around the sides of the plaza. Behind the spectators and on alleys leading to the plaza, vendors sell food and drink and small goods such as jewelry or pottery, as they also do at Jémez's summertime Corn Dance. The atmosphere is one of subdued festivity, modulated by a touch of religious solemnity, all confined within the space of the plaza.

When the action gets under way, it is in a similarly subdued manner. The dancers in the Spanish version are costumed in more or less the same fashion found in other matachines performances (with the exception of the white pillowcases worn over dark trousers), and their actions for the most part follow the usual pattern, with the notable exception of the high-stepping style of the dancers. As the dance begins, two chairs are set up for Malinche and Monarca to sit on while the dancers line up in two parallel rows. After a number of rounds of dancing to Spanish music played on guitar and two fiddles and broadcast through an amplifier, Toro appears. He is impersonated by a little boy in a cowhide cape with horns on his head; he leans forward on two sticks that act as his forelegs and give him an amusing, hunched-over gait. Two clowns with whips also appear as Toro dances through the two lines of dancers. Pulling on a white cloth draped around Monarca's wrists, Malinche leads Monarca through the two lines of dancers. As she weaves through the dancers, she dances briefly with each pair in turn. Meanwhile, the clowns occupy themselves attending to the kneeling dancers, straightening their ribbons, and fussing over them. Intermittently, older men, who are not wearing costumes, come from the ramada-shrine, carrying pouches into which they dip their hands and then touch the shoulders of the dancers in an anointing gesture. The effect is one of solicitous concern and respect that downplays the militarism that might be anticipated as a lingering trace of the *moros y cristianos* tradition. A similar gentleness marks the handling of the bull's demise, when after a chase by the two clowns, little Toro is captured and led away, rather than being killed as he is in other versions. After an hour, the dance ends with unexpected abruptness, without any clear sense of climax or conclusion, and spectators drift away to buy food or drinks from the vendors.[56] The whole performance is marked by an understatement and economy of motion that is the opposite of spectacle. While striking, the costumes are also homely and are constructed of items taken from ordinary life: communion dress, dark suits or trousers, gloves, scarves, pillowcases. The only extravagance is in the headdresses, which in contrast with the rest of the matachines' quotidian array, signal the ritual incorporation of nonordinary and mythical-historical material.

After a pause of about ten minutes during which the tightly packed spectators disperse briefly, another and larger set of dancers quietly begins to gather at the other end of the plaza, away from the ramada and its religious statues. A group of around sixteen dancers in Indian costume and wearing moccasins moves into the upper part of the plaza and the "Indian" version of the dance begins as images of the Spanish version still linger in the minds of spectators. Although the movements of this second dance are much the same as in the preceding version, the contrast between the two is stark. This time, Malinche is a young woman, not a little girl, and she wears a costume of white buckskins.[57] No longer the small and clearly subordinate child of the Spanish version, here Malinche is an adult who is a peer of the other dancers. The master-of-ceremonies now is dressed more or less the same as the other dancers, and so does not stand out from them as he did in the Spanish version.[58] On the end of the plaza farthest from the ramada-shrine, the dancers dance for an hour accompanied by drum and chant, rather than by the amplified fiddle and guitar of the Spanish version. The dance once again ends abruptly and unceremoniously, with the music and dancing simply coming to a halt. When the dancers are done, they are done, and they stop, thwarting the desire for climax and catharsis.

Although reintegration is generally thought to be a central aspect of rituals, providing the mechanism by which participants and spectators reenter the world of normative structure, at Jémez because neither version of the dance creates a strong separation of ritual from ordinary life—the dancers just quietly appear on the plaza and their dance just ends without much ado—reintegration from the liminal back to the quotidian is largely absent.[59] As a result, the effect of the liminal experience of the ritual lingers and carries over into the "return to the ordinary" that bifurcates the day, when in the lull that follows the morning's set of dances, families invite guests into their houses for lunch in honor of the Virgin of Guadalupe.[60] After lunch, another set of dances is performed, once again alternating Spanish and Indian versions, before the day's events come to an end on a similarly unceremonious note balanced between the ritual event and ordinary life.

Although Jémez has recently built a large new visitor's center, the Jémez matachines performance remains a relatively private event and is not advertised, as many other matachines dances are; as a result, few of the spectators are outsiders. One reason for this shunning of tourism has to do with the pueblo's small size and its inability to handle crowds, although it manages to accommodate a much larger audience at the summer Corn Dance, which is more of a tourist attraction. Perhaps the early December date of the matachines dance, which comes during a lull in the tourist season, makes it possible for Jémez to deflect outsiders in ways that preserve the intimacy that the rituals of the feast of Guadalupe demand: it would hardly be possible to maintain the day's tradition of feeding guests were the pueblo inundated by outsiders. Added to the relative remoteness of the pueblo, the decision not to publicize the dance means that audiences for the Jémez matachines dances are fairly small, easily fitting along the perimeters of the plaza; residents and neighbors predominate over outsiders, making the dance seem less of a tourist attraction than it is in other places.

What do these two performances say about the past and its place within the present? The "Indian" version, following as it does immediately on the heels of the "Spanish" version, seems to rebuff the earlier dance by replicating it, but with crucial twists. Perhaps most obvious is the distancing of the second dance from both Catholic ritual (accomplished quite literally by locating the dancers at the far end of the plaza away from the ramada-shrine) and Spanish settler culture (evidenced especially in the substitution of drum-and-chant for the Spanish music). The Indian version also offers an altered account of the conquest, particularly in its handling of Malinche. Within the cultures of the southwest, Malinche is a powerful icon of female sexuality, who also represents a clash of cultures (Spanish-native) and religions (Christianity-indigenous beliefs). The little girl in her communion dress found in the Spanish version of the matachines downplays the sexual symbolism of Malinche, while also aligning her with Catholic practices; in contrast, the young woman clad in buckskins of the Indian version reinfuses Malinche with her sexual potency and also presents a less docile, more independent representation of the character. But because the Jémez matachines dance refuses to choose one over the other, the effect of presenting two Malinches is to externalize and make visible the historical contradictions in her character, bringing to the surface those features of the Malinche legend that remain suppressed in other performances of the dance-drama that feature just the one, childish Malinche.

It is important to stress again that the Indian version of the matachines dance at Jémez does not replace or erase the Spanish version; instead, the Indian version offers a latter-day comment on the Spanish dance that presents another way of viewing the historical events underlying both dances. The genius of the Indian version is that it is less a rejection of a Hispano/Mexicano understanding of the conquest than it is a reorienting of it; by airing two competing interpretations of past events, the Jémez performance points to the indeterminacy of all historical narratives and their openness to reinvention. Jémez's two dances in this way offer a sophisticated commentary on the writing of history by recognizing the existence of competing histories, and by subtly critiquing the dominant narrative (portrayed in the Spanish version), while allowing both stories to coexist. While the Spanish dance carries the privileged status of the "original," the newer Indian dance defamiliarizes the mythic original by challenging its primacy and its claim to be a definitive historical narrative, even if the Indian version never quite topples that original. Within close temporal and spatial confines, the Jémez dances play out a contested history, without allowing either side the final say.

That refusal to provide a definitive history comes across in the rhythms of the Jémez performance. Although the matachines dance—at Jémez as elsewhere—is structured around a narrative, that narrative surfaces only for brief episodes during the dance. The exchange between Malinche and Monarca, the capture of Toro, these and other narrative moments occupy a small part of the dance and punctuate nearly unrelieved choreographic and musical sameness. As in other versions, the dancing in both Jémez versions by and large consists of a repeated series of stamping steps interspersed with bowing and kneeling, the whole having a rhythmic and mesmerizing effect that is enhanced by the music, which consists of a few set themes, played over and over again. In tandem with the music, the dancers fall into automatic and repeated movements that emphasize the submission of the dancers to the repetitive patterns of the dance. The effect of all this is to diminish the importance of the narrative, and with it the historical events it recounts; in so doing, both versions of the dance seem to suggest that conquest history, in whatever way it is being refigured, has been absorbed, subdued, and put in its place. The performance itself has triumphed over history. The *experience* of the performance for both spectators and performers in this way not only provides access to a hidden transcript that gives a different account of historical events than official sources do, but more boldly offers a way of resisting history altogether, by assigning its most charged and violent moments—Cortés's invasion, the missionaries' coercive conversion of the Puebloans—a minor role in the flow of time. The ritualized repetitions of the dance, with their encoding of a never-ending rhythm of human motion and endurance, relegate historical events to the status of minor disruptions that cannot halt or alter that continuum. Thus the most dramatic rewriting of history that occurs in the Jémez dances is a refusal to allow past events—no matter how violent and disruptive—to get the upper hand; those events—conquest, conversion—are instead submerged under a set of repetitive motions that seem as durable and as beyond the reach of temporal vicissitudes as nature. In the struggle between timelessness and topicality, the victory in the Jémez matachines dances goes to that which endures beyond historical disruptions.

While the matachines dances derive a large share of their meaning from the history of conquest and conversion in New Mexico, they also touch on local and contemporary issues as well, such as community history and structure, ecological and environmental concerns, relations to neighboring settlements, and other conflicts in the modern Río Grande Valley, as Rodríguez has shown. At Jémez as in other places where it is performed, the dance can serve as a point of community pride, can play out social hierarchies and relations (particularly in its assigning of performance roles), can help preserve a sense of cultural heritage, and can be used to defend the community's boundaries and interests against encroaching forces. One thing the matachines dance cannot do is exclude those forces entirely. In particular, it cannot exclude outside spectators, who perhaps inevitably have an impact on the dance's functions and meanings, and carry those functions and meanings beyond the borders of the communities that perform the dance.

These days, the past obliquely recorded in the matachines dance is claimed, if spectatorship can be understood as a form of possession, by others beyond the Puebloan and Hispano/Mexicano groups who perform it. Ethnic tourism is a booming industry in New Mexico, as it has been since the days of promotions sponsored by the Santa Fe Railroad to entice Eastern travelers to venture westward. Marta Weigle has described how Fred Harvey and the railroad joined forces to market the "Indian Southwest" by promoting the region as a tourist attraction in order to increase ridership on passenger trains. Among the many postcards produced as part of this marketing effort were images of matachines dancers, which were conscripted into the effort of helping market the Southwest as a tourist destination.[61] The role of the matachines in this effort was as an exotic and colorful spectacle that was as worthy of the visitor's gaze as red rock canyons or scrub-pine mountains, and just as readily accessible. The gaudily yet enigmatically costumed matachines dancer painted by Gerald Cassidy and reproduced by Harvey on postcards made for the 1922 Santa Fe Fiesta, positioned the dance within consumer culture, where it remains firmly located to this day.

While ethnic tourism is by no means an unmitigated good, it has to be credited with having helped preserve local dramatic traditions, such as the Christmas play known as *Los Pastores,* which in recent years has been widely revived in schools, parish halls, and community gyms across the state and has been staged on television and radio.[62] Touristic interests spurred the revival of a wide range of arts and crafts and have made New Mexico a center of artistic production where it is possible for artists to make livings by practicing traditional as well as modern trades.[63] The matachines dance has not been immune to a tourist-inspired revivalist impulse. The Arroyo Seco matachines, for example, was revived in 1985–86 by a local school teacher as part of what Rodríguez claims was "ethnocultural mobilization" around the issue of land and water rights in the area; in 1987, the Arroyo Seco dance was performed at the Museum of International Folk Art in Santa Fe, thus almost immediately bringing itself to a tourist audience.[64] While it is difficult to chart the precise impact of tourism on these revivals, at the very least the interest of tourists has heightened awareness among local communities themselves of the region's performance traditions and has encouraged groups to resurrect those that have died out, while also providing a wider audience for the various material and cultural messages the performance might be seeking to transmit.

To return, finally, to the question of American relations with a medieval European past, although the New Mexican matachines dance is understood by its participants to be a link to the past as well as an occasion for asserting claims on the present, and while its origins lie at least partially in the performance traditions of medieval Europe, for most participants and observers—aside from scholars of medieval drama who have a vested interest in the matter—the medieval legacy of the dance does not play a large role in its present meanings. That is, the values of the dance are not explicitly linked to a premodern European past that is seen as in some way lying outside of or grounding subsequent history. Instead, the dance's central meanings are understood as having been forged in the New World during the years of the conquest; while medieval Spanish origins are not denied, they also are not invoked in any concrete way. The dance thus tends to be taken as a thoroughly indigenous affair that springs from and has meaning chiefly within New World contexts. Even Mexicano/Hispano communities, which have good reason to link the matachines with Spain as homeland, generally downplay its medieval origins—although they are proud of its connections with Cortés and the early Spanish colonists—and instead view the dance as a narrative of their New World history, that is, as a narrative of Spanish settlement in Mexico and the southwestern United States. Puebloan communities, not surprisingly, tend to see the dance as developing from their own indigenous traditions, which while adopting European features, are assumed to preserve a record of resistance to the events of the conquest. Neither group shows much interest in the specifically medieval past that shaped the dance. With the matachines dance, there is no search for origins in a premodern moment, no nostalgia for a lost past. Indeed, the nostalgic impulse appears unable to gain a purchase on a performance that continues to play out a living history still relevant for its participants. In the end, then, the medieval past that the matachines displays is one that remains present. Perhaps that is the fate of all contested pasts, which, whatever their origins, refuse to be settled.

CHAPTER 2

Selective Histories
Albany's Pinkster Festival

According to an eyewitness account published in the *Albany Centinel* in 1803, on the Monday after Pentecost, while the pious population attended church, thousands of the less spiritually inclined gathered together on Pinkster Hill in Albany, New York, to begin a weeklong celebration. The crowd, so the account says, eagerly awaited the arrival of an "old Guinea Negro," known as King Charles, who after riding on horseback through town at the head of a motley procession, would be ceremoniously greeted on the hill.[1] Over the course of the next few days, people watched and participated in various games and sports, including the centerpiece of the festival, the Toto dance, which featured African music and dancing. The chief musician played a Guinea drum and was "dressed in a horrid manner—rolling his eyes and tossing his head with an air of savage wildness; grunting and mumbling out certain inarticulate but hideous sounds." On either side of him were two "imps," who were "decorated with feathers and cow tails" and who made "uncouth and terrifying grimaces" while playing smaller drums. Men and women danced to the drum music, with the "most lewd and indecent gesticulation," finally meeting at the climax of the dance and embracing "in a kind of amorous Indian hug, terminating in a sort of masquerade capture, which must cover even a harlot with blushes to describe." The other festivities included activities that "Raphael the master of painters could not delineate, not Milton, the biographer of devils, describe." During the week of the festival, all "restraints are flung off" and "every vice is practised without reproof and without reserve"; sexual decorum was also overthrown and even "the married negroes consider themselves absolved, on these occasions, from their matrimonial obligations." At the end of the festivities, King Charles ceremoniously descended the hill into Albany, going door to door with his attendants and demanding tribute, using "such a horrid noise and frightful grimaces, that you are glad to bestow something to get rid of him." Participants spent the rest of the week returning home and sobering up so that gradually "the city gets composed and business goes on as usual."

What this remarkable account describes is the celebration known as Pinkster, a springtime ritual performed throughout the Hudson Valley region, including in Albany, New York. While Pinkster had its start in the Pentecost celebrations of seventeenth-century Dutch settlers, by the late eighteenth century it had become chiefly an African-American festival. Then, in the first half of the nineteenth century, Pinkster disappeared, but was revived again in the middle of the twentieth in an entirely new guise as Albany's civic heritage festival.[2] How and why these successive appropriations occurred is the subject of this chapter. The written documentary record of Pinkster is frustratingly scant. We know about Pinkster only from a handful of brief mentions in diaries and other records; from two contemporary accounts from 1803, including the one from which this chapter's opening description is taken; from reports later in the century by antiquarians interested in local history; and from a long descriptive passage in a semiautobiographical novel by James Fenimore Cooper. With the possible exception of one of the 1803 accounts—which bears tantalizing traces of close intimacy with the performance—all of these references to Pinkster come not from participants but from outsiders, whose sometimes grotesque distancing from the performance (as seen in the account above) often reveals more about the observer than about the event being described.

Given these deficiencies of information, it is now difficult to know how Pinkster in its various forms might have functioned as a lived experience for those who participated in it. We can surmise, however, that for the Dutch settlers who imported the Pentecostal ritual, one of Pinkster's main functions was as a mechanism of social exchange, since in their hands the festivities apparently consisted primarily of house-visits among neighbors that reiterated bonds of social solidarity. For the African Americans who adopted the festival from the Dutch, and added to it their own African traditions, Pinkster seems to have been valued as a chance to represent themselves in ways that engaged with the Dutch settlers' terms, by partially collaborating with and appropriating what Mary Louise Pratt has called "the idioms of the conqueror" while also reshaping those idioms to new uses dictated by the local context of colonial and postrevolutionary New York.[3] At some point in the late eighteenth century, private house visits among a small coterie of Dutch colonists became public processions of African-American slaves and freemen, in a transformation that asserted the rights of the dispossessed to move freely through the streets and to occupy—however temporarily—a central place in the city. As the *Albany Centinel* account suggests, African-American Pinkster also served as a place where whites could vicariously participate in a licentiousness proscribed by their own cultural code and could define their own racial and regional identity.[4]

Selective recollections of the past have been important for all of the groups involved with Pinkster. In its earliest incarnation as a Dutch holiday, Pinkster flourished within the memory of religious traditions from the Old World that provided a comforting link to the homeland for Dutch settlers. As the holiday was taken over by slaves, another memory of Old World traditions—this time of the rituals of misrule that provided the disenfranchised groups of medieval Europe opportunities for welcome release from the daily routine of enforced labor while also licensing parodic and satiric attacks on dominant structures of rule—helped smooth the transfer of Pinkster from Dutch settlers to their African-American slaves by encouraging the former to permit a kind of festivity familiar to them from home. The memory of the past was also important for Pinkster's African-American participants, as historians of the African diaspora have argued, with the festival functioning as a vehicle for the reproduction of African ritual tradition. For the nineteenth-century antiquarians who gathered reminiscences about Pinkster, the performance was valuable precisely because it was already part of the past and offered glimpses of the quaint customs of early Albany. A similar investment in historical memory animates Pinkster's latest incarnation—its revival as a civic heritage festival designed to honor the city's Dutch past. Albany's Pinkster now features not a king but a debutante queen, and not African dancing and music but quaint Dutch customs. Although there have been attempts elsewhere to revive a specifically African Pinkster, Albany's present-day festival skips over the African-American incarnation of the event, resurrecting Dutch rituals instead, thus deliberately choosing only a partial version of the past to bring to bear on the present.

The remainder of this chapter examines the three embodiments of Pinkster in Albany from the seventeenth century to the present: the religious holiday celebrated by the city's Dutch settlers, the ritual of licensed misrule that slaves grafted onto the Dutch holiday, and the civic heritage festival of modern Albany from which all signs of the black celebration have been erased in a move that recalls Joseph Roach's comment that "forgetting, like miscegenation, is an opportunistic tactic of whiteness."[5] In all of these stages, as will become clear, the memory of a medieval European past has played a hidden role as the agent of both Pinskter's survival and its transformations.

Reproducing the Homeland

Dutch Pinkster was one of the items of culture settlers brought with them to North America, and it was in its way just as essential for their survival as the material goods they needed for shelter, sustenance, warmth, and transport. In 1609, two years after the English settled at Jamestown, Henry Hudson sailed up the river that bears his name and stopped at its headwaters near what is now Albany. A Dutch trading village grew up at the spot, attracting the first European immigrants to the area—most of them soldiers, traders, and adventurers sent by the Dutch West India Company to establish the fur trade.[6] In 1624 these settlers built a trading post at the headwaters of the Hudson and named it Fort Orange; after threats of Indian attacks in 1626 caused all but sixteen men to decamp for Manhattan, the fort languished as a mere outpost until a new wave of immigration in the 1630s and 1640s, when several hundred settlers arrived, sent by Kiliaen Van Rensselaer in hopes of establishing an agricultural colony. When the British took control of New Netherland in 1664, the boom in Dutch migration came to an end and a period of English-Dutch cultural accommodation began.[7]

Pinkster in colonial Albany initially was rooted in what could pass as a close replica of a northern European village. If societies need understandings of social relations to keep going, plausible stories of how the world works and where people fit into it, the story the Dutch told themselves with their built environment was that they had never left home. The town the early settlers carved out was a reassuring replica of a Netherlands trading village, replete with the beliefs and practices the Albany Dutch had brought with them from their native land; it would remain that way for a nearly a century. A map of 1696 gives a good impression of the traditional design of early Albany, showing a seven-sided town, surrounded by a three-quarter mile palisade wall, and with narrow lot frontages and houses set close together. Following medieval customs, the Dutch kept livestock that the town's herdsman drove outside the walls each day to a common pasturage.[8] The old guild system was continued, with the two classes of small and large burghers creating a hierarchical social order.[9] Albany also maintained close connections with the Netherlands via summer ships, and between 1651 and 1665 some forty-seven residents made return voyages.[10] Although by 1750, a few leading merchants had adopted English dress, language, and customs and nearly one-quarter of the inhabitants were of British descent, for a remarkably long time Albany retained its character as a Dutch community that looked and felt like a traditional low-country town of close-set brick buildings housing merchant families who as much as possible replicated a social and cultural order imported from the Old World. When the Swedish naturalist Peter Kalm traveled through the region in 1749 he registered this allegiance to the old ways, noting that the "inhabitants of Albany and its environs are almost all Dutchmen. They speak Dutch, have Dutch preachers . . . and their manners are like wise quite Dutch."[11]

This insularity marked the Dutch community in ways that help explain why Pinkster went almost unnoticed by outsiders until the eve of the Revolutionary War. As David Hackett's detailed study of early Albany's social organization and religious life has shown, the roster of merchant families in Albany remained stable for generations, with close family networks and widespread prosperity, particularly among elites. Between 1697 and 1757 even though Albany's population more than doubled, from 724 to about 1,800, most of the growth was internal, through the multiplication of Dutch families. The common pattern was for the children of the first immigrants to grow up, marry their neighbors, and raise large families. By the beginning of the eighteenth century, growing subsections of the town were bound together by blood ties. The Schuyler clan, for example, lived in nine separate households. The growth and intermarriage of these large families, their proximity of residence, and ongoing

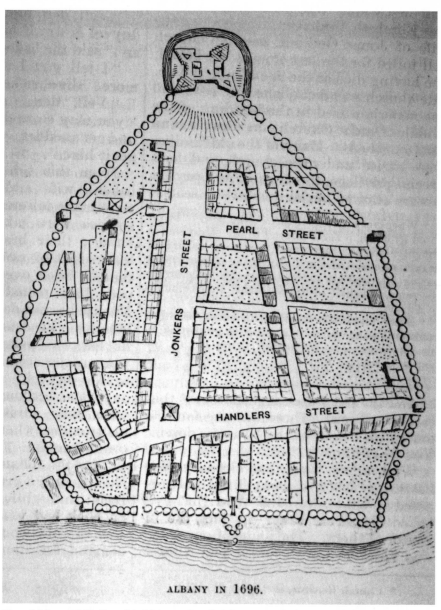

ALBANY IN 1696.

Map of Albany, 1696. From "A Glimpse of an Old Dutch Town," *Harper's New Monthly Magazine* 62 (March 1881). Courtesy of the Special Collections Department, University of Iowa Libraries, Iowa City, Iowa.

business relationships provided the basis for community stability as well as an unusually insular community.[12] As this account suggests, Dutch Pinkster was the ritual of an essentially closed society, shared only with members of the Dutch settlers' households.

The impetus for the expropriation of Pinkster by African Americans was established in the slaveholding practices of the Dutch. The Dutch colony ran on slave labor, and in the eighteenth century slaves, supplied to the Albany settlers by the Dutch West India Company, accounted for about 10 percent of Albany's population.[13] William Strickland in 1794 observed that most Dutch farmers owned twenty or thirty slaves and were completely dependent on them.[14] Slaves were acculturated culturally and linguistically, many speaking Dutch, not a pidgin or creole, as is evident from advertisements for the return of runaway slaves. Other signs of acculturation included the adoption of Dutch names, marriage and baptism within the Dutch Reformed church, and celebration of Dutch holidays, including Pinkster.[15] Despite this acculturation, Albany slaves were on the lowest ranks of the social hierarchy and were subject to separate laws and punishments designed chiefly to keep them close to their master's house and to prevent disorder.[16]

Although Pinkster in all of its later forms was secular, it was initially tied to religious practices. Most of early Albany's Dutch residents were members of the Dutch Reformed church, whose rituals and organization played a dominant role in the town's social and cultural life, as Hackett shows: the social hierarchy in Albany was exemplified in the seating within churches, which was elaborately arranged according to wealth (ownership of certain seats), position within the church government and the common council, generation, gender, and race; wealthy elders dominated the best seats, others were seated in lesser positions according to age and gender, and the gallery was reserved for slaves.[17] Liturgical time drew townspeople to religious services on Sundays, Wednesdays, and occasions of special religious significance, which made for a steady round of churchgoing. The liturgies recorded for 1665 show that the Reformed church congregation attended services on almost one out of four days a year.[18] Despite the relative austerity of the Reformed liturgy, there were Dutch celebrations associated with New Year's, Shrove Tuesday, Easter, Pentecost, and Saint Nicholas Day (December 6), as well as weddings and funerals. Two-day Easter (*Paas*) celebrations continued into the 1780s, and were reputedly popular among slaves; the festivities featured colored eggs and *Paas* cakes, a form of pancakes, cooked on one side and then flipped over, which were generally made by the slaves.[19]

This, then, is the context for Pinkster's first appearance in America: a stable, tightly knit settler community with strong ties to the homeland, hierarchically organized, slave-owning, and with a ritual year oriented around religious holidays. While linked to the religious occasion of Pentecost, Pinkster was also apparently a vernal festival of renewal that celebrated springtime; the "pinkster flower" (a blue iris) and the "pinkster blummachee" (an azalea) were often associated with the holiday, and Pinkster Hill, the spot in Albany where the celebration was held, was known for being covered with flowers in the springtime.[20]

Although we do not know much about Pentecost celebrations in New Netherland, the record is fuller for Europe. Pentecost, or Whitsun, was one of the most important holidays of the pre-Reformation liturgical year. In medieval Europe, it was the great occasion for summer *ludi,* with celebrations often linked via wooing games and courtship rituals to sex and procreation. Whitsun was also a traditional time of freedom from contractual manorial labor obligations; the plowmen of King's Ripton, Huntingdonshire, for instance, claimed that their right to immunity for eight days at Pentecost was a privilege dating from the twelfth century.[21] This customary association of Whitsun with cessation of labor was echoed in Albany in Pinkster's function as a completion date for work contracted in May or early spring, a fact that probably contributed to its festive spirit and ensured its popularity. In Europe, Whitsun was also linked to dramatic activities; in the Netherlands, a processional religious drama known as the *Ommegang* was commonly performed on the Sunday before Pentecost under sponsorship of the Guild of the Crossbowmen, who were possibly aided by the local Chambers of Rhetoric. The procession included companies of archers, drummers, and pipers, fifty-two craft guilds, and fourteen wagons with tableaux vivants depicting central events in the life of Jesus and the Virgin Mary, with important citizens and the clergy coming behind on foot. The procession, which took place in the morning, was followed by a mystery play in the afternoon.[22] In the seventeenth century in the Netherlands, secular festivities were also associated with Pinkster, including the choosing of a young girl as *Pinxterblom,* who was decked with flowers, silver, and gold in a May fertility ritual.

As with the case of Pentecost celebrations in Europe, in its context within the Dutch colony of Albany, Pinkster was part of a church-dominated ritual year and provided the chance for warm-weather recreation and festivity. It also offered a cultural link to the homeland in the form of an annual reminder of its traditions and served as a marker of a specifically Dutch identity distinct from that of other settlers, something that might have been especially valued in times of encroachment from New Englanders or other European settlers. Although Donna Merwick claims that Pinkster was celebrated by the Dutch in New York "to the fullest extent, even as the medieval church intended,"[23] there are so few references to Dutch Pinkster that it is hard to reconstruct a detailed picture of the festivities; this lack of references might be due to the Anglocentric nature of the historical sources, which ignored Dutch rituals, or to Dutch perceptions of the thoroughly ordinary and unremarkable nature of their celebration of the festival.[24] Whatever the reason for this neglect, if ideologies flourish to the degree that they go unnoticed, then we might well conclude that the ideological work of Dutch Pinkster was an unapplauded success.

African-American Pinkster

While Dutch Pinkster was the product of a hierarchical, stable, and self-contained culture that was a close copy of its European parent, African-American Pinkster was the product of the compound interculture seen by scholars like Paul Gilroy as characteristic of the societies of the Atlantic rim, an interculture that was shaped by the intersecting peoples, histories, and behaviors created by the imperial economies of the seventeenth century and beyond. Formed by the history of the slave trade linking Europe, Africa, and the Americas, the Atlantic rim, as Gilroy observes, is a transgeographical culture without national boundaries that lives on syncretism and lateral networks.[25] In this culture of permanent in-betweenness, identity is shaped by migratory forces and in reciprocal relations with other cultures.

The first known mention of the intercultural creation that was African-American Pinkster was in 1789, when Alexander Coventry remarked in his diary entry for Whitsunday that his slave Cuff was "keeping Pinkster, a festival or feast among the Dutch." Coventry added: "It is all frolicing to-day with the Dutch and the Negro. This is a holy day, Whitsunday, called among the Dutch 'Pinkster,' and they have eggs boiled in all sorts of colors, and eggs cooked in every way, and everybody must eat all the eggs he can. And the frolicing is still kept up among the young folks, so that little else is done to-day but eat eggs and be jolly." Coventry's diary two days later observed that people were "still frolicing Dutch Pinkster."[26] Coventry's wording suggests that Pinkster was still primarily a Dutch festival in 1789, but one in which blacks also participated. This picture is reinforced by William Dunlap, who noted in 1797 while traveling to Passaic Falls, New Jersey, that "the settlements along the river are Dutch, it is the holiday they call pinkster & every public house is crowded with merry makers"; Dunlap added that "blacks as well as their masters were frolicking."[27] Like Coventry, Dunlap seems to be describing a primarily Dutch festival that attracted black celebrants as well. A rare insider's glimpse of the participation of African-Americans in Pinkster comes from Sojourner Truth, who was born in Ulster County, New York, around 1797; a true citizen of the interculture, she was said to speak English with a Dutch accent. Her *Narrative* describes how—after she escaped in 1826 by walking away from the Dumont farm where she was enslaved and finding refuge with a sympathetic white family, the Van Wageners, who had known her from infancy—she longed to return to the Dumonts to join her former companions "enjoying their freedom for at least a little space, as well as their wonted convivialities" during the Pinkster holiday.[28] As she remembers it, the "frolicking" and "merry-making" noted by Coventry and Dunlap were an occasion for communal festivity and the reproduction of social bonds among cohorts as well as for welcome festivity, and her life with the Van Wageners seemed in contrast dull and uneventful.

Although the documentary record is silent on the question of how Pinkster became an African-American celebration, the gradual breakdown of the traditional Dutch community in Albany offers some clues as to how what began as selective black participation in a Dutch festival became a complete takeover of the celebration. Between 1749 and 1771 the town's population quadrupled from 10,634 to 42,706, with most of the new population being European-born but not Dutch.[29] As the Dutch monopoly on the fur trade was replaced by a competitive commercial economy, patriarchal rule by leading merchants who were also church elders yielded to a more heterogeneous popular politics. At the same time the Dutch Reformed church gave way to other Protestant congregations and religion became less a source of unity than of divisiveness. In the 1770s, facing the threat of British invasion, Dutch leaders—who, according to Hackett, increasingly spoke English and dressed in the English manner—joined with leaders from the growing Scotch-Irish and English communities, shifting the basis for local political unity from Dutch ethnicity to American citizenship.[30] The loss of Dutch hegemony was signaled in the early 1790s when a new capitol building was constructed at the head of State Street and the Dutch church was moved from the intersection of State and Market soon thereafter. By 1800, the Presbyterian church was the most influential in Albany.[31] In the wake of these changes, old rituals no doubt suffered. Certainly it is the case that new communal rituals were developing in Albany in the late eighteenth century, including a Fourth of July celebration, which seems to have been designed to cement the town's common American and Christian ties, while effacing English-Dutch divisions.[32] For a Dutch elite seeking to hold on to power within a newly heterogeneous community that it no longer unquestioningly dominated, festivities like the new Fourth of July celebration might well have come to seem more appropriate than the old-fashioned and ethnically marked Pinkster.

At the same time as Dutch hegemony was diminishing and the Dutch were moving toward assimilation with the English, the African-American presence increased. By 1790 Albany had the largest black population in the region: 3,929 slaves and 170 free blacks. This increased population brought fears of rebellion, echoing events that had occurred earlier in New York City.[33] In Albany in 1793, the same year the city passed a law forbidding blacks to be on the streets after 9:00 P.M., a fire burned down Leonard Gansevoort's stables and much of the city. Two African-American women, Bet and Dean, were accused of arson and another slave, named Pompey, was hanged for his alleged role.[34]

Dutch assimilation and a growing black presence in Albany perhaps set the stage for the transfer of Pinkster. However it occurred, by 1800, Pinkster was a predominantly black festivity, as documented in two contemporary accounts, both of them dating to 1803. One of the accounts is an anonymous letter published in the *Albany Centinel* and then reprinted in the New York City *Daily Advertiser* on June, 29, 1803. The other is a verse narrative called "Pinkster Ode," written under the pseudonym of "Absalom Aimwell," also published in Albany. Although offering contrasting accounts of Pinkster, the *Albany Centinel* letter and the "Pinkster Ode" not only reveal a good deal about white fascination with Pinkster but also offer glimpses of the disguise, disidentification, and other covert actions taken by African Americans in order to adopt someone else's ritual and make it their own, tailoring it to fit the needs of their specific social structures and economic interests. As a cultural performance, African-American Pinkster obtained its leverage from partial engagement with the dominant culture—inhabiting gaps and spaces in it, or making forays into it at strategic spots, as Stuart Hall claims subordinate cultures often do—from which it gained the foothold needed to launch itself.[35]

The *Albany Centinel* letter locates Pinkster's dissident effects in what the letter views as exotic and saturnalian rites. The letter begins by describing preparations during the week preceding Pinkster when the "negroes patrol the streets in the evening more than usual, and begin to practice upon the Guinea drum." They also, we are told, erect a tent encampment on Pinkster Hill, and build arbors made out of stakes set in the ground and woven through with branches to create "airy cottages" shielded from the sun. These "cottages" are arranged in a semi-circle so as to form an amphitheater in front of the royal arbor and are stocked with cakes, fruit, beer, and liquor. The writer mentions that these arbors signal springtime in contrast with "the forbidding nakedness of the surrounding hills." On the Monday after Pinkster, the crowd gathers on Pinkster Hill to await the arrival of King Charles, after his procession through town.[36] In a deft melding of ritual gift-demand with commercial rent-collecting, when he arrives on the hill Charles goes around to all the tents collecting rent or tribute of one shilling from every black man's tent and two shillings from every white's; the tent of anyone refusing to pay is torn down. The festival that follows includes African-derived music and dancing that the writer describes as lewd and uncouth. From the perspective of the letter-writer, the entire event is one in which ordinary standards of propriety give way to widespread licentiousness.

As its title suggests, "A Pinkster Ode for the Year 1803: Most Respectfully Dedicated to Carolus Africanus, Rex: thus Rendered in English: King Charles, Captain-General and Commander in Chief of the Pinkster Boys," reveals a rather different attitude toward Pinkster.[37] After four stanzas of homage to springtime, the poem turns to praise of "Charles the King," who "like Israel's mighty Saul, / Is nobly born, well made and tall." The poem draws attention to the gap between Charles's hereditary status and his present situation: "Tho' for a Sceptre he was born, / Tho' from his father's kingdom torn, / And doom'd to be a slave; still he / Retains his native majesty." The "Ode" goes on to describe the music associated with the festival (banjo, drum, pipe, tabor, flute, and fyfe) and to recall how the "Pinkster boys" march up the hill and assemble under a shady tree where they are led by Charles, who wears "Pinkster clothes" (which James Eights recollects some sixty years later as having consisted of a multicultural medley of British brigadier's scarlet jacket, tricornered cocked hat, and yellow buckskins)[38] in the "Guinea dance." Charles then addresses the "boys," in a speech that stresses respectability, good behavior, and forbearance, as well as liberty: "This day our Bosses make us free; / Now all the common on the hill; / Is ours, to do with what e'er we will . . . let's taste and see / How sweet a thing is liberty." Lest this yearning for liberty be taken too far, however, the writer makes sure Charles adds, "Let us with grateful hearts agree / not to abuse our Liberty . . . Yet nobly let us still endure / the ills and wrongs we cannot cure." Toward its end, the "Ode" devotes a series of stanzas to a world tour of different races and nations, including French, Germans, Scottish, Hawaiian islanders, Laplanders, and others, then returns to Pinkster Hill, which it constructs as a fantasy of inclusiveness: "Every colour revels there, / From ebon black to lilly fair." The "Ode" brings us back to the local context by mentioning the nearby "Africs' burying ground" with the tombstone: "Here lie Dinah, Sambo wife; / Sambo lub him, like he life; / Dinah die 'bout sik week ago; / Sambo massa tell he so." The final verses of the "Ode" describe the end of the day, as the sun sets and most people go home, while a few stay to revel all night.

Although they offer tantalizing glimpses of the Pinkster rituals, what the *Centinel* letter and the "Ode" are best at showing are the contradictory meanings Pinkster had for whites. Both texts presumably come from and represent white (and probably English- rather than Dutch-American) attitudes toward the ritual event, albeit from different angles. The tone of the *Albany Centinel* letter is censorious yet voyeuristic in its emphasis on the lewd, uncouth, and alien behavior of the celebrants. The "Ode," in contrast, manages to mingle abolitionist sentiments (for instance, its carpe diem line "Rise then, each son of Pinkster, rise / *Snatch fleeting pleasure* as it flies," which seems to suggest a call to arms in its ambiguous use of the word "rise") with grotesque racial stereotypes (the singing of the "the ebon lassie" and the oblique comparison of the participants to "*orang outings*"). Certainly the writer of the "Ode" is much more involved in and sympathetic to the festivities than is the anonymous letter-writer whose perspective is distanced, objectifying, and condescending. Yet for all its sympathies, like the *Centinel* letter the "Ode" shows considerable deficiencies of interpretation and is unable to imagine what Pinkster might have meant for its participants, focusing instead on its effect on white spectators.

The apparent inclination of many whites to see Pinkster as a "show" to be watched and assessed is not surprising given the growing co-optation of racial and ethnic performances by the commercial theater early in the century. It is suggestive that just a year later, in 1804, in New York City on Pinkster Monday there was a special theater performance that included a "pantomime interlude" called "PINXTER MONDAY or HARLEQUIN'S FROLICS," a performance that moved the outdoor ritual of Pinkster to the stage.[39] James Fenimore Cooper's novel *Satanstoe,* written in 1845, which includes a lengthy description of Albany's Pinkster apparently drawn from Cooper's memories of his childhood in Albany, also describes a theater performance featuring whites in blackface that took place soon after Pinkster. This linking of Pinkster with pantomime and blackface theater underscores, as Geneviève Fabre notes, the theme of blacks entertaining themselves and in so doing providing entertainment for whites, and also reveals one reason for white interest in Pinkster in the early nineteenth century.[40]

Another reason for white interest in African-American Pinkster, as the abolitionist sentiments of the "Ode" imply, had to do with growing opposition to slavery in the Northeast. The killing of Crispus Attucks in Boston in 1770, when British troops fired into a crowd of demonstrators, had helped link anti-British protests with antislavery protests. Soon afterward the first antislavery society in the United States was founded by Quakers (in 1775), and in 1787 Britain established the colony of Sierra Leone for blacks who had fought on the British side in the War of Independence. Perhaps more important for Pinkster, in 1799 the New York state legislature passed a law providing for the gradual elimination of slavery, although slavery would not be banned outright in New York until 1827. At a time when slavery was more and more debated, Pinkster could hardly have failed to attract attention for its at least momentary staging of black freedom.[41]

While white attitudes can be reconstructed in some detail from the *Albany Centinel* letter and the "Ode," we have few clues as to what Pinkster meant to its participants. Accounts by whites provide only a limited scope for conjecture about this, even in the case of the "Ode," whose author is sympathetic in a way that perhaps suggests an insider's perspective.[42] Barring the unlikely discovery of participants' accounts of Pinkster, we can only hazard guesses, but we can assume that Pinkster's meanings for blacks engaged in some way with the cultural history of New York's African Americans, their current social relations, and their personal identities. Like coronation festivities, Pinkster was no doubt useful in community building and was an event at which, as Melvin Wade has said of coronation festivities, "black communities celebrated their existence as social systems."[43] Certainly a considerable amount of structured group effort was expended during Pinkster, in setting up Pinkster Hill for the festivities and in organizing the performance events. In addition to what the "Ode" and the *Albany Centinel* letter reveal about the organizational efforts for Albany's Pinkster, other accounts show that slaves on Long Island came to New York City to sell sassafras, roots, oysters, and clams in order to raise money for Pinkster festivities; such activities suggest a level of commitment to the holiday that argues for its importance for participants.[44] The choosing and honoring of a "king" that is a feature of the Albany procession and the collecting of tribute from participants and nonparticipant householders similarly signal the significance of the festival for blacks' social organization, since both provide ways of acquiring real and symbolic capital.

Pinkster's appeal for black participants must also have been tied to its conscious reinvention of African tradition. Cooper's *Satanstoe* describes this privileging of Africanness, though without understanding its cultural import, in its remark that for American-born blacks, the African-born are "ambassadors from the land of their ancestors" who bring with them old customs.[45] Cooper's recognition of the importance of Africa for blacks reflects the way that in postrevolutionary America, as Fabre observes, "black ceremonial life constructed an image of Africa as the homeland and a land of freedom, despite all historical claims to the contrary."[46] By privileging Africanness, Pinkster made visible and also legitimated the black presence in white America, providing a link to an honored African past. But emphasizing African heritage ran some real risks, given its implicit threat to the legitimacy of white rule and white cultural dominance.

This threat is most apparent in Pinkster's bold invasion of public space. Although the social space allotted for black festive culture in northeastern America was often marginal—fields, open fields near a spreading tree, burying grounds, or a farm—Albany's Pinkster was a far more centrally located event.[47] First in the procession through town (up State Street to Bleecker Hill), then on the prominent and symbolically rich site of Pinkster Hill, and finally in the door-to-door demand for tribute that marked the end of the festivities, Pinkster aggressively moved into the white domain, bringing it under black control for the duration of the festival.[48] For a short time—as Charles lorded it over Pinkster Hill—Pinkster made it possible to imagine an alternate social order, one in which the dispossessed took charge while those who normally wielded power were reduced to lurking indoors, dreading the "horrid noise" that would force them to pay up. The shantytown of tents and wooden arbors on Pinkster Hill represented a takeover of white public space, converting it into a place where otherwise forbidden social mingling and licentiousness could occur.

Pinkster Hill was full of connotations that would have intensified the meanings of the week's festivities. It was a vernal spot, where people went to gather flowers; it was Albany's public forum, the location of the Old Capitol; and it was a place of punishments and executions. On Pinkster Hill, the world of nature met civic order, and punishment and repression lurked just beneath the surface, offering a reminder of the power of whites that no amount of inversionary symbolism could deny. For whites, the hill's association with punitive forces might have been reassuring, with its suggestion that black power could easily be controlled. For blacks, however, the hill was perhaps the most loaded place on which to stage a symbolic rebellion: by building arbors where gallows were raised, celebrants could defiantly yet covertly challenge white rule.

Pinkster Hill's nearness to two other sites—the military graveyard and an old black cemetery—also probably deepened the festival's meanings, as Fabre notes. While obviously serving as reminders of the fleeting nature of life and of the loss of past generations, the cemeteries concretized the pull between America and Africa. Fabre argues that the military graveyard recalled blacks' heroic participation in the project of nation-building; if that was the case, as seems plausible, the military graveyard might also have served as a sign of a new "American" identity forged for blacks as well as whites by the Revolutionary War. In contrast, the black cemetery might well have been, as Fabre suggests, a reminder of blacks' separate status and of their links to Africa, not America (African origins were often noted on the grave epitaphs);[49] the black graveyard might also have recalled oppression, suffering, and loss in the New World, as the lines from "Dinah's tombstone" quoted in the "Ode" suggest. As with Pinkster's link to punishments, the two graveyards probably resonated differently for blacks and whites, in ways that allowed oppositional meanings to co-exist within the performance.

Finally, Pinkster's proximity to markers of Albany's Dutch roots and to the power-center of the town also must have shaped its meanings. Pinkster Hill stood near the intersection of Market and State streets—the location of the Dutch Reformed church and the historic center of the town closely identified with former Dutch dominance.[50] As the participants in Pinkster moved into and took over this central location, they momentarily displaced the status quo from its historic hub of dominance in a mock seizure of civic control. With Charles installed as king of the festival and, by virtue of geographic location, de facto city leader, the revelers at Pinkster enjoyed temporary symbolic co-optation of the town's structures of rules. It is hard to envision a more visible demonstration of the rebellious threat at the heart of Pinkster than this seizure of the town's center.

Why, then, would Albany's authorities have allowed Pinkster to invade that charged site? Part of the answer derives from the power of custom, a power that was conferred on the African-American celebrants of Pinkster when they appropriated the festival from the Dutch. Because Pinkster had long been celebrated on the hill, even apparently from the days when the festival was a Dutch holiday and people went to the hill to gather flowers, the potential meanings of black usurpation were disguised under customary behavior. In other words, African-American Pinkster wasn't something new, it was instead a version of something familiar, and that very familiarity might have covered up the degree to which the celebration had been reshaped. The link to the town's Dutch past might have contributed to tolerance of the festivities by Albany's increasingly non-Dutch population in another way as well, by styling those festivities as remnants of the customs of a slightly exotic but now displaced settler culture. It seems plausible that the Dutchness of Pinkster, which commentators remarked on long after the ritual had been taken over by African Americans, was a contributing factor in white tolerance of the black ceremonial in the late eighteenth and early nineteenth centuries, when Albany's Dutch hegemony was fading away.

When we turn from the location of Pinkster to its participants we can see similar tactics of disguise and conflation of cultural meanings that opened the performance to multiple readings depending on the observer's social positioning. The ceremony's star, King Charles, was, according to accounts, of large stature ("well made and tall," the "Ode" claims) and of African royal birth (a Guinea man from Angola and "nobly born" according to the "Ode"). James Eights, a white doctor reminiscing about events he had seen in his youth at the end of the eighteenth century, describes "Charley of the Pinkster Hill" as having been purchased by "one of the most ancient and respectable merchant princes of the olden time" (Volckert P. Douw, of Wolvenhoeck, one of Albany's most prominent citizens) and as being "tall, thin and athletic; and although the frost of nearly seventy years had settled on his brow, its chilling influence had not yet extended to his bosom."[51] As this description suggests, Charles seemingly spoke to both whites and blacks alike. Commenting on his popularity, Fabre claims that he "commanded respect, wielded authority, and acted as mediator between two racial worlds"; but Shane White argues that white interest in Charles was tinged with discomfort at the idea of African Americans as leaders.[52] For blacks, Charles perhaps embodied all the things they were denied—freedom, power, and authority; for whites, he modeled the attributes of the ideal slave—strength, respect, docility, and source of condescending amusement. This combination of attributes is neatly captured in a recollection published in *Harper's New Monthly Magazine* in 1856–57 that describes how the powerful but grandfatherly King Charles put the author, when he was a boy, on his shoulders and jumped over a five-foot-high bar before getting "gloriously drunk" on free drinks shortly thereafter.[53] Charles seems to have been successful in the Pinkster role, which he apparently kept for many years, precisely because—whether consciously or not—he was adept at combining and manipulating cultural symbols into shapes that could be interpreted to please a wide range of people black and white. Charles, so accounts suggest, was not just a master of ceremonies, but a master of cultural semiotics as well.

Charles also conflated racial and national identities by deftly manipulating what Gilroy, speaking about the "compound culture" of black settler communities, has described as "wilfully damaged signs."[54] Charles's very identity as Pinkster king turned on just such damaged signs: he was an African-born, Dutch-speaking black, performing in a Dutch holiday, and wearing a British brigadier's scarlet jacket, a tricorn hat, and yellow buckskins.[55] Everything

King Charles Racing on Ice. From "A Glimpse of an Old Dutch Town," *Harper's New Monthly Magazine* 62 (March 1881). Courtesy of the Special Collections Department, University of Iowa Libraries, Iowa City, Iowa.

here is cunningly askew, with no sign unambiguously intact. While some ob- servers might be inclined to view this twisting of markers of identity as hap- penstance, Gilroy's emphasis on purposefulness urges us to consider the possi- bility that at least some degree of intentionality was at work. Charles's brigadier's jacket, in particular, seems an inspired appropriation, at one and the same time expressing patriotism (look what we Americans did to those British) and sending a warning (watch out for slaves who may become mas- ters). What could be a better double-sided message about the changeability of fortunes in ongoing struggles of dominance and subordination?

Gilroy sees the politics of black "compound culture" as "low frequency" yet utopian, with an impulse toward transfiguration. That this utopian im- pulse could be recognized by outsiders, even if for self-serving ends, is made clear in Cooper's account of Pinkster in *Satanstoe.* Cooper moves the festival, which he calls "the great Saturnalia of the New York blacks," to New York City and sets it in 1757, but his description is probably based on recollections of his childhood in Albany, where he was born in 1789.[56] Cooper's description is striking in a number of ways, particularly for its reading of Pinkster within regional race relations. The Pinkster segment begins as Corny (Cooper's protagonist) goes with his friends Jason and Dirck to Pinkster field "which was now quite full of people, as well as of animation." Jason, who has never seen Pinkster before, since he comes from Connecticut where the blacks are "ground down in the Puritan mill," is "confounded with the noises, dances, music, and games" of nine-tenths of the city's blacks and others from forty miles away "collected in the thousands in those fields."

As the account continues, Pinkster's meaning for blacks and whites is explored by Cooper. For blacks, in Cooper's narrative, the festival offers a chance to display their traditions for others as well as for themselves, and in so doing to renew their identities as African. As for whites, we are told that hundreds of them are there as "amused spectators," including children come to see their nurses' entertainments and adolescent white girls under the care of old black women, one of whom "jabbered away, explaining the meaning of the different ceremonies of her race, to a cluster of very interested listeners." Corny and his friends next stop to watch a "party of native Africans" for whom the festivities "seemed to have revived their early associations [i.e., memories of Africa] and they were carried away with their own representation of semi-savage sports." Cooper's novel imagines that American-born blacks were mesmerized by this vision of their African heritage, so much that they "gazed at this group with intense interest, regarding them as so many ambassadors from the land of their ancestors, to enlighten them in usages, and superstitious lore, that were more peculiarly suited to their race" and even tried to imitate the African-born. In Cooper's account, Pinkster offers whites a similar chance for self-definition. One possibility is modeled by Jason, who unlike Corny and the other New York whites, "often expressed his disgust, at the amusements and antics of the negroes, declaring they were unbecoming human beings." As Jason's reaction reveals, for Corny (and presumably Cooper), appreciation of Pinkster represents white New York sophistication and a nonpuritanical attitude toward pleasure. It also symbolizes a utopian vision of race relations, albeit one skewed by white complacency, as is evident when Corny lectures Jason on the New York system of slavery, which he claims treats "both races as parts of a common family." Like the author of the "Ode," Cooper stresses Pinkster's ability to bring together all races and classes, but in Cooper's hands this cohesive quality becomes a sign of New York superiority, as does the ability to enjoy Pinkster.[57] Jason, the New Englander, is shocked and disgusted by Pinkster, while the New Yorkers are styled as tolerant sophisticates; Pinkster thus becomes a way of defining white regional identity and solidifying New York's self-image of liberalism, in opposition to straight-laced New Englanders. In Cooper's hands, Pinkster becomes not just a fantasy of race relations ("both races as parts of a common family") but also a defense of regional identity.

Cooper's account—like the "Ode" before it—also suggests that the exotic otherness of Pinkster was part of what fascinated white commentators. The "antic" dancing, Guinea drum, African rituals, and the whole feel of the event including its tone of sexual freedom attract white spectators in Cooper's novel and presumably in real life, if the sentiments of the *Albany Centinel* letter can be assumed to represent more than just one person's view. In this regard it is no accident that Cooper sets his scene of flirtation among young whites at the site of Pinkster. *Satantoe's* image of blacks "collected in thousands in those fields, beating banjoes, singing African songs, drinking and most of all laughing, in a way that seemed to set their very heart rattling within their ribs" suggests that Fabre is right in arguing that Pinkster served as a place where whites could experience pleasures their own cultural code would not allow them to act out.[58]

But whose traditions, whose past, did Pinkster enact? An earlier generation of scholarship would have been likely to frame a response to that question in two diametrically opposed ways. One response would have argued that African traditions had been thoroughly wiped out in America by lengthy captivity in Africa, the middle passage, and the plantation system in the New World. From this perspective, a performance like Pinkster could only be seen as an imitation—often amusing, occasionally threatening—of customs that had European origins in such festivities as Lords of Misrule and had been shaped by European Americans. This assumption of European origins underwrote the view of early chroniclers like Jane Shelton, who asserted that in African-American ceremonies like Pinkster: "The white customs were carefully followed."[59] (The obvious problem with this interpretation is that it relegates participants in these festivities to the role of passive subjects almost completely taken over by a dominating white culture to which they can offer little resistance.) The second response, offered by advocates of cultural nationalism, would have argued that far from being erased, preservation of African traditions had been an important part of the survival mechanisms of slaves in the Americas and that New World coronation festivities like Pinkster clearly had African roots.[60] For these scholars black festivals were not imitations of white rituals, but rather celebrations of black self-awareness that used African cultural forms, especially songs, dances, musical instruments, and games that derived from Africa.[61]

More recent scholarship has adopted a middle position between these extremes, emphasizing the cultural hybridity of festivities like Pinkster. In a study characteristic of this approach, Sam Kinser has argued that syncretic processes began as soon as slaves from different African groups were thrown together on slave ships, resulting not in an erasure but rather a blending of their original cultural practices.[62] Most of the slaves brought to northeastern America were from the western coast of Africa, especially Guinea, with the West Indies forming a "distributing point" for slaves for Americas.[63] Such regional localization, combined with the compression effect of channeling slaves through the West

Indies, encouraged the blending of western African cultural traditions that were dispersed throughout the African diaspora in the Americas. Since rituals similar to Pinkster appeared among blacks throughout the New World, especially in Cuba, Louisiana, Brazil, Peru, and the Virgin Islands,[64] in sites subjected to very different kinds of colonization, it seems plausible that common West African traditions shaped them all. In Pernambuco, Brazil, in 1706, for instance, the coronation of a black king highlighted the popular plays known as *Congos*. Many Brazilian blacks also celebrated Twelfth Night (Kings Day) with a festival called *Rei do Congo* in which they elected and crowned a king and queen of the Congo (unlike the northeastern coronation festivals, the southern versions featured queens as well as kings).[65] And as early as the sixteenth century the nearly ten thousand blacks in Mexico were organizing themselves into *cofradías*—sometimes described as "nations"—mutual aid societies that fostered self-help and sponsored performances, including coronation rituals.[66]

Because the height of Pinkster and other coronation festivals in northeastern America coincided with the peak years of the northern slave trade, and since a number of the men chosen as kings and governors at these ceremonies had African names and were probably African-born and of royal lineage (these included King Pompey of Lynn, Massachusetts; governors Quash Freeman and Tobiah of Derby, Connecticut; governor Jubal Weston of Seymour, Connecticut; and governors Cuff and Quaw of Hartford), a fairly direct attachment to a not-so-distant African past seems to have been an important part of the rituals.[67] One chronicler captures the linguistic as well as the cultural connection with Africa when he remarks that at the Newport festivals "all the various languages of Africa, mixed with broken and ludicrous English, filled the air accompanied with the music of the fiddle, tambourine, the banjo, drum, etc."[68] Coronation festivals also seem to have lasted longest where the black population was densest and where contact with the West Indies was the most direct; in northern America, that meant in New Haven and in Rhode Island.[69] In light of this evidence, it appears likely that coronation festivals functioned on one level to reinstate patterns of African authority in America, an authority that was patriarchal and regnal. As Wade has observed, the festivals stressed "Africa as homeland, African ancestors as authority figures, and patriarchy as social organization," a pattern echoed by Albany's Pinkster.[70]

But while Pinkster and other coronation festivals show links to Africa, they also conform to European traditions, especially to patterns of ritual inversion well known in premodern Europe. Medieval Whitsun festivities contained a number of elements that resembled those of Pinkster as celebrated by African Americans. At Whitsun, it was a common custom to go into the countryside before sunrise and return with flowers and greenery to deck streets and houses. May ales or May games followed in the next two months, celebrations dedicated to communal life, summer, and contributing to parish funds.[71] There is evidence of actual coronations or knightings at royal Whitsun celebrations, which might have led to, or at least prefigured, the "king games" or elections of mock kings that were a feature of popular festivity in the later Middle Ages.[72] In those popular festivities, mock kings were chosen to rule over the ceremonies in a carnivalesque ritual of inversion that could lead to real disruption, as apparently happened among the apprentices of London in 1400 who had gathered to elect kings among themselves and ended up rioting.[73] A tradition of largesse was also associated with Whitsun celebrations, as indeed with other folk performances. Great lords were expected to open their households to minstrels and folk performers and to reward them with payments of money or with food and drink; similar largesse was anticipated for parish games such as May Ales, with cash donations demanded by performers.[74] While it is unlikely that a direct link connected these medieval performance features to Pinkster, they might have provided a set of memories within which Pinkster could be understood by European-descended whites, memories that would normalize Pinkster as a "traditional" form of festive release and thus defuse its threat.

This normalizing would have been welcome given that one of the social functions of Pinkster and related festivals was to license misrule by giving free play to the carnivalesque themes of plenty and excess, of carnality and sexuality, and of the world-turned-upside down or, if not inverted then at least made ambiguous.[75] Besides authorizing mechanisms for self-rule through the election of a king or governor in an overt usurpation of white right-to-rule, these festivals allowed African Americans to participate in activities otherwise off-limits to them, such as the right to congregate in large groups, parade through the streets, fire guns and wear uniforms, drink, and escape labor. These were the same activities that as early as 1680 various slave statutes sought to prevent: e.g., running away, drunkenness, theft, riot, property destruction, assaults on whites, and disturbing the peace (particularly through nighttime street disorders).[76] In response to fears of uprisings, curfews were imposed on blacks, Indians, and mulattos throughout northeastern America, and members of these groups were also barred from joining the militia, a fact that adds a rebellious edge to the wearing of military uniforms and the firing of salutes in African-American festivities. Indeed, the point was not lost on whites, who at times tried to rein in these dissident practices with their threats of actual revolt; the Salem Town Records of May 16, 1768, for instance, tried to prevent slaves on election day "from wearing swords, beating drums, and making use of powder."[77] As was the case with medieval European status-reversal festivities, those of the New World were often associated with fear of rebellions and threats to public order.

Pinkster and other African-American festivals attracted a diverse mix of people, including whites, as *Satanstoe* and the two accounts from 1803 show, because they provided opportunities for white participation in carnivalesque excess while also affirming their sense of moral and cultural superiority. The latter can be seen in references such as those found in the *Albany Centinel* letter to the fantastic clothing worn by the African Americans and their "uncouth" and "indecent" behavior that included boisterous shouting, laughing, singing, and feasting, which often, we are told, ended in drunkenness. The former can be seen in 1768, when the Hartford militia, apparently imitating the lavish costumes of black election parades, wore fantastic dress while escorting the white governor in a procession through town, and in 1859, when Newport, Rhode Island, hosted a parade of "Antiques and Horribles," a carnivalesque procession that included blackface marchers.[78] As these occasions suggest, whites seem to have been inspired to adopt for themselves the revels they had watched and mingled in at black festivities. White cooptation was efficacious because by inscribing within itself a potential threat—a threat its own internal contradictions had produced—the dominant ideology was able to further its own reproduction.

Both blacks and whites might have had reason to imagine that the ritual of Pinkster worked to their advantage. Whites could interpret the festivities as a sign of indulgence toward slaves in the form of granting them a holiday treat, thus affirming white slaveholders' and landowners' sense of their own generosity, or as a cheap and effective way of appeasing their slave and free workers, perhaps defusing built-up tensions created by the slave-owning system. If Pinkster kings could be seen by whites as agents of white dominance, blacks could view them as forms of black social control that operated relatively autonomously, given the constricted circumstances—a form of self-government that helped develop patterns of African-American leadership and so contributed to the early organization of black civic life.[79]

Whatever the appeal of Albany's Pinkster, and despite its success at displacing, refashioning, and transferring a Dutch ritual into the black domain, it did not survive for long into the nineteenth century. Internal forces were one reason for its waning. As White notes, antiquarian accounts suggest that Pinkster in Albany became increasingly commercialized and began to feature exhibitions of wild animals (including a Bengal tiger), rope dancing, circus riding, and clown-play.[80] As a result, Pinkster began to resemble other forms of commercialized popular entertainment, thus losing some of its old distinctiveness. These internal changes were matched by external realignments of sentiment that made Pinkster less popular as economic expansion was accompanied by the growth of mechanic and Methodist beliefs among laborers, less affluent journeymen, and shopkeepers, beliefs that Hackett argues emphasized "usefulness" and productivity, as well as self-sufficiency and respectability.[81] These new creeds had little place for the antiwork ethos and irreverent spirit of Pinkster. Eights's reminiscences suggest that after the third day of the celebration, when "the sable throng" departed, Pinkster was entirely left to "the free enjoyment of the humbler classes," at which point the festival dissolved into drunkenness, "wrangling discord," and fistfights that leave "bruised eyes, and bloody noses unnumerated."[82] Such antics probably did not accord very well with the new orientation toward a work ethic and civic sobriety.

Anti-Pinskter feelings came to a climax in 1811 when the Albany Common Council passed an ordinance banning erection of booths, tents, or stalls within the city limits for the purpose of selling food or alcohol; gathering together in large groups for gambling or dancing; and marching or parading during the "days commonly called pinxter." As White notes, this seems less like hostility to African Americans than antipathy toward an earlier popular culture that was fast losing its appeal.[83] But the language of the ordinance suggests a distaste for the riotousness Eights describes. It is probably not just a coincidence that in 1813 Albany's elite church members (English and Dutch Calvinists) supported the passage of a state "Act for Suppressing Immorality," and formed committees to watch out on the Sabbath for immoral behavior, especially among young men.[84]

African-American attitudes toward festivities like Pinkster were also changing. In 1828, for example, *Freedom's Journal* criticized African-American parading in Brooklyn that the writer saw as "foolish exhibitions of ourselves," as well as a waste of money in the buying of cast-off garments of the military so the marchers could dress up as generals, marshals, and admirals.[85] When other venues were found for the development of African-American social and political power, festivities like Pinkster lost their appeal. Although their legacy survived in a few other places—rural Mississippi in the 1860s; the Georgia Sea Islands and Rockford, Illinois, in the 1930s; and Harlem in the 1970s, where blacks elected "mayors" as part of the surviving tradition of dealing with social and political obstacles—for the most part coronation festivities no longer served a purpose.[86] As "respectable" blacks and whites began to shun Pinkster, its rituals were absorbed by the minstrel shows that were emerging as popular cultural forms. Albany's festival was last held in 1822, according to one account, and Charles died two years later.[87] For the next century and a half, after its performative impulses had been relocated in the commercial theater, Pinkster would survive only as a nostalgic memory, a recollection of quaint folkways that had been part of Albany's early history.

Rewriting the Past: Albany's Tulip Fest

Although long gone as an African-American ritual, Pinkster has been reinvented in Albany as the Albany Tulip Fest, an annual event held in May on Mother's Day weekend. The two-day festival is billed as a celebration of springtime and of Albany's Dutch heritage; it features reenactments of Old World traditions like scrubbing the streets, a tulip flower show, a *Kinderkermis* (a children's street fair) and Pinksterfest, which is now described as a celebration of spring. Instituted after World War II, the Tulip Fest is sponsored by the City of Albany's Urban Cultural Park Program Department, with backing from various corporate sponsors. The main thrust of the Tulip Fest is to link civic pride, ethnic heritage, and tourism in one attractive package. Whether deliberately or by accident, in the process it eliminates all traces of the disorderly African-American celebration of Pinkster, jumping over those decades of the ritual's life and recapturing an imagined Dutch ancestor.

The festival's deliberate linking to the city's Dutch origins is signaled in the opening ceremonies during which an official proclamation is read aloud by the mayor preceding a symbolic scrubbing of State Street; the scrubbing is billed as the historical reenactment of a Dutch tradition and features the Dutch Settlers' Society. The street scrubbing is followed by the Tulip Luncheon, a farewell event for the former year's queen and court. The new Tulip queen is crowned the next day in Washington Park after a procession through the park and is then honored with a receiving line and punch-and-cookies reception. On Saturday evening there is a Royal Tulip Ball over which the queen and her court reign.

Modern Pinksterfest, which reproduces traces of the ceremonial and economic activities of African-American Pinkster, includes craft and food vendors, bands and other entertainment and is held on Saturday and Sunday in Washington Park; there is also a bicycle race, a fair for children, and other family-oriented entertainments. In 1996, according to publicity information from the Albany Urban Cultural Park Visitors Center, there were ninety-five craft exhibitors, forty food vendors, and forty information booths for nonprofit groups, with more than two hundred volunteers staffing the event. In 2002, historical reenactments were on the program, when the Center for Heritage Education and Tourism created a War of Independence encampment as one of the events of the Tulip Fest. The encampment featured costumed performers in scenes of camp life, home life, and on the battlefield, thus managing to link Albany's local history with a story celebrating American national progress.

The Tulip Fest is at its most successful as a recuperation of the past in its echoing of the vernal aspect of early Pinkster. Even though the festival is organized around the tulip—nowadays a more readily recognizable link to Dutchness than the "pinkster blummachee"—it still captures Pinkster's traditional link with flowers and greenery. The festival is timed so that the masses of tulips planted in Washington Park, the site of the festival, are in bloom. Tulips are, indeed, at the heart of the festival, which had its origins in an editorial that ran in May 1949 in the Albany *Knickerbocker News* proposing that the tulip be made Albany's official flower and that an annual tulip festival be held each spring in Washington Park. This focus on the vernal aspect of Pinkster, while echoing one of the festival's earlier emphases, also represents a retreat into an unobjectionable and universalized heritage in which inoffensive nature stands in for a depiction of ethnic and racial histories that would inevitably be more contentious.

Despite this retreat into the safe haven of a springtime celebration of nature as culture, the dissident past has not been entirely erased from the present-day festival. Surprisingly, the Tulip Fest remains a coronation ritual, although of a markedly different kind than the one that featured King Charles. In their current guise, the coronation ceremonies mingle debutante party with beauty contest; but vestiges of African-American Pinkster can still be glimpsed. The first year of the Tulip Fest featured a king and queen, but the king was dropped within three years for lack of interest. Today's coronation festival is centered entirely on women and includes a queen and her court—five young women from Albany County between the ages of seventeen and twenty-one. Much of the coronation ceremony revolves around the judging, parading, crowning, and fêting of the queen and her attendants. Pinkster's homage to patriarchy's prized attributes of hierarchy, deference, and physical power have thus been replaced by a celebration of competitive female beauty, perhaps a more relevant source of cultural reproduction for the twenty-first century.

Despite its any-city outdoor-festival feel, the Tulip Fest also maintains some distinctively local links, particularly through its attempt to emphasize the city's Dutch heritage. In addition to the street-sweeping ritual, "Dutchness" is emphasized in the choice of names for the events—Pinksterfest, *Kinderkermis*—as well as in such additional entertainments as a tour of the historic house of Abraham Ten Broeck, an organized walking tour through an old Dutch neighborhood, and a "Dutch heritage worship with old Dutch customs" held at the First Dutch Church; the church service is followed by a reception featuring Dutch pastries. The festival also includes men and women in Dutch costume, some of whom perform traditional dances.

The drastic reshaping of Pinkster in its current incarnation, which involves a bypassing of its earlier ritual significance in order to recuperate what is seen as Albany's "Dutch heritage" as conveyed through the symbol of the tulip, demonstrates not just the infinite malleability of history and the selective work of cultural memory, but also the strong appeal of a sterilized version of the past. Gone is the transgressive license of African-American Pinkster; gone, too, the pious family rituals of Dutch Pentecost, neither of which, so it seems, captured quite the image of Albany and its past that the Tulip Fest's organizers wished to project. Despite this refusal to engage with the actual past, Pinkster's reshaping can nonetheless be seen as an attempt to understand the past and to make it relevant to present needs. As Richard Schechner has noted, "restored behavior" of the sort found in the Tulip Fest can offer individuals and groups the chance to become not just what they once were but—something better—what they wish they had been.[88] The Tulip Fest is appealing because it offers the chance to shape the world into what participants would like it to be, against the world as it was and is. If the civic boosterism and whitewashing of Pinkster seem dubious representations of history, they nevertheless speak to desires to find a usable past, a past that suits the needs of the present. Yet despite the boosterish aspect of the Tulip Fest and its obvious fabrication by city leaders, the fest—with its queen instead of king, springtime holiday air, and opportunity for mingling of people from all walks of life—does indeed echo the past, in ways that do not completely obliterate earlier Pinksters. If the desire for a nostalgic and well-scrubbed past is evident in Albany's recreated Pinkster, so too are the traces of an actual history.

Outside of Albany, attempts have been made to revive a specifically African-American Pinkster, but without much success in reclaiming its dissident force. One of these is sponsored by the nonprofit Historic Hudson Valley, which in a professed effort to call attention to the history of northern slavery re-creates Pinkster at Philipsburg Manor, a restored three-hundred-year-old Dutch farm where twenty-three slaves lived and worked until state law banned slavery in 1790.[89] The contemporary festival incorporates Dutch children's games like ninepins and stilts, baked goods, and country dancing, and blends with them African traditions of storytelling, drumming, dancing, and selection of a Pinkster king. Despite its emphasis on resurrecting African-American traditions, the Philipsburg festival does little to capture the oppositional aspects of early African-American Pinkster, but indeed how could it? Much like Albany's Tulip Fest, the Philipsburg festival perhaps inevitably conveys a sanitized and idealized version of the past that in this case stresses racial harmony and the equitable sharing of cultural traditions.

What can also not be re-created in the modern version of Pinkster are the festival's medieval European roots. For the current manifestation of Pinkster in Albany's Tulip Fest, the only past associated with the festival is that of a vaguely sketched notion of colonial Dutchness. But during the years of its origins and transfer to African Americans, Pinkster's links to medieval performance traditions served a much more important function as a set of memories within which the celebration could be understood and hence allowed to exist. When Pinkster was transformed from a decorous Dutch holiday into a boisterous celebration of African-American power, a cultural memory of the traditional inversionary and carnivalesque festivities of the disenfranchised was available to ease the way for the weeklong misrule of Pinkster. Understood by the Dutch and other European colonists as just another form of popular festivity, African-American Pinkster flourished within what was perceived as an allowable time for activities that on another occasion might have seemed undesirable if not downright dangerous. The waning of Pinkster, while attributable to a variety of more direct factors, might also have owed something to the fading memories of that model of traditional medieval misrule. When revived in the twentieth century, Pinkster was shorn of much of its earlier history, including its medieval European and African hybridity, and was instead fashioned into a vaguely historicized event that was connected to an indeterminate Dutch past defined primarily by quaint folkloric practices and colorful costumes and represented via one iconic specimen of the natural world—the tulip. Tulip Fest is a reminder of the power of performative historiography to write the history it wants to write, even if that rewriting cannot entirely erase the cultural residue of an at least partially determining past that continues to have an impact on the present.

CHAPTER 3

Philadelphia's Mummers and the Anglo-Saxon Revival

On January 3, 1876, the *Philadelphia Public Ledger* reported that the "Fantasticals or 'Shooters' were out in force during the whole day, and caused much boisterous amusement. Indians and squaws, princes and princesses, clowns, columbines and harlequins, negroes of the minstrel-hall type, Chinese and burlesque Dutchmen, bears, apes, and other animals promenaded the streets." What the *Public Ledger* described was a holiday performance in which gangs of young men disguised themselves in "fantastic" costumes, often also blackening or masking their faces, and paraded through the streets stopping at taverns and demanding free drinks, firing guns, playing raucous music on homemade instruments, and boisterously—sometimes violently—celebrating the New Year. In existence at least since the early 1800s, this disruptive and impromptu street theater would by the start of the twentieth century be transformed into the highly organized and city-sanctioned Mummers' Parade performed today.

This transformation offers a lesson in the power of semantics and in the ways in which print culture can influence performance. In the late nineteenth century, as newspaper accounts co-opted holiday revels for the pleasure of readers, commentators began to describe Philadelphia's New Year's street maskers—once called *belsnickles,* callithumpians, fantasticals, or shooters—as mummers. This semantic shift points to a cultural change not just in the nature of the performances but also, and more important, in public perceptions of them. As Philadelphia's "shooters" were turned into "mummers," a word that deliberately recalls connections with the real and imagined festive rituals of medieval England, their boisterous holiday performances were conscripted by a loose alliance of forces—including city government, commercial interests, and reformers seeking to better the lot of immigrants by reviving traditional arts and crafts—into the service of assimilation to a nationalism that was increasingly defined as Anglo-Saxon. It is no coincidence that this semantic shift occurred during the years of the great wave of immigration to the United States from eastern and southern Europe that created an anxious search for ways of "Americanizing" new immigrants whose cultural traditions were not those of Protestant northern Europe.

Philadelphia's New Year's parades make evident some of the conflicts that were part of the shaping of an "American" national identity in the late nineteenth century, struggles that turned on the competing claims of different racial, ethnic, and class groups to define "America" and that involved the revival of an idealized Anglo-Saxon past. The mummers so vividly described by the *Public Ledger* offer a prime example of invention of the self through the taking on of the identities of others (Indians, Chinese, and Dutchmen); they also offer an example of the intervention of groups interested in channeling that inventiveness in a particular direction. If, as Eric Hobsbawm has argued, nations shape themselves into republics and consolidate their power in part by inventing rituals and ceremonies that help create a national history, then the story of how Philadelphia's "shooters" became "mummers" through a process of inscription within print culture shows how rituals can be reformed by using the past to shape the present.[1]

The current form of the Mummers' Parade signals the success of those reformist efforts. Today the parade is an elaborate and carefully orchestrated spectacle in which organized groups of extravagantly costumed dancers, comics, and musicians "strut" up Philadelphia's Broad Street on New Year's Day, stopping at designated spots along the route to perform. Their end goal is City Hall, where assembled judges and television cameras await them and prizes for the best performances in various categories are awarded. The parade is the result of year-long practice and preparation on the part of the mummers, many of whom have roots in south Philadelphia, the historical home of the New Year's revelers. Although the modern parade is anything but spontaneous, it still manages to provoke controversy, and disruption still lurks beneath its surface; despite the efforts of reformers, it seems that at least some features of the parade's earlier incarnations have survived to challenge the official spectacle. To look at the history of the Mummers' Parade, then, is to see a partially successful rewriting of a performance tradition, one that aimed to reform the present by turning to the medieval past.

New Year's "Shooters" and Popular Festivity

Although late-nineteenth-century reformers would attempt to settle the question of origins by claiming that the New Year's revelers were heirs to a tradition of medieval English mumming, the actual story is more complicated than that. While the precise beginnings of Philadelphia's holiday rituals remain unknown, the immigrants who initially settled in the city in the seventeenth century were collective heirs to a long tradition of Christmas festivities. Among these were the Scandinavian custom of celebrating Epiphany with a parade of masqueraders; the British rituals of holiday house-visits, masking, and mummers' plays; and the German practice of *belsnickling*. It is likely that all of these European festive activities influenced Philadelphia's New Year's revels to some degree. The important point for the later history of holiday revelers is that while there are, then, grounds for assuming an historical link to an English tradition of mumming, that tradition represented only a partial genealogy of Philadelphia's revelers. The reformers who coupled the revelers with an Anglo-Saxon heritage ignored other possible originary myths in their quest for an acceptable past for the holidaymakers.

For much of their early history, Philadelphia's revelers were in fact linked to the German tradition of *belsnickling*. *Belsnickling* featured a man-woman with a darkened face disguised in a fur-skin coat or hat impersonating a demonic version of St. Nicholas (*pelz-nickle* means "furry St. Nick"). The practice was common in German settlements on the East Coast and is fairly amply documented in Pennsylvania from the 1820s on. Shaking cowbells attached to his belt or garments and brandishing a whip or club, the *belsnickle* went house to house frightening children and giving small gifts. William Haines, who at Christmas in 1845 disguised himself in "a huge shaggy cap" and put on "a mask and flowing beard," as we know because he was arrested after having gathered a "great crowd around him in Chestnut Street" seems to have been playing within the *belsnickle* tradition.[2] Until about 1830, when it was supplanted by the terms *fantasticals* and *callithumpians*, *belsnickling* was the usual word used to describe Philadelphia's revelers, suggesting that most commentators up until that time viewed German customs as the source of Philadelphia's holiday rituals.[3]

Although the early revelers were categorized as *belsnicklers* not mummers, it is important to note that the distinction was one of word choice not practice. In practice, the two traditions tended to merge, as surviving accounts suggest, and activities that fit the pattern identified for medieval English mumming were apparently a part of Philadelphia's holiday festivities from at least the seventeenth century.[4] A diary of 1686, for instance, mentions a Christmas mummers' play; another diary of 1781 describes the firing of guns in the night and loud music on New Year's Eve that perhaps accompanied a procession.[5] The records of a Quaker family suggest that it was considered proper to give holiday disguisers a few pence, to invite them into the house, to serve them food and drink, and to pretend not to recognize them.[6] An incident involving two women, Dorothy Canterill and Sarah Stiner, who in 1702 were charged with dressing as men and "walking and dancing in the house of John Simes at 9 to 10 o'clock at night," is sometimes taken to refer to mumming, although the details are too sketchy to be able to say with any certainty what was involved. Along with the women, Simes himself was charged with keeping "a nursery to Dobotch ye inhabitants and youth of this city . . . to ye Greef of and disturbance of peaceable minds and propigating ye Throne of wickedness amongst us." Another record from the same year points less ambiguously to mumming: a John Smith was charged with "being Maskt or disguised in womens' aparell; walking openly through the streets of this citty and from house to

"Bell Snicklin'." From "A Day in the Ma'sh," *Scribner's Monthly* 22 (July 1881). Courtesy of the Special Collections Department, University of Iowa Libraries, Iowa City, Iowa.

house" on December 26, in violation of "the Law of God, the Law of the Province, and the Law of nature, to the staining of holy profession, and Incoridging of wickedness in this place."[7] Masking, cross-dressing, noisy processions, house visits with ritual performances and demands for money—all of these echo practices associated with medieval English mumming.

One of the most detailed accounts of these holiday rituals can be found in the reminiscences of Samuel Breck, who was born in Boston, then lived for thirty years just outside Philadelphia.[8] In 1830 when Breck was fifty-eight years old, he described the "Anticks" whom he remembers disruptively entering households in Boston as late as 1782, using the license of holiday custom: "They were a set of the lowest blackguards, who, disguised in filthy clothes and ofttimes with masked faces, went from house to house in large companies, and *bon gré, mal gré,* obtruding themselves everywhere, particularly into the rooms that were occupied by parties of ladies and gentlemen, would demean themselves with great insolence." Breck recalls that he had seen mummers enter his father's house, when his father and friends were playing at cards, and "take possession of a table, seat themselves on rich furniture and proceed to handle the cards, to the great annoyance of the company. The only way to get rid of them was to give them money, and listen patiently to a foolish dialogue between two or more of them." That "foolish dialogue" appears to have been a performance of what folklorists have identified as the hero-combat play, with its character of the quack doctor:

> One of them would cry out, "Ladies and gentlemen sitting by the fire, put your hands in your pockets and give us our desire." When this was done and they had received some money, a kind of acting took place. One fellow was knocked down, and lay sprawling on the carpet, while another bellowed out, "See, there he lies, / But ere he dies / A doctor must be had." He calls for a doctor, who soon appears, and enacts the part so well that the wounded man revives. In this way they would continue for half an hour; and it happened not unfrequently that the house would be filled by another gang when these had departed.

Breck goes on to note that there was no refusing them admittance, since custom "had licensed these vagabonds to enter even by force any place they chose." Although Breck does not use the term *mumming,* he does link the "Anticks" to medieval English traditions, referring to them as "a remnant of the old Mysteries of the fourteenth and fifteenth centuries."

Exactly what medieval mumming consisted of has been a matter of some debate. The British custom of mumming can be traced to the late Middle Ages, but has been most amply documented by folklorists who have collected more recent, but perhaps derivative examples, such as the Scottish Hogmanay "guisers," the English soulers, pace-eggers, wren-boys, and other folk performers.[9] In these ritual performances, a group in disguise (usually a disguise involving gender-reversal) and wearing blackface or masks goes house to house at holiday time; inside, they perform a play, sometimes accompanied by a riddling game in which the hosts try to guess the identity of the disguised players—a correct guess may be followed by unmasking at which point the hosts treat the mummers to food and drink.[10] The play that was sometimes performed as part of the ritual was apparently of the hero-combat type that included a ritual death-rebirth scene. Although some scholars have argued that such plays are a product of the nineteenth century, others have found evidence of links to medieval performance traditions, noting, for example, that the fifteenth-century English play known as the Croxton *Play of the Sacrament* features a quack doctor and his assistant who offer to heal a Jewish merchant whose hand was torn off when he touched the communion wafer.[11]

Even in the absence of surviving play texts, the written record offers a fair amount of information about medieval Christmas rituals, often in the form of prohibitions against them. Apparently in response to the real or perceived threat posed by mummers to law and order, between 1440 and 1560 a number of English cities, including London, Bristol, Chester, and probably other towns whose records no longer exist, forbade anyone to walk about masked during the Christmas season.[12] Permissible disorder figured in Christmas festivities in the character of the Lord of Misrule, Abbot of Misrule, Christmas Lord, or whatever other local name this master of the revels went by; these lords of misrule can be found in the royal court, in the employ of the Lord Mayor and sheriffs of London, at university colleges, and in the Inns of Court. Role-reversal seems to have been a key aspect of lords of misrule: where their status can be determined, they were drawn from younger, lower, junior ranks; then, in the course of the festivities, they were allowed to lord it over the usual authorities. Early-sixteenth-century churchwardens' accounts from Norfolk, Suffolk, and Essex record sums handed in by such figures of misrule who gathered money during their activities; we do not know what those activities consisted of, although they probably involved processions with costumes and music and may have included games and performances. As Ronald Hutton observes in his account of mumming's place in the traditional British ritual year, the parallel in the ecclesiastical world was the boy bishop, whose presence is recorded in the surviving accounts of a number of medieval cathedrals, including Salisbury, York, St. Paul's, Exeter, Lincoln, and Hereford.[13] At Salisbury, the boy bishop was elected by the choirboys from among themselves and led services on the day before the Feast of the Holy Innocents (December 27); at St. Paul's, he was chosen by the senior clergy and preached a sermon, three of which survive. Around 1500, boy bishops appear in the records of some of the major abbeys, including Bury St. Edmunds, Westminster, and Winchester. Boy bishops also played a role in parish affairs on the Feast of St. Nicholas.

In an entry for the year 1551–52, Henry Machyn's *Diary* offers a vivid account of the arrival of the king's lord of misrule (George Ferrers) in London on January 4. According to Machyn, a great scaffold was erected at Chepe for the "kynges lord of myss[rule]" who coming from Greenwich landed at the Tower accompanied by "yonge knyghts and gentyllmen a gret nombur on [horseb]ake sum in gownes and cotes and chynes abowt ther nekes, every man havyng a balderyke of yelow and grene abowt ther nekes." The group went in order to the Tower Hill: first men carrying a standard of yellow and green silk with St. George on it; then men with guns, squibs, trumpets, bagpipes, and other instruments; then "a gret company all in yelow and gren, and docturs declaryng my lord grett, and then the morse danse dansyng with a tabret" and twenty men on horseback; followed by the lord of misrule along with fifty men of the guard in red and white, then a cart carrying the gibbet and the stocks, all accompanied by a trumpeter, herald, and doctor of the law. On arrival at Tower Hill, a proclamation was made in praise of the lord of misrule's progeny and the greatness of his household; the lord then drank from a hogshead of wine at the scaffold and offered drinks to everyone else before going to the Lord Mayor's house for dinner. In an entry for 1558, Machyn describes another lord of misrule who rode into London from Westminster on January 1, with herald, drums, trumpets, and men disguised in white.[14]

Although its routes of passage have been obscured, this European performance tradition anticipates the various rituals of misrule involving masking, "rough music," house-visits, plays, and disguises that can be found in many parts of the New World.[15] Structurally, the performances are quite similar: all feature young men in masquerade who come to a dwelling making noise, "playfully" threaten the inhabitants, and are bought off with gifts of food, drink, or money. The *Philadelphia Pennsylvanian* of January 2, 1834, in a column titled "Le Charivari," makes explicit the link between Old World rituals of misrule and Philadelphia's holiday maskers when it describes how "the Lord of misrule for a week past has been paramount; and the valorous watch has been effectively cowed. On Christmas Eve, it appeared as if Pandemonium had been opened, and that the imps, elevated with spirits, had been allowed to come on a picnic to Philadelphia." Transplanted to cities like Philadelphia, European traditions of misrule continued to serve the same social functions—as rites of passage, as rituals of communal regulation, and acts of role reversal—as they had in the Old World, even if new urban contexts were inevitably reshaping those traditions.

Rituals of misrule are usually interpreted as symbolic and expressive modes of communication that at least momentarily affirm the values of conviviality, help redistribute wealth and power, and enforce social discipline through the practice of mutual surveillance, even if they also on occasion lead to violence. Thomas Pettitt has described how aspects of Christmas mumming could in medieval England spill outside the traditionally licensed misrule of the festive context to acquire a function at other moments of revolt or unrest.[16] As Pettitt observes, the collector of the money in mummings often appeared as the "treasurer" of a rebellion; rebellions usually featured a leader (captain, general, counselor, the king) who paralleled the leader at festivities; distinctive clothing (badges or disguises, including blackface or gender inversion) was central to both rebellions and festivities as were "rough" music and fire (bonfires, torches); and, finally, the two basic movements of mummings—their "visit" to a household and their procession through town—both appeared in popular revolt (the visit could be exploited by rebels for coercion or the presentation of demands). Even when mumming stopped short of protest, it still often aimed at asserting the rights and identities of the performing groups—a feature that in many authoritarian contexts could seem by its very nature rebellious.

The radical potential of rituals of misrule was not lost on nineteenth-century Philadelphians. In her study of street parades, Susan Davis shows how Philadelphia's labor movement made extensive use of misrule in the form of parades. These militant strike-parades belonged to the same milieu as the New Year's shooters, as Davis shows, arising out of the same south Philadelphia neighborhoods and attracting the same participants.[17] Davis has also described resemblances between the military burlesques that mocked the militia system and the New Year's shooters in the first half of the nineteenth century.[18] A form of political charivari that resembled earlier European forms of vernacular protest, mock-militia parades mounted a visible opposition to forced participation in the public militia and to compliance with laws in general. In one burlesque in 1825, which took place at the militia officers' election, the Eighty-fourth Regiment in protest elected John Pluck, an ostler at a tavern stable, as their colonel. Pluck was described in newspaper accounts as poor, ignorant, physically ill-formed, and as having long been the butt of neighborhood taunts. Mounting Pluck on a spavined white horse, dressing him in a woman's bonnet, and arming him with outsized sword and spurs, the Eighty-fourth paraded through the streets behind their "leader" in a motley and disorderly procession that deliberately inverted the orderliness, uniformity, and solemnity associated with military parades. In the eyes of the public, as perhaps for participants themselves, protest parades and New Year's revels tended to blur together as descriptions in newspapers emphasizing the fantastical costumes and absurd appearances of protesters indicates. Moreover, like the bands accompanying mock militias, New Year's revelers were called "callithumpians," a designation that stressed the real or perceived connection between them.[19] And both sorts of street performances were popular in the same plebeian south Philadelphia neighborhoods, as Davis notes.[20]

Given these historic and contemporary associations of New Year's revels with popular protest, it should not be surprising to learn that Philadelphia's newspapers for the period before the Civil War are full of descriptions emphasizing the riotous activities of New Year's maskers and complaining about violence revolving around the festivities of the Christmas season.[21] The *Philadelphia Daily Chronicle* of December 26, 1833, protested that "riot, noise and uproar prevailed, uncontrolled and uninterrupted in many of our central and most orderly streets. Gangs of boys howled as if possessed by the demon of disorder." The *Public Ledger* of December 25, 1844, described what seems to have been a milder celebration of young men who gathered in Chestnut Street, a fashionable part of town: "Some, more fantastic in their taste and extravagant in their expression . . . tricked out in burlesque garb and whimsical costumes, while musical costumes from the trumpet to the pennywhistle enlivened the ear with sound, if not melody and harmony." Three years later, however, the *Public Ledger* of January 2, 1847, was chronicling more outrageous behavior: a "callithumpian band . . . accoutred grotesquely and with blackened faces . . . with rams horns, bells and kettles . . . shocked the very moon with their enactments."[22] In the following year, the *Philadelphia Evening Bulletin* of January 1, 1848, ran a story under the headline "Terrible Scenes on New Year's Eve" that described how the city on the previous night had been "disgraced by numerous drunken brawls and riotous scenes." At Second and South streets, the account continued, "intoxicated rowdies" caused a disturbance in an oyster cellar and stabbed the owner who took a gun and shot two Southwark watchmen by mistake; there were other casualties from pistol discharges (someone's hand was blown off). A few years later, the *Evening Bulletin* of December 27, 1853, enumerated the arrests of revelers, among them fifty disorderly young men, who were accused of tearing down signs, overturning buckets of coal ashes, destroying public lamps, and fighting.[23]

Although it is difficult to know how much credence to give to newspaper accounts of holiday aggression, Davis argues that news stories from the 1830s through 1850s, while perhaps skewed toward destructive, and hence more newsworthy, activities, provide an accurate record of the city's youth gang and labor problems during these decades and that many New Year's processions did indeed turn violent.[24] We know that the maskers sometimes fought each other, challenging rival troops with their wooden swords, as in 1857 when fantasticals dressed in white costumes, plumes and hats, blackface, and gold earrings stabbed a German workman to death.[25] Maskers' processions also made tours of taverns, demanding free drinks and starting brawls if they were denied. Participants and bystanders were injured, sometimes seriously, and revelers were on more than one occasion arrested and fined. Philadelphia's rapid growth in these decades into a major manufacturing center that attracted migrants from the surrounding countryside and from abroad helps explain the class and economic relations underlying holiday revels and their aggression. As industrial capitalism grew in the city, so too did economic disparity, and a shrinking group of elites began to control an ever-expanding share of wealth and property. Overcrowding, an increase in wage-labor, and the growth of the propertyless poor all contributed to social unrest. The city also had a large surplus labor force working—when the laborers could get work—for low wages; especially vulnerable to the caprices of the economy, these workers were socially unstable and insecure.[26] Many Philadelphians faced grim and inescapable material circumstances; not surprisingly, Philadelphia's streets in the mid-1800s were full of symbolic and real acts of protest as street theater and mob violence shared public space.[27]

Despite its antiauthoritarian flavor, however, much of the New Year's violence appears not to have been directed toward the property or persons of elites, but instead was localized within working-class neighborhoods. In the course of the nineteenth century, as the city expanded rapidly, neighborhoods acquired separate identities based on ethnicity or industry, and conflicts over territories developed. Because the city lacked open and central space for large public gatherings, as Davis notes, the streets themselves became the site for theatricality. Although separation of the different populations was never complete, which meant that poor people's activities were always to some degree visible to elites, the city was nonetheless stratified by class and ethnicity, providing elites with a buffer against the lower-classes' riotous entertainments.[28] When working-class districts were declared out of control year after year during the Christmas season or when Southwark was described as a demonic region, elites were drawing symbolic distinctions between themselves and the poor that heightened the threatening alterity of the very men on whom elites depended for the running of their factories and businesses.[29]

Unlike the Luddite rebels in northern England, however, who disguised themselves as mummers in order to avoid detection and to appear to be the impersonal agents of ritual retribution as they ceremonially purged their communities of polluting objects, revelers in America took another route. Rather than protesting the exploitative practices of manufacturers and civic authorities whose demand for cheap labor was largely responsible for the predicament of the working and nonworking poor, the holidaymakers used New Year's festivities to define their own group identities and to create solidarity for themselves by mocking other dispossessed outsiders, particularly Irish immigrants and blacks.[30] Davis notes that brawling was used to carve out and protect neighborhood territories and more often occurred if boundaries were crossed, citing the example of an occasion in 1854 when the night watch was summoned to stop "rough music" at William Myers's tavern on Ridge Road; when the watch arrived and attempted to intervene, the owner, clientele, and band all turned on the officers and drove them away.[31] Thus while disguised rioters engaged in street brawls in poor neighborhoods in Southwark, elites remained safe and could even enjoy watching fantasticals dance for crowds in the Chestnut and Eighth Street theater districts.

While working-class revels provided amusement for higher-status social spectators, they also had entertainment value for readers as well, in a cross-media migration that had consequences for their later reshaping as "mummings." The *Philadelphia Inquirer*'s "Local Intelligence" column for December 25, 1861, for instance, suggests how the revels had become a source of pleasure for spectators and readers alike: "At night, Chestnut Street and Eighth Street presented a carnival of fun, and those who were not crowding the theaters and exhibitions walked backward and forward, ready to enjoy the jokes—practical and verbal—that were rife, to gaze upon the illuminated lanterns, with their grotesque processions, and listen with delight to the husky toot of tin horns." Were newspaper accounts like this one echoing or shaping respectable public opinion? Probably a bit of both. But in either case, an important result of the annual commentary offered by newspapers was that it captured and fixed on the page performances that were quintessentially unscripted and spontaneous. While the revelers themselves performed a relationship with history, that relationship was largely unconscious, complex, and amorphous. When co-opted by print culture, however, that history became available for reworking in more deliberate ways. As holiday revels were transported into the privileged representational space of literate elites, they were set up for later appropriation and reshaping by civic authorities and reformers. It was at this moment, perhaps, when they became fixtures in newspaper accounts, that it first became possible to think of Philadelphia's revels as "folk rituals"—a designation that is usually only applied by someone other than the "folk" participating in the ritual—and that "shooters" were launched on the path to becoming "mummers."

Taming the Revels

The transformation of Philadelphia's New Year's revelers into mummers is intertwined with a changing context after mid-century that encouraged greater order and control of holiday festivities. Post–Civil War assaults on working-class culture, a growing alliance of commerce and government in producing festivity, the spread of mass media, and the physical remaking of the city to accommodate industry, automobiles, and more people, all combined to change the nature of street festivity. These forces worked hand in hand with the restyling of Philadelphia's New Year's revels as mummings, as the parade gradually became tamer, more heavily policed, and more organizationally complex.

New Year's revels may have remained a perceived problem for public order in mid-century, but for the first time something could be done about the mayhem since the city had acquired a professional police force in 1854, thus enabling greater civic control of street festivities than had been possible under the earlier, less effective system of the watch.[32] In addition to mounting a stronger police presence, civic authorities used licensing of performers as a way of maintaining order. The antimasquerading law that had been passed by the Pennsylvania House of Representatives in 1808, albeit with little effect on the New Year's revelers, was lifted in 1859, thus granting legal status to the mummers and opening the way for further regulation of them.[33] The *Inquirer*'s account of the New Year's parade in 1861 suggests the general orderliness that now prevailed. Its New Year's Eve report describes how the year's end

> was marked in this quarter with less racket than usually greets the dying year. Efficient police arrangements have greatly checked the wild riot of former days on such occasions, and pistols no longer flash in the face of every passing pedestrian. . . . A few clubs of fantasticals paraded with discordant music from one headed drums, cracked horns, and penny whistles, but there was no approach to a general saturnalia. . . . Occasionally a report from a fowling piece or a revolver told of a year going to the scene of the mighty past, but such discharges were comparatively few.[34]

For the next few years, holiday festivities were apparently fairly tame, because many men were at war and other amusements competed with the parades. The *Inquirer* of December 26, 1864, comments that:

> Christmas Eve was celebrated in the usual old fashioned Philadelphia style . . . the prominent thoroughfares were completely thronged with seekers after fun. All ages, all sexes, all classes, and all creeds were well represented. . . . Numerous parties of young men and boys, fantastically dressed and armed with tin trumpets, perambulated the streets, testing the power of their lungs on their primitive musical instruments, and thereby making a constant jargon of discordant sounds that would have been unbearable on any other occasion than Christmas eve.

Significantly, there is no mention of rowdy activities beyond the din of tin horns. Competing amusements that year included theater (with performances of the "Octoroon" at New Chestnut Street Theater and "Metamora, the Last of the Wampanoags" at the American Academy of Music), the circus, Signor Blitz, and the Ethiopian Minstrels.[35] Church services and private parties in homes filled out the bill.

During the 1870s, crackdowns on the revels led to a pervasive sense that the nature of the holiday festivities was changing. In 1872, Christmas masquerading was forbidden entirely, and the holiday was celebrated in churches and at benevolent societies but not in the streets. The *Inquirer* of December 24, 1872, remarked that "no such demonstrations as characterized Christmas eve in years gone by will to-night be permitted." The mayor stationed police on Eighth, Second, and other crowded streets, and it was vowed that "no unseemly or disgraceful conduct such as has made Eighth Street famous on former Christmas eves, will be allowed" much to the pleasure of Eighth Street merchants. The same paper on the following day observed that "a description of the Christmas eve scenes and incidents on Eighth Street formerly made an important feature in the Christmas items of the newspapers—the crowds and what they did, the masqueraders and their pranks"—but that last night there were no masqueraders, no pranks, no crowds, no horn-blowing on Eighth Street as there had been in times past, thanks to the police presence.[36] The *Evening Bulletin* reported in 1875 that the tradition of New Year's shooting seemed to be on the wane and the *Inquirer* in 1878 explained why:

> Years ago Christmas eve on Eighth Street meant a carnival of disgrace and disorder, but Mayor Stokley soon changed all that by stationing reserves at close intervals, and ordering the arrest of all turbulent or ill behaving persons. His Honor was down at his office during the greater part of last evening to give his personal attention to this matter. There were many parties of masqueraders to be seen about the streets, but they were orderly in their conduct.

One consequence of such mayoral attention was the "almost absolute absence of the pistol-shooting and tin horn blowing nuisances this year." Lest there be any doubt as to the *Evening Bulletin*'s feelings about that, the column adds: "It is to be hoped that the nuisances will not be revived."[37]

After the late 1870s and in response to pressure from elites, the city began to require parade permits, effectively doing away with the spontaneous, unplanned quality that had been the hallmark of the earlier revels.[38] Voluntary associations and clubs, which were usually built around neighborhoods and so segregated by class, and which had been part of life in nineteenth-century Philadelphia, gradually merged with the mummers, providing a year-round structure for the various groups of paraders.[39]

Such changes shaped holiday festivity and street theater into more respectable forms.[40] Especially as labor's power grew and hence became a more serious threat, as manifested in the Great Strike of 1877, elites sought stronger control of the streets, using them for their own rituals of self-display. Civic and commercial events such as the Centennial Exhibition (1876), the Bicentennial (1882), and the Centennial of the Constitution (1887), all of which were successful tourist attractions as well as skillful acts of civic myth- and history-making, began to occupy the public stage of the city, as elites adopted the theater of the streets for themselves. Extravagant department store parades designed to introduce consumers, especially women, to commodity culture also began to be mounted, claiming the streets as an extension of capitalism's domains and squeezing out the right of disenfranchised groups to use thoroughfares as places of entertainment and social protest.[41]

In 1884, the *Evening Bulletin* noted that "over two hundred permits were granted yesterday, and to clubs bearing all sorts of odd names, represented by all sorts of people, from boys of eleven in ragged attire up to the young man with the showy plaid and the glaring glass pin in his shirt-front."[42] As this account suggests, the New Year's revels had by 1884 taken the shape of a more or less organized—yet still motley and diverse—series of parades involving various clubs, each now appearing with its own band and props or floats. The *Public Ledger* of January 1, 1885, ran a first-page story called "New Year's Eve Masqueraders," describing how thousands of people turned out to celebrate. With the reserves on duty, there were few arrests. While crowds waited around Independence Hall for midnight bell ringing, "the time was enlivened by the appearance of several small parties of 'fantasticals,' among whom the usual New Year Indians, Chinamen, Yankees, policemen, negroes, washerwomen, etc., were conspicuous." The story described how "one or two clubs, among which was the Keystone New Year Association, composed of young men, made a fine display, and attracted much attention and favorable comment from the spectators." An account in the same paper the following year suggests a similar mix of the organized and the spontaneous: "Bands of masqueraders paraded the streets in every direction. Many of these companies were organised 'socials' and 'New Year's Associations,' but the greater number were evidently impromptu bands gotten up with little system and at small expense."[43]

Newspaper accounts from the last decades of the nineteenth century show the increasing bureaucratization of the parade. The *Inquirer* on December 31, 1886, listed the clubs that "turned out" for New Year's: Wilmer W. Banner Club, Golden Crown, Golden Star, Silver Crown, Keystone, 47 Coons, George Beatty, Southwark, William Penn, and others. Masqueraders appeared at Eighth and Chestnut around nine thirty, and one organization after another "passed the Mayor's Office and gave three cheers for 'Bullitt Bill.' " There were also "transparencies" in the line, some "rather grotesque." One was of a team of horses drawing a horse car and under it written "We live over the Schuylkill, and this is the way we get home, unless we take a sleeper on the cable: shoot the rails into the air." The "Swampdoodlers" of the Twenty-eighth Ward came along with the motto: "Mud and brickyards everywhere, but not a place to stand; who'll put down a plank walk? Don't you forget it, we're happy all the time." Chestnut Street was crowded with "parading bands of merry masqueraders." The streets below South Street were lined with "pedestrians en masse in beautiful and fantastic garbs," worn, the paper adds, by some who could ill afford them. The paper also offered a glimpse of how the clubs operated that night, noting that the Wilmer W. Banner Club—"each member dressed fantastically"—"left the club room, on Third Street, between South and Bainbridge, at 9:30 o'clock and marched up Third to South," crisscrossing the area and then finally marching up Broad to Industrial Hall, "where the Mystic Club ball was in progress." Police patrolled the streets all night "and they kept a careful watch for pistol firers and horn blowers." At midnight, paraders, "accompanied by bands of music and followed by crowds of sight-seers," arrived near the State House.

When the parades became better organized they also attracted crowds of spectators who turned out to watch; at the 1889 parade, the "best order was maintained, and all the police had to do was to look on and enjoy the mirth-provoking sights," according to the *Inquirer*.[44] The *Public Ledger* offers details of what those sights were. Dark had hardly fallen when "strangely attired" men and boys emerged onto the streets and stole to previously agreed-on places and formed into clubs with banners and music. About 211 permits for parading had been issued (over 111 more than the previous year). Some of the clubs "revelled in names as singular as the attire of the members was grotesque. The 'get up' of many of the masqueraders can only be classified as gorgeous." Tin-horns, trumpets, kazoos, and the occasional shot contributed to the sounds of the night. Many clubs paraded all evening but only at midnight did masqueraders come in full force. The Golden Crown Association passed Independence Hall headed by a band and led by "a handsomely-robed Indian chief." There was also a Robinson Crusoe on horseback and a float displaying a boat occupied by two people representing an elderly "colored" couple "who were 'holding forth' to the street that 'marriage was not a failure.'" The Keystone Club, Gibbon New Year's Association, Bright Star Club, and "all the principal organizations turned out in large numbers, and the costumes worn were, in many cases, of the handsomest description."[45]

As this comment about the outfits worn by the Keystone Club reveals, the parades had by century's end become expensive, as performers increasingly hired costly costumes. In 1893, when fifty-six clubs secured permits from the police department to march,[46] the *Philadelphia Times* protested the increasing expense, worrying that many shooters "will doubtless catch the 'grippe' for imprudent exposure to the weather after dancing in heated halls during the early hours of the morning, and others will be poor in pocket for weeks because of the money squandered in hiring costly costumes. For several hundred dollars a man may be a very imposing king for a day and wear more circus

New Year's Mummers on Chestnut Street. *Harper's Weekly* 32 (January 1888). Courtesy of the Special Collections Department, University of Iowa Libraries, Iowa City, Iowa.

jewelry than the Czar of Russia." The article goes on to complain that in the early years there was just as much merriment but less display and expense, and lamented that "many of the paraders spend too much money for vain show, and deprive themselves of necessaries to gratify a foolish desire to outshine their fellows. The tendency to extravagance should be abated; just as the reckless pistol-firing and the excessive drinking have been eliminated."[47] That last sentence suggests the extent of encroachments on the revelers' activities; the authorities wanted not just to maintain public order but also to intervene in the private decisions of the revelers—weighing in as the participants decided how much, quite literally, to invest in their rituals.

Accounts of the 1893 parade show just how elaborate the organizational structure had become. Expectations were that the parade would be "the finest ever seen in this city."[48] Fifty-six clubs secured permits from the police department, and many valuable prizes were being offered by businesses. The mummers were watched by thousands on Broad, Chestnut, and surrounding streets, with groups of judges stationed at many points along the way. The costumes were fancier than ever before, costing hundreds of dollars and requiring weeks of work. Illustrations and captions in the *Inquirer* on Monday, January 2, suggest the range of the costumes, which included the Grand High Muc-a-Muc; the Skirt Dancer (a blackface woman); the Three-Eyed Dude; Collars and Cuffs (in blackface); The Happiest Fellow (a clown); A Good-Natured German; The New Matamora (Indian); and an Old Uncle Tom. Captains wore huge trains or wings held by "pages" and danced and pirouetted. The Clements parade reputedly cost seven thousand dollars and featured 200 mummers as well as two bands. The Julius Kleinguenther Social Club was equally lavish, with 188 maskers and two bands; some of the members were costumed as Aztec chieftains. The White Caps, a comic club, were dressed in rags as "pickaninnies." The Early Risers Club was disguised as a chain gang in striped suits. The *Inquirer* reported that for the first time "a colored club," the Golden Crown, paraded, adding that their "numbers and costumes rivaled many of the white clubs" and that they "did not need to black their faces but they did use rouge lavishly." Although most of the clubs followed the new rules, at least one club paraded without a license: the Growlers Club, which was connected to a "downtown political club," and which—perhaps in symbolic protest against the new strictures—paraded in prison suits.[49]

Although the local authorities succeeded in creating order, the greater organization and expense led commentators to lament the loss of the former innocence of the revels and to predict the imminent demise of the custom. The *Call-Philadelphia* for 1893, for instance, claimed that twenty years ago the shooters cost little money, their costumes being whatever they could throw together, but with the inducement of prize money, the costumes had become expensive and heavy: the captain's costume alone for the Thomas Clements club cost six hundred dollars to hire. Moreover, the account continues, the clubs were busy for a whole year and had the added expense of hiring a hall.[50] The *Public Ledger* on January 1, 1895, explicitly contrasted past with present practice in a capsule history of the parade:

> This is the *fin de siecle* conclusion of the old custom, that dates back beyond the memory of the present generation, when the fantasticals, garbed in the simplest disguises, were confined entirely to the mystic region known as the "Neck," visiting one farm house after another. They were always welcomed, one band leaving as another entered, but the custom ceased to be peculiar to the Neck shortly after the Schuylkill Rangers' tragedy, about 1852, when the Hornkeiths were killed in Gray's Ferry Road. The costuming gradually became more elaborate and the clubs of masqueraders sprang into existence all over the city.

In a long column on "Ringing in the New," the *Ledger* in 1897 sounded the same theme, commenting that the "shooter" is on the wane, having reached a zenith five or six years ago, and that public revelry has been replaced by private balls. The article goes on to describe the origins of "shooters" in the Neck and to link the growing use of the term *mummers* with the demise of the old revels: " 'New Year's Shooters' is the first name these masquerades got, and the only name they should get. They have been called 'Merry Mummers,' etc., but they are 'shooters' just the same."[51] By 1899, the *Inquirer* was predicting the abandonment of New Year's parading, noting that in 1899 only 29 clubs applied for permits while ten years earlier 211 clubs had paraded.[52]

Perhaps in part because New Year's parading was seen by the end of the nineteenth century as a dying ritual linked nostalgically to the city's past, civic leaders decided to conscript it in 1900 into a massive extravaganza intended to mark the new century and to put Philadelphia on the map. The city council's plan was to have the various New Year's clubs cooperate with the city in putting on an annual Mardi Gras of one large parade in the center city. Reports of those negotiations suggest that the clubs retained a good deal of clout: the city council wanted the parade to take place at night on New Year's Eve, but the clubs insisted it be on the morning of New Year's day. The clubs also demanded prize money, threatening to refuse to parade as one group otherwise (it was thus the clubs that instituted the commercialization of the ritual, not the city).[53] The city agreed to both demands and on January 1, 1901, the first civic-sponsored mummers' paraded was held, featuring three thousand men. The captains of the clubs wore costumes with huge trains; there were also men in women's clothes who danced and cavorted and "some of the exhibitions were ludicrous in the extreme," according to the *Public Ledger*. The *Ledger* averred that "perhaps there were too many Indians and too many negroes to suit, but many of these were in such queer toggery that laughter was compelled." Mummers dressed like hoboes and devils; there were some African Americans (and some women—but only in the African-American clubs); there were men costumed as Topsies, Zulus with shaggy red hair, and Mexican half-breeds.[54] According to the *Ledger,* the judges' stand with the mayor and various politicians was on the west side of City Hall; prizes ranged from three-hundred-dollar first prizes down to fifty dollars for sixth place. At the end of the day, the *Philadelphia Record* exulted that "there is nothing in this country to compare with it," adding that the parade was "worth a million to the city."[55]

Mumming and the Anglo-Saxon Revival

Between the riotous festivities of prewar shooters and the civic extravaganza of 1901, is a hidden story, one in which reformers and revivalists played important parts. In their hands, holiday revelry was reshaped as an Anglo-Saxon tradition that could successfully incorporate non-English immigrants and meld them into "Americans" by imagining their holiday festivities as latter-day manifestations of early English traditions.

What happened to the mummers in part fits the pattern of reinvention described by Hobsbawm, in which a break with tradition acts as a spur for revivalism. This was the case with English Christmas folk carols, for example, which ceased to be created in the seventeenth century but were revived by middle-class collectors in the new settings of church, guild, and women's institute and then spread into popular venues. Such revivals, Hobsbawm claims, are a way of disguising historical ruptures or breaks, and hence tend to insist on a particular tradition as "alive" rather than "invented."[56] In Philadelphia, what was revived was not precisely the activities of the New Year's revelers, but rather the idea of mumming, which offered a useful way of describing (and reshaping) the rowdy revels of the holidaymakers: hence the attempt to recast the shooters, fantasticals, and callithumpians as mummers.

An early example of the linking of Philadelphia's revelers with the British folk tradition of mumming can be found in the *Philadelphia Sunday Dispatch* of December 27, 1857. The account begins with the assertion that the kind of "mummery" described by Sir Walter Scott "was practiced in Philadelphia within recollection." The writer claims to have

> frequently seen gangs of young fellows parading the streets of a Christmas eve, with their shirts outside of their lower garments and their faces blackened over. They would visit houses, and, after going through a series of "mumming," as it was called, they would put the master of the place under contribution for money or drink, and then go somewhere else to go through the same foolery. We have a glimmering recollection, too, of some of the uncouth rhymes recited by these Mummers.

The account locates the origin of these customs in "the time of the Restoration in England, when it was fashionable to poke fun at 'Oliver Cromwell and his

"Mummers at Christmas in Olden Time." Drawn by E. H. Corbould. *Illustrated London News* (December 1866). Author's collection.

long copper nose.'" "In our own city," the writer continues, "the Mummers were finally voted a nuisance, and all doors being shut against them, the Mummers became metamorphosed into Calithumpians, and these noisy Christmas-keepers now go about at night creating all sorts of discord, and 'making night hideous' with their yells." Two things should be noted about this account. The first is the reference to Sir Walter Scott, which suggests the influence of the Anglo-Saxon revival, with its construction of an idealized version of medieval England. The second is the claim that Philadelphia's revelers had *started out* as folkishly droll mummers, but then changed into the noisy and discordant callithumpians still plaguing the holiday. The obvious implication is that even though the "foolery" of the early mummers was a nuisance, it was more alluring than the current debased activities of the callithumpians because it was linked to British folk customs. In the logic of the *Dispatch* account, the way to reinvent Philadelphia's holiday revels as mummings is through a return to their "true" origins in premodern English customs.

When, some twenty-five years later in 1881, Maurice Egan described the crowds of men and boys who dressed themselves in fantastic costumes and roamed the Neck and lower part of the city all night on New Year's Eve as engaging in a custom that was "doubtless a remnant of the old English Christian 'mumming,'" he was making a similar choice about how to view the maskers' antecedents. By styling this rowdy activity a "remnant" of the "old English

Christian 'mumming,' " Egan legitimized it and claimed it as part of a specifically Anglo-Saxon cultural history. In so doing, he and other commentators shaped a particular attitude toward Philadelphia's New Year's revelry and created a way for elites to embrace it.[57]

By the 1870s and 1880s, Anglo-Saxonism had become a kind of patrician nationalism among the upper-classes in the northeastern United States and was linked to the growth of nativist sentiments, as happened in Philadelphia. In 1854, the Act of Consolidation established the present-day borders of the city and a nativist Whig mayor was elected. Among his acts was the reorganization of the police department, which restricted hiring to native-born whites (a short-lived policy, but one that exacerbated ethnic tensions).[58] Although Philadelphia's percentage of foreign-born residents was the smallest of any northern city, averaging just 25 percent of the total population between 1870 and 1920, the city did not escape ethnic strife.[59] Nativist sentiments grew during the 1880s, and the local press called for immigration restriction, especially of "those undesirable classes whom foreign governments are only too glad to get rid of."[60] In 1893, the *Inquirer* asked, "Are we becoming a mongrel nation?"[61] As an article from the *Public Ledger* in 1903 makes clear, the objects of concern were immigrants from southern Europe.[62]

Although it could be used for conservative ends, the medieval revival of nineteenth-century England had a progressive side in the hands of men like William Cobbett, Thomas Carlyle, John Ruskin, and William Morris, who viewed the revival of handicrafts and other traditional cultural forms as an important mechanism for dissent. Morris's ideal society, for example, sketched in his utopian novel *News From Nowhere,* was modeled on a romanticized medieval past and featured a decentralized, agrarian communism without classes, states, private property, or money in which the arts are performed or created anonymously and locally with no large-scale or commercialized productions. In the United States, a similar anti-industrial movement developed independently but contemporaneously, shaping the ideology and practice of the progressive settlement schools begun in the 1890s under Jane Addams, Ellen Gates Starr, and other reformers.[63] These schools aimed at educating poor, urban children and adults, and establishing social centers, libraries, and other cultural activities in working-class communities. Addams and Starr were followers of Ruskin and Morris, and so not surprisingly championed the traditional crafts as a way of preserving the ethnic traditions of immigrants. Under the impact of nationalism, however, preservation of ethnic traditions was discouraged, since it seemed to clash with the goal of assimilation into the mainstream of American society. The result was the privileging of an Anglo-Saxon past as other ethnic traditions were disregarded. At Hull House, for example, a "labor museum" was opened in 1900 to train Italian women in skilled occupations; six trades were taught—woodworking, bookbinding, textile production, "grains," pottery making, and metalworking—all skills lifted from a

Morris-style medievalism.[64] The Hull House emphasis on preindustrial crafts reveals how the medieval past was seen to offer a route to assimilation, as, more explicitly, does the settlement of Italian immigrant-farmers in Tonti-town, Arkansas, in what was described as "the most amazing modern replica of a medieval republic."[65]

More important for Philadelphia's mummers, performances were also susceptible to being co-opted by medievalist impulses.[66] Early folk-life festivals grew out of the settlement schools, and although these festivals had the goal of reviving local traditions and identities, they were quickly conscripted into the service of nationalism as well.[67] Rather than preserving local traditions, folk-life festivals sought the reconstruction of a pure, preindustrial Anglo-Saxon tradition uncontaminated by other cultures. Such festivals were strongly anti-immigrant in their celebration of an Anglo-American culture and a retreat into an imaginary preindustrial past.[68]

Also linked to the revivalist spirit were the pageants organized under the auspices of the Americanization movement that aimed to reinvent the traditions of the early republic.[69] The Hudson-Fulton Festival of 1909, for instance, which was intended to commemorate Henry Hudson's discovery of the Hudson in 1609 and the inauguration of steam navigation on the Hudson in 1807 by Robert Fulton, was also designed to "promote the assimilation of our adopted population" (and hence was supposed to be "educational" not "commercial"). The festival cost $1 million, and attracted 2 to 3 million spectators. It attempted to re-create memorable scenes from the history of the state and city, while also parading as many representatives of other nationalities as possible, in the interest of merging them with the new image of America.[70] The festival was an obviously didactic event, designed to convey a particular image of New York's past and to assign immigrants a specific place within it.

Newspaper stories in Philadelphia in the 1880s and 1890s echo these revivalist themes in their fascination with the festivities of early England and an inclination to see those English festivities as the source for Philadelphia's New Year's revels. An account in the *Public Ledger* on December 25, 1884, reveals this interest. "Christmas Festivities in Queen Elizabeth's Girlhood" describes how the Lord of Misrule burst into the great hall of Hatfield House, a "fierce and ferocious" fellow with green mustache and ogre's face, carrying a staff topped with a fool's head. His crew, the article continues, included giants and dwarfs, dragons and griffins, hobbyhorses and goblins, Robin Hood and the grand Turk, as well as bears, boars, fantastic animals, and fantastically costumed men and women. The Lord of Misrule proclaimed Christmas to Twelfth Night his reign and commanded all revelers to act as children. Two years later, the *Inquirer* on December 25, 1886, ran a small piece titled "The Lord of Misrule" that once again recounted Christmas festivities in the "Time of Queen Elizabeth." The account describes a mumming and notes the presence of such characters as the Lord of Misrule, Robin Hood, giants, dragons, hobbyhorses, goblins, and grand Turks as well as participants in fantastic consumes. (The *Inquirer* also offered recipes for a fourteenth-century Yuletide Game Pie.) In the same vein, an article in *Harper's New Monthly Magazine* in 1891, describing the celebration of a saint's day by a London guild, suggests what premodern mumming was envisioned to have been: the article recounts the various events of the day, including the procession to church of the whole livery company followed by a banquet in their hall and the election of new officers for the year; after that, "the loving-cup goes round, and the mummers come in to perform plays and interludes, dressed up in such fantastic guise as makes the women scream and the men laugh and applaud."[71]

In the *Moravian,* on January 1, 1863, a Philadelphia correspondent reminisced about an "old custom, now discontinued," he saw when he was a boy, of children parading as " 'mummers,' " that is, squads of five to ten men dressed "fantastically," who "visited the houses of those who they imagined would receive them kindly" where they recited verses, sang humorous songs, or acted a drama, and were rewarded by pennies or cake.[72] Three years later, the *Sunday Dispatch* of December 23, 1866, noted that most customs of Christmas Eve derived from English and German ancestors have passed away, the last being "mummers' sports" which were still in vogue within living memory and which featured mummers dressed in a "grotesque manner," who "went from house to house, where they enacted a mock play, entitled 'Alexander and the King of Egypt,' or recited humorous poems. No doubt the discontinuance of this custom arose out of the annoyance it subjected those to who had no fancy for such sport" since permission to enter was often given reluctantly and the mummers often stayed too long. On December 24, 1876, the *Sunday Dispatch* explained that "Mummers exist among us in degenerated forms as 'Fantasticals' or 'Calithumpians'—men who render the night hideous by their yelling, drum-beatings, and horn-tootings, and by the day disgusting by their outrageous masking and foul disguises." The *Dispatch* goes on to note that "the Mummer formerly occupied a prominent place in the old-time Christmas revels, enacting those rude and irreverent mysteries, and miracle-plays which have been superseded by charades, parlor-games, dancing, and other refined amusements." The *Doylestown Democrat,* on January 6, 1885, devoted a long piece to a description of mumming, described as "one of the English customs which obtained a foothold in Philadelphia" and was performed as recently as fifty years ago. The *Democrat* recounts how the mummers dressed in fantastic costume and went from house to house reciting certain rhymes in expectation of a handout. The source for their rhymes, the account claims, was the "English Christmas masque of 'St. George and the dragon,' " which had been Americanized by replacing St. George with George Washington.

The *Philadelphia North American,* on December 21, 1913, echoed this preoccupation with the issue of origins, claiming that:

The mummers, direct from anciently merrie England, have been shouldered off by Philadelphia's Christmas on to its New Year. In the early part of the nineteenth century the mummers appeared on Christmas eve, instead of New Year's eve, and they went from house to house, after the homely English fashion, singing their waits' songs and seeking dole of pence and cakes—and got it. That practice lasted on up to twenty years ago, although transferred to December 25. During the last two decades the magnificent New Year pageant has developed on a scale that leaves humble petitioners at doorsteps too much beneath the mummers' dignity.

The article goes on to suggest that Philadelphia's mummers created Americanized versions of traditional figures from English mummers' plays, noting how a man named Eph Horn ("in after years famed as the most popular nigger minstrel") organized a band of mummers that belonged around Sixth and South streets, and "supplemented the character of George Washington—the patriotic substitute for the British Saint George—with our own peculiar Coonery Cracker, with Beelzebub and with the Prince of Egypt—all mummers' roles which held sway for years in the streets of Philadelphia."[73]

These attempts at linking Philadelphia's revelers with the tradition of English mumming can be seen as part of a process of reproducing popular behaviors in new contexts. Reinvented as descendants of English mummers, the New Year's revelers were invested not only with respectability, but also with an acceptable tradition of holiday festivity thought to derive from Anglo-Saxon custom. Not insignificantly, the Englishness evoked in this new description of the mummers' origins provided a convenient way of assimilating, or at least masking the difference of, non-English immigrants. The diversity of the groups participating in the New Year's festivities—and their disruptive force—could be hidden under a history grounded in the medieval past. Philadelphia thus solved its problems with working-class immigrants—at least on the symbolic terrain of the parade—by conjuring up a myth of common origins in Anglo-Saxon history, a myth that worked to turn everyone into Anglo-Americans and to mute the antiauthoritarian tendencies of the paraders.

What is remarkable, given the effectiveness of those efforts, is how much of the nineteenth-century paraders' disruptiveness still survives in clandestine fashion even today.[74] Under the institutionalized extravagance and organizational overdetermination of the modern parade, which has been held every year since 1901 except for two years during the depression when clubs could not afford costumes or the city prize money, old themes of affirmation of conviviality, redistribution of goods, and social discipline can still be seen. The emphasis on conviviality has, if anything, been increased since the nineteenth century. Mumming is now an institutionalized activity centering on the parade, but it has been temporally expanded to last for much of the year. While the parade itself is public, the mummers' activities are for the most part private affairs located in their clubhouses, where members meet year-round to raise funds, work on costumes, and practice their routines—and not incidentally strengthen bonds of family, affinity-group, and neighborhood. Conviviality is often cited by present-day mummers as a motive for joining a club. Mummer John Lucas, captain of the Golden Sunrise Club (a Fancy club) has accounted for his participation by saying: "This is my vice." "Some people drink, some gamble and some men chase women, but this is my thing, and my whole family joins in." Bill Speziale, captain of the Joseph A. Ferko String Band claims that "it's the greatest hobby there is." "I was born into it,'" says Edward Connor, "'I love it. It's part of my life."[75]

The enshrining of the Mummers' Parade as an Anglo-Saxon tradition and its institutionalization as a civic event have not severed its attachment to the working-class and largely Irish and Italian-American neighborhood of South Philadelphia where it continues to flourish. For most of the year, the activities of the mummers are confined to that neighborhood, where many of the participants live and where the clubhouses are located. Even those participants who live elsewhere spend a fair amount of time in South Philly, practicing and working on costumes in the clubhouses. It is only on New Year's that the mummers leave the neighborhood, as they march up the spine of the city to the dignified precincts of City Hall—the governmental and financial center of the city. The neighborhood feel of the parade has also been preserved, thanks to the fact that although the Mummers' Parade was first televised in 1947, by Philco Station WPTZ, and although three-quarters of the 2 million people who watch the parade do so via television, it has not become a major television event—the duration of the parade as well as the vagaries of Philadelphia weather make the television networks unwilling to reserve airtime for the event—much to the disappointment of some participants, who would like what they view as the city's "treasure" to find recognition in other places as well. Typically the parade appears in clips on local and regional news broadcasts, but goes unnoticed in the rest of the United States.

Similarly, while the organizational armature of the parade seems to replicate the structures of modern corporate capitalism and thus might appear to acquiesce to existing socioeconomic paradigms, it also operates in part as a mechanism for redistributing wealth and power in ways that echo the redressive tendencies of the earlier shooters. The current parade is characterized by an extremely elaborate organization of Fancy, Comic Clubs, and String Bands into divisions and associations, an organizational structure that is tightly guarded and sorted into a visible hierarchy.[76] While the clubs are in part arranged according to performance type—the Fancy Clubs have big floats, the Fancy Brigades stage theatrical performances, the Comic Clubs do comic routines, and the String Bands perform musical-dance numbers—they also occupy rungs on a status ladder, with the String Bands, which many consider the elite clubs, at the top and Comics at the bottom. The parade is expensive for the clubs, which pay for the elaborate costumes through a strict regimen of dues

Philadelphia Mummers' Parade, 1984. By permission of the Mummers' Museum, Philadelphia, Pennsylvania.

and fundraising. It can also be lucrative for the winners, however, since the city awards around $300,000 in prizes each year and some clubs find other ways to make money (such as the Ferko String band, which hires itself out for performances during the year).[77] These financial tactics replicate the gift demands of earlier mummers and effect a similar transfer of wealth. Redistribution works more strongly, however, at the level of symbolic capital, since the rewards of mumming are less financial than prestige-based. In this regard, the excess that is one of the most striking qualities of the modern parade, with its extravagantly gaudy costumes and its surplus of manpower—both of which might initially appear to be a squandering of resources—can be seen as a rational investment calculated to reap the rewards of a symbolic economy. That symbolic economy stands in obvious opposition to, even if it also intersects with, the actual economic order of late-capitalist America, and so functions as a constructed realm of socioeconomic justice in which the traditional havenots briefly gain the upper hand.

Social discipline continues to be meted out by the parade as well, in part by shutting some groups out of the parade and in part by impersonating various "others," although both practices have lessened in recent years in response to public criticism. Until recently, women and blacks were largely excluded from the parade but were often parodied in absentia via impersonation. The black-faced "wench" and "dude" were popular mummers' characters before the 1964 ban on blackface, and other ethnicities continue to be impersonated, while male to female cross-dressing remains popular. The mostly white, male mummers thus prolong an earlier performance tradition of establishing their identities by displaying what they take to be their differences from others.

If the parade still bears traces of its past in these and other ways, it also shows a concern for preserving that past in forms that reach beyond ritual performance. The Mummers' Museum, which was built in 1976 and which serves as a visible sign of the parade's link to the neighborhood, attests to a growing self-consciousness among participants about the historicity of the parade and to a desire to convert what is by nature an ephemeral and ever-changing event into stable artifacts and records. Although the mummers tend to think of the museum as theirs, it belongs to the city. Established by the city along with several other museums (including the African-American Museum), the Mummers' Museum was built on publicly owned property with city funds and continues to receive funding from the city each year.[78] Though funded by the city, the museum speaks to the mummers' own eagerness to preserve the history of the parade, not just by continuing to perform in it but by putting pieces of it on public display. Filled with samples of costumes (unusually extravagant specimens have pride of place), memorabilia, props, and documents relating to the parade, the museum serves as a tourist attraction and as an archive of information, much of it gathered and donated by participants themselves. Like the newspaper articles that in the nineteenth century conscripted the New Year's revelers into print culture, the museum represents another attempt at transplanting performance into a more determinate medium, one that can display and make permanent a particular version of the history of the parade in ways that the fluid and open-ended performance cannot.

The museumizing of the Mummers' Parade has not, however, diminished the parade's experiential qualities or its value to participants; if anything, it has intensified them. What might be more disruptive to the tradition of New Year's parading is the construction of a new center for the arts near City Hall on Broad Street (which in a sign of the intended sociocultural repositioning has been renamed the Avenue of the Arts). The center aims to buff up what is perceived as the tarnished image of downtown and to encourage residents of the suburbs to venture into the city. In addition to its symbolic claiming of the urban streets once possessed by popular culture, the Arts Center has also materially altered the cityscape in ways that might also reshape the parade; for the first time, in January 2000, the parade was routed up Market instead of Broad, a departure from tradition that altered the usual viewing and marching route. It is too soon to know in what other ways the Mummers' Parade will be influenced by this new shrine to entertainment and its middlebrow, suburbanite culture, but the Arts Center seems likely to have an impact on the parade's populist appeal.

While it is hard to imagine that the medieval past could ever again act as it once did to refashion Philadelphia's New Year's revels in ways palatable to dominant groups, the story of the shooters' refashioning as mummers after the parade's near demise at the end of the nineteenth century suggests a resilience and adaptability that perhaps bodes well for the future of the parade. A sense of connection to the past remains widely shared among current participants. "I'm a traditionalist," one mummer has said. "I believe that it's our responsibility to make sure that this tradition continues not just for ourselves, but for our children and future generations."[79] At the same time, linking of the parade to early English holiday rituals continues to shape local perceptions and to provide an ideological underpinning for the revels. In an article entitled "Mummers Trace Spirit of Revelry to 11th Century," which appeared in the *Philadelphia Bulletin* on January 1, 1978, Richard Southern's *Seven Ages of Theater* was used to trace, once again, the origins of Philadelphia's mummers to medieval theatrical traditions. This article suggests that as performative historiography the Mummers' Parade still profits from a sense of continuity with Anglo-Saxon traditions, which anchor it in a desirable historical past and endow it with a cultural respectability that remains efficacious even today.

CHAPTER 4

Reinventing Tradition
Brooklyn's Saint Play

Each July, in a ritual repeated annually for most of the past century, an Italian-American community in the Williamsburg section of Brooklyn, New York, spends two weeks celebrating the combined feasts of Our Lady of Mount Carmel and Saint Paulinus. The festivities include various outdoor entertainments, religious services, and street processions of which the undisputed centerpiece is the performance known as "the dancing of the *giglio*." In this performance, some 250 male participants lift and "dance" with two massive aluminum and papier-mâché structures—a tower (the *giglio*, pronounced "jeel-yo," often affectionately shortened to "the jeel") and a boat. Their progress through the streets is understood to dramatize the story of Saint Paulinus, a fourth-century bishop and patron saint of Nola, a town about twenty miles north of Naples. In the most widely accepted version of the legend as it is told in Brooklyn, Paulinus is said to have offered himself in exchange for a widow's only son, who had been captured by Saracens raiding southern Italy. When he and the other captive Nolani were released from slavery in northern Africa by a Turkish sultan impressed by Paulinus's self-sacrifice, they returned by boat to Nola where they were greeted by delighted townspeople waving lilies (*gigli*). The program for the feast distributed by the church of Our Lady of Mount Carmel claims that the first *giglio* was built by the Nolani in Paulinus's honor and has been carried in Nola every year since then in remembrance of the saint's generous act.[1]

According to the received history of the performance, in the early years of the twentieth century Italian immigrants from Nola brought the *giglio* ritual with them to New York City, where it was performed in various Italian neighborhoods. Today, however, despite occasional attempts at revival in other parts of the city, the Brooklyn *giglio* is the lone survivor of this once more widespread tradition. This selective survival points to what is one of the most important features of the *giglio,* and the one that helps make sense of its cultural meanings—the fact that it is a resolutely local performance, overlooked by much of America and unknown even to most New Yorkers. The benefits of this neglect are many, including that the performance has never attracted enough attention to warrant censoring, reshaping, or indeed much in the way of self-justification by its participants. Instead, the ritual has quietly survived demographic changes in the neighborhood and the pressure of a homogenizing mass culture. This survival has a number of causes, including the support the *giglio* has received from the parish church, but one of the most important sources of the *giglio*'s resilience in Brooklyn is the insistence of the local community that the performance provides a cultural link to a premodern European past that stands as a solution to problems of ethnic identity faced by the Brooklynites. As we shall see, however, the *giglio* does not so much preserve an actual past as reinvent a strategically useful version of it, one in which the supposed medievalness of the performance figures as a positive, even if only vaguely sketched, value that stands as a sign of the longevity of the tradition (and hence signals its importance) while offering a way of smoothing over tensions that might otherwise be aroused by a performance strongly marked for ethnicity, as the *giglio* is. In these and other ingenious ways, the *giglio*'s success offers a lesson in creative reinvention and in the constructive recycling of historical performances.

To a remarkable degree, the materiality of the *giglio* precedes its meanings and functions. The *giglio* is an attention-getting structure: a tall white-and-blue tower ornately decorated with bas-relief images of saints, *putti*, flowers, and religious symbols and topped by a statue of Paulinus, who wears a cloth robe that billows out behind him in the wind once the lifting starts. At the base is a platform for the band and a singer; the whole tower is wired for sound with large speakers hidden behind the façade. Beams protrude from all sides of the tower's base; during the dancing, men crouched four deep beneath each beam lift the *giglio* on their shoulders. Although descriptions of the *giglio*'s size vary and are susceptible to inflation by local pride (church publicity describes it as 105 feet tall and weighing four tons), it is emphatically big and easily soars far above the tallest building in the neighborhood. The phallic associations of the statue are hard to overlook, but just as important is its expression of a deep longing for attention and respect. In its gigantism, the *giglio* makes a claim for public recognition and esteem, attributes its sponsoring community has otherwise found to be in short supply.

The dancing of the *giglio*, which takes close to four hours to perform, is an elaborately orchestrated, processional music-drama performed in the streets in the midst of thousands of cheering and clapping spectators. At the command of a leader known as the *capo*, the 125 or so men (known as *paranze*) under the *giglio* simultaneously straighten their legs and thrust the *giglio* into the air, supporting it on their shoulders. With a peculiar stiff-legged gait and to the accompaniment of the band and singer, they then march with the tower a short distance (usually no more than thirty feet), executing various maneuvers ordered by the *capo*, including bouncing the *giglio* up and down, turning it around, and even moving it backward. After two or three minutes of dancing, the *capo* gives the command to release the *giglio*, which crashes back down onto its supports as the *paranze* bend their knees and drop it from their shoulders. Although the men's faces are contorted from the effort of lifting the heavy structure, the whole effect is surprisingly graceful and the *giglio* does indeed appear to dance through the streets, the statue of Paulinus bobbing and swaying on top.

While the *giglio* is being danced down the street from one direction, around the corner on an intersecting street the boat—which holds another band and singer along with the men playing the roles of the Turk and his entourage, who are dressed in turbans and carry scimitars—is lifted and danced by another group of men following the orders of their *capo*. Beginning out of each other's sight, the men heft the boat and tower in a characteristic stop-and-go movement over the course of the four hours of the performance, until they meet at last in front of the church, where in a symbolically charged and emotional moment the *paranze* from each crew clasp hands and embrace.

This description of the Saint Paulinus festival will undoubtedly sound familiar to anyone aware of the street theater of medieval Europe. Like the Corpus Christi and Whitsun cycles extant from northern England in the fourteenth through sixteenth centuries, the French Passion plays, the *autos* of medieval Spain, Italy's saints' processions, and the many other dramatic performances that were the hallmark of the public, festive culture of late medieval Europe, the Brooklyn *giglio* combines dance, music, narration, and impersonation into a complex ritual performance that plays an important role in the life of the local community.[2] It is striking, in fact, how much the *giglio* resembles the textbook definition of medieval urban religious drama: though church supported, it is a community production with actors and many spectators drawn from present or former residents of the neighborhood; it is performed annually on the occasion of a saint's feast and thus is part of a cyclical calendar of ritual religious performances, yet depends on overtly secular elements as well; it is a source of community pride and helps shape the community's identity; and it offers material as well as symbolic benefits for participants, the local church, and the neighborhood. One would have to look hard, particularly in the United States, to find a more vivid example of an extant medieval urban drama. From this perspective, then, Brooklyn's *giglio* can be seen as a rare survivor, a fascinating holdover from a ceremonial public culture that was largely obliterated centuries ago by the combined forces of religious reform, industrialization, and encroachment from other cultural forms. For two weeks each July, it seems, the Williamsburg section of Brooklyn becomes—like the more famous colonial town in Virginia that shares its name—a kind of living-history site, not one reconstructed by history buffs and civic authorities, but a place where a genuine tradition still flourishes after all these years.

But appearances can deceive. Despite its seeming replication of medieval performance modes and despite the local myth of its origins, the history of Brooklyn's *giglio* is one of imagined origins, fitful and disruptive transmission, and creative shaping to meet new needs. The version of the *giglio* ritual that is performed in Nola can be traced back to the sixteenth century—no earlier—although it probably existed in some form before that and is clearly a legacy of the many local theatrical traditions that once existed throughout Europe and that combined religious fervor with dramatic entertainments. But the Brooklyn version shows breaks with those traditions, particularly in many of its features that are clearly adaptive strategies aimed at helping the immigrants survive in a difficult new environment.

Part of the challenge of assessing the cultural meanings of the *giglio* ritual is to understand its relations with tradition—and to understand what we mean by that term. The most influential discussion of tradition, by Eric Hobsbawm, has tackled the subject from the oblique angle of spurious aspirants to that state. Hobsbawm's study of invented traditions describes the surprisingly large number of traditions that turn out on closer inspection to be nothing of the sort, dating back not to time immemorial but to a modern bureaucrat's bright idea.[3] The public ceremonials of the British monarchy, for instance, which are usually thought to descend from an ancient past, were in fact invented in their modern form in the nineteenth century to serve nationalist ends—and then that inventedness was immediately suppressed and forgotten. As is the case with these royal ceremonies, invented traditions typically aim to establish continuity with a suitable historical past so as to structure, in Hobsbawm's words, "at least some parts of social life as unchanging and invariant." Hobsbawm argues that traditions tend to be invented during times of change and innovation; once created, invented traditions proclaim themselves as traditional through processes of formalization and ritualization that are characterized by reference to the past, often by imposing repetition. The obverse of invented traditions, in Hobsbawm's scheme, are what he calls the "old ways" or traditions that have survived without disruption into the modern age and that act as strongly binding social practices with ties to a still living past.

The complexities of the relations of Brooklyn's *giglio* to the past go a long way toward revealing the limitations of these binaries. The *giglio* is patently not a true "old way," since there are obvious breaks and discontinuities in its history as well as fabrications about its longevity and about the past with which it claims connection, but it does share the hallmark quality of the customary "old ways" in being a strongly binding social practice with real ties to the past. For that reason, the *giglio* cannot be called an invented tradition either, despite the fact that it contains invented elements and that it tends to use history as Hobsbawm asserts invented traditions always do, as "a legitimator of action and cement of group cohesion."[4] Not quite custom or invention, not quite *echt* or *ersatz*, the *giglio* might best be described as a reinvented tradition that has links to actual historical practices, but that in the face of disruptions has had to reinvent itself to suit its new circumstances.

The most pressing impetus for reinvention was the move across the Atlantic from Italy to New York, which landed the *giglio* in a new cultural context in which both religion and ethnicity had radically altered meanings. Transplanted to the United States during the peak period of immigration from Italy in the 1880s to 1920s, the *giglio* performance not surprisingly became caught up in that era's debates about immigration, assimilation, and nationalism. As a folk performance linked to Catholic ritual it was scrutinized by both Catholic elites, for whom it seemed culturally primitive and apt to project the wrong kind of religiosity, and non-Catholic outsiders—some of the earliest eyewitness accounts of Italian-American festivities come from Protestant reformers and social workers intent on bettering the lot of immigrants through assimilation. In the early years of their importation to New York, Italian-American festivities like the *giglio* attracted voyeurs and cultural tourists interested in the "colorful" activities that went on in the Italian ghettoes. What is perhaps unexpected is the extent to which many of the same tangled issues of ethnicity and identity from that era continue to revolve around the *giglio* today.

The past remains of crucial importance to the *giglio* performance, but what that past is and what it means is not at all simple or self-evident. One way of describing the *giglio* would be to say that by holding to the image of the *giglio* as part of a long and unbroken tradition stretching back into the medieval past, Brooklyn's Italian-American community works to preserve its identity in the face of growing cultural homogeneity and demographic changes. This is what might be described as the official message of the *giglio*, the version that shows up in church publicity about the feast and in idealized accounts of the meaning of the performance. This version holds considerable appeal for participants and spectators alike, since the *giglio* performance obviously demonstrates nostalgia for historical roots and for many participants is about the remembered past that serves as a ground for the present and a way of connecting generations. One function of the *giglio*, then, is to make available to the present a usable past, one in which a reinvented medieval tradition becomes a securing point for a fast-eroding community identity.

But as a complex cultural performance, the *giglio* sends other messages as well, to both participants and spectators. Most of those messages are about consequences: the consequences of allegiance to a specific European past, of holding to an ethnic identity in the face of a melting-pot ideology, and of publicly performing that identity for a larger—and ethnically and religiously diverse—audience. The dancing of the *giglio* thus offers glimpses of the meanings of ethnic identities and cultural tradition in the context of a modern United States driven by the conflicting ideologies of assimilation and multiculturalism. The performance also comments on the consequences of work, since the dancing of the *giglio* creates, no matter how briefly, an alternate material and symbolic economy that in the earlier years of the century spoke directly to the economic circumstances in which most of the participants found themselves. Even now, when those economic circumstances have changed for many participants, the *giglio* continues to comment on what it means to be a laborer and an immigrant in a large American city. The *giglio* performance offers the spectacle of one man ("the guy with the stick," as one participant has aptly put it) directing the hard physical labor of a hundred men whose individuality is merged into the collective effort needed to move the tower, an effort that is expended, it seems, on nothing.[5] This labor is understood by participants to involve a kind of voluntary redemptive and honorific suffering, but it also symbolically rewrites the terms of the worker's position in a capitalist economy. In these and other ways, the *giglio* is a striking expression of the complex structures of feeling that shape attitudes toward working-class ethnicity in the United States, an ethnicity that in this case relies on a notion of communal roots in a medieval past as a bulwark against the present.[6]

Seeking Origins

That the Brooklyn *giglio* diverges from the Nola "original" in a number of ways should be no surprise, given the temporal and geographic distance between the two, but the details of that divergence merit consideration nonetheless, since they handily throw into relief the implications of the reinvention undertaken by the Brooklyn version. Secure within its social and historical milieu in a way that the Brooklyn performance can never be, the Nola version is able to risk a degree of competition and excess that have been erased from Brooklyn's *giglio,* while also taking for granted elements that must be continually reiterated in Brooklyn.[7] The Nola version shows the distance that the Brooklyn *giglio* has traveled and reveals the disruptions and creative adaptations that resulted as the performance was imported into America.

The city of Nola, with a population of around thirty-five thousand people, is located about thirty kilometers from Naples, behind Mount Vesuvius. It is an ancient city, and traces of the Etruscans and Romans, its earlier inhabitants, can still be seen in street pavings and buildings. While for most of its existence the city was dependent on agriculture, it also had a strong civic structure. Today, it is a prosperous bedroom community of Naples as well as a center of regional government.

Written records of Nola's *giglio* performance attest to its apparent notoriety for centuries. The earliest known description of the ritual in Nola can be found in the history of Nola written by the sixteenth-century philosopher Ambrogio Leone, who was born there. Leone's account describes an eight-day festival during the course of which there occurred a procession through the city featuring a large torch shaped like a column, lighted and decorated with sprigs of grain, which was carried by farmers. This torch was so large, Leone claims, that it could not be lifted by just one man and was called a *cereo,* or "candle." The farmers and their candle were followed by artisans and other lay groups with other candles. After these came the monks and priests, with the bishop last, carrying in his hand the reliquary containing relics of San Paolino. Accompanying the bishop were local dignitaries as well as the chief citizens and other townspeople, all on foot.[8]

During the seventeenth and eighteenth centuries, pageants using large decorated structures became popular throughout Italy, and in Nola the "candles" were replaced by huge "machines" (globes, pyramids, ships, and other shapes, according to a 1747 description by Gianstefano Remondini) decorated with flowers and the emblems of the artisans who constructed them.[9] They were called *gigli*, Remondini says, a term thought by the Italian scholar Franco Manganelli to be related by sound to the word *cilii*, the dialect term in Salerno for *ceri* "candles."[10] The sound shift from *cilii* to *gigli* apparently resulted in the embellishment of the legend that has the townspeople waving lilies to greet their saint's return. By 1850, a new character had appeared: the Turk, a popular figure in southern Italian folklore. In a technological innovation, papier mâché was now used for the *gigli*. In 1866, Francesco de Bourcard described the "bella festa" during which Nola celebrated its bishop and protector Paulinus and commented in particular on the size of the "pyramids," which according to him towered over the town's highest buildings. The *gigli* that Bourcard saw were adorned with flowers, ribbons, and papier-mâché statues; on the first level of the structures were orchestras, while on the second, men and women stood. Bourcard claims that the *gigli* were constructed under the sponsorship of the guilds, although they moved through the streets accompanied by clergy.[11] If Bourcard's description can be believed, then the feast as performed today in Nola has changed remarkably little since he saw it in the nineteenth century.

As this interest in the performance by the literate classes suggests, Nola's ritual was by the nineteenth century, and perhaps even earlier, no longer a purely local affair but one that had begun attracting tourists. In 1856, Charles Dickens's journal *Household Words* published an eyewitness account by one such tourist—who was possibly Dickens himself.[12] The account starts with the English traveler's arrival in Naples, with a description of the crowds assembled around the Naples train station waiting to go to Nola, including foreigners like the author himself and a woman so ill with malaria that she seems to the author to be on the verge of death, but who wants to see the *gigli* nonetheless. As the train approaches Nola, the author glimpses "a large, irregularly-built city on a vast plain, with a background of mountains." Joining the passengers who fight their way through the throngs to the principal street, the author exclaims over a pretty steeple he glimpses and is told it is one of the *gigli*. Up close, he sees that it is made from a framework of wood interlaced with canes and that it consists of a series of towers one upon the other, tapering away, all decorated with architectural ornaments, flowers and evergreens, drapery, paintings, and statuary, while at the corner of each tower floats a flag. A hundred feet in the air, the top holds a saint of the group of artisans who made the tower. Around the platform of the tower is a full brass band, while on the upper reaches stand men and boys. There are nine such structures, the author discovers, each constructed by a specific guild of craftsmen, which hangs its emblems on the tower. The *giglio* derives its name, the author believes, "from some fancied resemblance to the flower of that name, the lily."

The festival begins, the author continues, when the *gigli*, carried on the shoulders of fifty men, assemble in the plaza before the *Sottintendente*'s house. The exertion "appears to be tremendous, even to raise the structure from the ground," and the author marvels that four hundred or five hundred of the strongest porters from Naples vie for the chance to be lifters, even though all they receive is a *piastre* each, plus all they can eat and drink. Led by hundreds of priests and singing boys, the *gigli* move for three hours through the town, going a few feet before stopping to rest, and finally returning at last to the piazza on the west end of town where they began. The author wrangles an invitation to the *Sottintendente*'s house, and using the occasion to ask about the origins of the custom is told that it dates to the time when Saint Paulinus "wrought the miracle on our bell" by running his finger through the bell; the hole still remains. The night before, the author tells us, in a ritual that he missed, thousands came to town and engaged in the custom of musical duels in which competing parties send one another challenges to sing (the challenges are usually full of gibes and ridicule of the others); the competition goes on for hours and sometimes ends in violence. On the day of the festival proper, the author estimates that some fifty thousand people are crowded in the town, most of whom devote themselves to eating, drinking, and dancing after the procession ends and before riding on horseback or in carriages into Naples to parade about. For those who stay in Nola there are horse races to watch. Perhaps once upon a time, the author speculates, the religious element dominated, but now pleasure reigns in this thoroughly secular event. At ten thirty that night, the author arrives again in Naples, where he finds the Nolani still driving about and shouting or seated at tables along the streets eating and drinking.

Although the author of the *Household Words* article never reveals his motives for traveling to Nola to watch the festival, we can surmise from what he finds worthy of remark that in his search for material to fill the magazine's pages and to entertain readers, he is drawn to the pleasurable exoticism of the event, particularly its atmosphere of exuberant excess, which he discovered in the singing competitions, the feasting and dancing, and the efforts involved in lifting and processing through the streets with the nine *gigli*. Our writer is by and large content to take the festivities at face value and to remain a detached and superficial observer of the scene. Not surprisingly, his account presents an easy, uncomplicated relationship with cultural tourism: no questions are asked about the significance of the festival for its participants; no qualms are expressed about the effects of an outsider's presence.

The Nola performance may have reached its touristic peak with this nineteenth-century account, despite the efforts of the many Nola residents who have a strong interest in making known the history of the town's *giglio* festival. Along with scholarly historical studies, collections of historical references and editions of early photographs of the festival aimed at a popular readership have been published in recent years.[13] Tourists are actively courted and there is also considerable publicity about the festival, including an official website of the event. These promotional activities do not, however, appear to have helped the Nola festival attract many spectators from outside the region, and the festival remains largely a local affair.[14] The group of tourists for whom Nola's *giglio* holds the most appeal is Brooklynites, for some of whom the Nola festival has attained cult-status, although the number who actually attends it is small.

Those Brooklyn residents who manage to see the Italian "original" of their ritual may be taken aback by the differences between the two, which are pronounced. Those differences point to the extent of reinvention in Brooklyn's version and suggest some of the reasons for the need for changes in order to adapt the performance to a New World context. The broadest of the changes is that in Nola the *giglio* festival is organized around centripetal forces that the local context can easily absorb (and perhaps even needs), but that would be distinctly unwelcome in the Brooklyn setting. Unlike Brooklyn's, Nola's performance stresses multiplicity, competitiveness, and innovation. It features not one but eight *gigli,* plus the boat; its sponsors are not the local religious authorities, but various guilds, although it has the support of church and civic authorities as well; the lifters are not from the community, but are hired from out of town. The performance begins when the *gigli,* which have been stationed for the week at various spots throughout the town where they can be admired, are gathered in a line against one side of the *piazza duomo.* On the first Sunday after June 22, a *ballata,* or dance, in the piazza in the morning begins the day's performance during which the *gigli* and the boat are danced among the spectators packed into the piazza. The *ballata* is followed by a competitive procession through the streets that starts in the afternoon and continues through the night, well after many spectators have gone home to bed. The performance ends the next day in the piazza, where each team performs various maneuvers and lines up in front of the town hall for the final judging and a chance at the substantial cash prizes paid to the winners. As in the nineteenth century, singing contests and joking insults are part of this procession as the eight teams of men try to carry their *gigli* as quickly as possible through town without rubbing up against any buildings as they negotiate the tight turns in the streets. Rather than working as a harmonious group as the Brooklyn lifters do, the eight teams in Nola—which are comprised not of local townsmen but of athletic lifters drawn from farther afield—compete against each other. Rather than moving within a constricted space that signals dispossession of the

Festa dei gigli, Nola, Italy, June 1997. Photo by the author.

larger public domain, the Nola *gigli* roam freely through the city's streets. Rather than being carefully treated as enduring monuments that are painstakingly disassembled and stored each year, the Nola *gigli* are destroyed and rebuilt anew for each festival, with each construction team seeking to outdo the others with its decorative arts. Those involved in the Nola *festa*, it seems, can afford to risk competition, the incorporation of outsiders, novelty, and wasteful destruction because they are confident of their ownership of the place in which the event occurs.

Where the two versions of the *giglio* performance converge is in their current insistence that the festival celebrates the return of Saint Paulinus from being held in captivity by barbarians; according to popular tradition in both Nola and Brooklyn, Paulinus was responsible for freeing Nolani who had been carried off by barbarians. He was welcomed on his return by townspeople carrying flowers and escorted in procession to the bishop's palace. The historical Paulinus who is invoked as founding father of the *giglio* was Pontius Meropius Anicius Paulinus, who was born circa A.D. 353 into a wealthy Roman family in Bordeaux, France. He became consul of Nola in 387, came under the influence of Saint Ambrose and Saint Martin of Tours, and was baptized in 389; he was ordained four years later. A cultured man, he wrote lyric poetry and corresponded with Jerome and Augustine, while also finding time to oversee extensive building projects in Nola and serve as bishop there from 409 to his death in 431. The source for the legend behind the *giglio* feast comes from

Gregory the Great's *Dialogues,* which were written nearly a century after Paulinus's death. Gregory describes how Vandals attacked Nola, shortly after Paulinus had become bishop of Nola, and kidnapped many of its inhabitants. To save a widow's only son, Paulinus offered himself as a slave in his place. While in captivity, Paulinus prophesied the upcoming death of the Vandal king (a prophecy that matched the king's dreams). Learning of the prophecy, the king ordered Paulinus brought to him and as a reward, or perhaps out of fear of his powers, freed Paulinus and the Nola captives, gave them boats, and sent them back to Nola.[15] Although many of the details evoked in the *giglio* ritual are present in this account, Gregory does not mention the triumphal return of Paulinus to Nola that is celebrated in the *giglio* ritual. Gregory's Vandals presumably became the Turks of today's festival sometime during the Christian-Moorish conflicts of the sixteenth century.

As an anchor for the Brooklyn *giglio* festival, Paulinus's legend holds obvious appeal. Not a miracle-worker like that other saint of Italian immigrants, Manhattan's San Gennaro, Paulinus instead promises that hard work and self-sacrifice will be rewarded and that ethnic clashes can be overcome. It is in fact difficult to conjure up a more perfect saint for the circumstances faced by the Italian immigrants to Brooklyn. Whatever attractions Paulinus held for the Nolani, they must have been magnified many times over for the early-twentieth-century immigrants to Brooklyn thrown into a harsh world of ethnic hostilities and economic hardships.

This perhaps explains why, while both versions are organized around the same legend, only in Brooklyn is that legend a structural part of the performance. Despite their shared stock in the Paulinus myth, the Nola and Brooklyn versions differ in the degree of their investment in it. In Nola, where the performance is not sponsored by the church, not linked to another church feast, and not conceived of in sacrificial terms, the Paulinus myth serves as background rationale for the performance, but contributes little to its cultural meanings. In Brooklyn, the Paulinus myth is fundamental to the meaning of the performance for its participants. Another way to put the difference is to say that, in Nola, the festival is primarily a footrace, while, in Brooklyn, it's a drama. This is not to claim that races do not encode dramatic action, since they do. But for the Brooklyn *giglio* the narrative of exile and return and of ethnic hostilities amicably resolved that is part of the Paulinus story matters in a way that it does not in Nola. The foregrounding of that narrative is one of the most obvious and important ways in which the *giglio* has been reinvented to suit its New World context.

Reinventing Traditions

To go from Manhattan to Italian-American Williamsburg over the Williamsburg Bridge is to experience an intense sense of dislocation. Although only a few miles in distance, the journey marks a shift from densely packed sidewalks full of hip young urbanites to half-deserted and trash-strewn streets; from soaring glass and steel buildings to small brownstones and storefronts with metal grates on their doors; from apparent wealth to seeming poverty; from residents and passersby whose ethnic backgrounds are masked by a patina of cosmopolitanism to signs everywhere one looks of distinctively defined cultural heritage—in clothing, in overheard snippets of conversation, in polyglot signs in store windows. Today three more or less distinct ethnic enclaves make up Williamsburg: Italians, Hassidic Jews, and Hispanics, who are chiefly Puerto Ricans. It is one of the poorest districts in Brooklyn, with a median family income of less than $10,800 in 1979.[16] More recently, low rents have been a magnet attracting artists to the neighborhood, and a limited degree of gentrification has taken place. But even though the Brooklyn *giglio* is performed in a borough of the metropolis of New York City, it for the most part goes unnoticed by the millions who live near it.

The geographic space of the performance is crucial to understanding its reinventive tactics. The "Italian Williamsburg" section of Brooklyn in which the *giglio* is performed was settled in the late nineteenth and early twentieth centuries by immigrants from Naples and its surrounding towns. Cut in half by the Brooklyn-Queens Expressway whose girders tower overhead, the community hides beneath and to the east of it, tucked away where Manhattan cab drivers have trouble finding it. Although pride in "the old neighborhood" animates the *giglio* festival, the community is also sensitive about what Joseph Sciorra, a folklorist with local ties who has written extensively about the festival, calls the neighborhood's identity crisis. Sometimes it is referred to as Greenpoint, sometimes as Williamsburg, neither of which seems to participants to accurately represent their community. One feast official quoted by Sciorra remarks that "when you say that the feast is in Greenpoint, people think *Polish.* When you say Williamsburg, they don't want to come."[17] Publicity for the feast gets around this problem by avoiding naming the neighborhood, defining its location with the broadly inclusive term *Brooklyn.*

The feast official's comment aptly points to the complicated attitudes toward ethnicity in the United States, attitudes that the *giglio* festival has had to contend with, like it or not. In recent years, as the image of America as a melting-pot nation has come under attack from those challenging the assimilationist drive to erase distinctive ethnic identities and those seeking to limit immigration in order to protect an "American" identity felt to be at risk, ethnicity has become a conflict-ridden cultural value, both desired and despised. On the one hand, ethnicity is associated with such positive values as cultural heritage, group cohesiveness, and tradition. On the other hand, it is often linked to social divisiveness, cultural isolationism, and resistance to progress. The dancing of the *giglio* demonstrates this confusion surrounding ethnicity, which oscillates between attraction and repulsion, "othering" and identification.

What is remarkable about the *giglio* ritual, however, is that it displays not just the considerable involvement of Italian-American culture in its own self-construction but also an ethnicity that promises to lead not to social discord and national fragmentation, as is often feared, but rather to cultural harmony and inclusiveness. That the *giglio* as ritual theater manages this trick is to a large degree the key to its continued survival and a testament to the adroitness with which it has been reinvented.

Any assessment of how the *giglio* performance intersects with contemporary structures of feeling about ethnicity has to start with an understanding of the history of Italians in the United States. The message of ethnic vitality and tolerance that the *giglio* now communicates was forged, ironically, out of early-twentieth-century opposition to immigration and is grounded in socioeconomic discrimination and ethnic hatreds. The section of Brooklyn where the *giglio* is performed was densely settled by Italian immigrants during the intense forty-year span of immigration from Italy to the United States that occurred between 1880 and 1920. Although Brooklyn was home to only 225 Italians in 1870, the numbers swelled rapidly to a reported 27,119 by 1900 and to 137,970 by 1920. After slowing to a trickle in the 1930s and 1940s, a second wave of immigration began after World War II as people left war-torn Italy. By 1980 there were 307,044 Italian Americans in Brooklyn, out of some 12 million in the U.S. population at large.[18]

The experience of the early Italian immigrants, most of whom came from Sicily and southern Italy, was marked by a lack of economic opportunity and hostility from those already settled in the States. Without capital to buy land or start businesses and often uneducated and illiterate, the rural agricultural workers who arrived from southern Italy were shunted into ill-paid and dangerous work, usually in heavy industry and construction in northeastern cities.[19] Philip Foner notes that immigrants from eastern and southern Europe were subjected to the same "white supremacy" theories that shut blacks out of labor unions and denied them access to bargaining that might have improved labor conditions and wages.[20] In a typical diatribe, Edward A. Ross, writing in *The Century Magazine* in 1914, claimed that the "dwarfishness" and mental defects of Italians made them poor laborers.[21] Italian immigrants were in fact often blamed for causing the very ills they suffered and were widely attacked in the popular press for depressing wages and lowering socioeconomic standards for American workers.[22] An anonymous author summed up the prevailing attitude when he complained in *The World's Work* that America was being swamped by "the undersized, illiterate overflow from half-medieval Naples and Sicily."[23]

In the face of these social and economic obstacles, Italian immigrants depended for their survival on a group solidarity fashioned out of affective regionalism and the maintenance of a shared cultural tradition that flowed naturally from an immigration pattern in which residents from specific towns and regions in Italy relocated in one particular spot in the States, as the Nolani did in Brooklyn. Although early reformers tried to address what was widely described as the "Italian Problem" by encouraging Italians to move to rural communities and become farmers, the majority of the Italian immigrants remained rooted in the urban northeast where there was a demand for unskilled and semiskilled industrial labor.[24] The consequence was that Italians were much more ghettoized than immigrant groups such as the Germans and Irish, who had arrived earlier and benefited from greater economic opportunity and hence more social and geographic mobility.[25] Whatever their problematic social and material effects, these patterns of immigration look rather better from a perspective that values cultural history, since they kept Italian regional culture alive in distinctive enclaves within American cities. But while cultural traditions provided Italian immigrants with a welcome buffer against social and economic hardships, with their emphasis on maintaining family and a closed community, such traditions often appeared to slow assimilation. Addressing this perceived problem, a *Guide for Immigrant Italians,* published in 1911, exhorted the immigrants to join "American" clubs and read "American" papers, while giving up "all 'campanilish' " sentiments.[26]

Religious street festivals, which were based on the popular cults of the Virgin and devotion to the local patron saints of each village, were the most visible manifestation of the regional culture Italians brought with them to the States.[27] Ambivalence about ethnicity was part of the response to these festivals from the outset. They were a source of embarrassment to American Catholicism and to the Italian-American clergy who tried to ban them—in part because the festivals (and the *festa* societies that supported them) challenged the authority of official Catholicism and siphoned off money that might otherwise have gone to support the church. They were also perceived as public advertisements for Italian cultural difference at a time when such difference was a distinct liability and when cultural integration and the "Americanizing" of all sorts of "others" was a concerted national project. But despite the fact that nativism was on the upswing and anti-Catholic, not to mention anti-Italian, sentiment was strong, these religious festivals thrived, serving as key cultural events for the people within the communities that sponsored them. It is important to note that these festivals also attracted the attention of outsiders, acting as entertaining spectacles for non-Italians. In the early years of the twentieth century, upper-class residents of West Harlem, for example, amused themselves by strolling over to the Italian East Side on Sundays and holidays to watch the festivities and to enjoy the colorful behavior of the Italians.[28] This sort of cultural voyeurism continued throughout the century and indeed survives today, echoed for instance in a promotional flyer published by Our Lady of Mount Carmel Church which proclaims that the *giglio* performance "must be seen to be believed," a phrase that seems to acknowledge and even encourage outsiders' voyeuristic impulses. What must be emphasized is that these displays of ethnicity were never private rituals but, because they took place on the streets of the city, always involved spectators from outside the immediate community. They were thus particularly susceptible to differing interpretations and divergent cultural meanings. One reason the Brooklyn *giglio* has proven so enduring and so successful is precisely that it has been able to mediate between insiders and outsiders, displaying an ethnicity that speaks to both groups—a topic I shall return to later. Perhaps that ability was forged in the early years of the *giglio* celebration in America, when it was forced to deal with not only the needs and desires of participants but also the reactions of spectators whose opinions mattered.

The history of the *giglio* in Brooklyn is marked by disruptions and tensions that would on the surface at least seem to belie the performance's longevity. The first Our Lady of Mount Carmel Church was built in 1887 at North Eighth Street and Union Avenue as a local church for the Italian immigrants who had been shut out of St. Cecilia's Church, which was controlled by the Irish and German Catholics. In 1903 the mutual aid society, *Società M.S. [Mutuo Soccorso] San Paolino,* was incorporated and danced the first *giglio* performance in Brooklyn. At the same time, other *giglio* festivals were celebrated in Astoria in Queens; in Harlem on 106th and 108th Streets; and in Cliffside-Fairview in New Jersey. In the 1920s and 1930s Italians from the various neighborhoods visited and participated in the different feasts, and a competition among neighborhoods developed, reproducing in a limited way the competitiveness of the Nola version. That competitiveness was short-lived, however, as all of the *giglio* celebrations except for Brooklyn's died out. The Brooklyn celebration itself was discontinued in the 1940s during the war years and when the original church was destroyed to make room for the Brooklyn-Queens Expressway, which bisected the community. In a crisis at the end of the 1940s, tensions between assimilation and preservation of a visible ethnic identity came to the fore: the church urged abandoning the ritual in order to help the community become more American while the mutual aid society argued on behalf of preserving tradition (money was also rumored to have played a role, with a struggle between the church and the society over who would control the profits). This disruption did not prove fatal, however, and the *giglio* performance was started up again in the 1950s by a new society, the *Società San Paolo,* made up of second-generation Italian Americans. In 1954 Our Lady of Mount Carmel Church assumed control of the feast, which was moved from June 22 to mid-July and was merged with the Feast of Our Lady of Mount Carmel. In 1958 the dancing of the Turk's boat was added to the Brooklyn feast, providing the dramatic basis for the present performance.[29] As this brief history suggests, a consistent feature of the Brooklyn *giglio* throughout the century has been its entanglement in controversies over maintenance versus loss of cultural difference, with its ownership contested by church and community. The 1958 addition of the Turk's boat opened the way for inscribing those controversies within the performance,

Giglio, Feast of Saint Paulinus, Brooklyn, New York, July 1996. Photo
by the author.

which could then enact a satisfying resolution of the "problem" of ethnic difference.

The insularity of the *giglio* community in Brooklyn suggests one reason for
its success in dealing with the cultural problems to which it so creatively responds. In contrast with the citywide Nola version, in Brooklyn the perfor-

mance is a small-scale neighborhood affair, in which collaboration and continuity dominate.[30] To be a lifter means to be linked to the neighborhood by residence there or by family or other ties of close affiliation. Participation in the
performance is thus essentially closed to outsiders, unless they somehow become insiders. The neighborhood focus is underscored by the ritual known as
the "*capo* line of march," which occurs on the first Sunday of the festival; a
procession accompanied by a band winds through the neighborhood on the
morning of the first "lifting," stopping at the doors of the former and present
capos to take them to the performance site. This procession not only links
households in the neighborhood, but while honoring the *capos* also provides
continuity between present and former performances of the ritual—as each
capo is added to the procession, the memory of the year in which he led the
giglio performance is recalled, with the result that the current year's celebration takes its place in a long line of performances.

Once the actual dancing of the *giglio* begins, collaboration is stressed in a
number of ways, most obviously through the united effort that is required for
the lifters to raise and move the *giglio*. The weight and height of the structure
demand carefully coordinated teamwork; if one side of the structure were to
be raised or lowered too quickly, it could easily topple, destroying it and harm-
ing the band members riding on top as well as the spectators gathered closely
around. Continuity is most visible in the ritual object itself. Only one *giglio* is
danced and it is sponsored by the entire community. Instead of being destroyed each year as the *gigli* are in Nola, Brooklyn's *giglio* is carefully disassembled and stored in the church basement until the next summer. Although
the *giglio* is refurbished from time to time, its style remains substantially unchanged from year to year and molds for the bas-reliefs dating from the time
of Ramoldo Martello, the chief *giglio* builder from 1929 to 1970, continue to
be used. As a consequence, the *giglio* that is lifted in Brooklyn today looks
nearly identical to photographs of the *giglio* from sixty years ago. In Brooklyn,
then, under pressure from a history of hostile social and economic forces, the
performance has come to dramatize the themes of membership, continuity,
and unity—rather than rivalry, innovation, and competition as in Nola.

While this emphasis on continuity and collaboration is certainly understandable in light of the animosity faced by the early Italian immigrants and
their need for group solidarity in order to survive, it is perhaps more surprising
that these themes endure in the present performance context as well. Among
contemporary participants, the *giglio* performance is consistently regarded as,
and asked to be, a point of stability in a rapidly changing world that is seen as
threatening to wipe out ethnic differences and erase tradition. Whatever the reality of this perception, it is widely shared by members of the community. As
one woman who lives in the community has said, "Other neighborhoods
evolved and changed way before we did. Their ethnic population changed.
People cut out sooner . . . [Williamsburg] is still more *intact* than the other
neighborhoods." A man who has lifted for many years and has served as *capo*

similarly has remarked that "the neighborhood is really held together with this feast. . . . If it weren't here, I don't even know if I'd be here."[31] As these comments reveal, for participants the *giglio* ritual is an important way to perform—and by performing, to preserve—a community-based ethnic identity. In order to accomplish this performance of a shared and traditional identity, the Brooklyn *giglio* cannot give expression to the competitive and innovative impulses that inform the Nola version since to do so might endanger important ideals of neighborhood unity and shared identity.

Where the Brooklyn *giglio* encounters the greatest difficulty in sustaining this image of communal harmony is along gender lines. The peculiarly male aspect of the *giglio* performance today causes a degree of defensiveness among the male participants and is a troubling issue for many women, who are concerned that they are shut out of their community's most important event. This exclusiveness is attributable not only to paradigms of patriarchy but also to the history of Italians in the United States. Among early Italian immigrants, men far outnumbered women: from 1869 to 1910, some 78 percent of the immigrants were male in contrast to other ethnic groups that had a more balanced sex ratio.[32] This imbalance occurred as a result of an immigration pattern in which Italian men typically came to America alone, on the assumption that their stay would last only long enough for them to earn sufficient money to take back to the families they had left behind. The early performances of the *giglio* were shaped not only by this sex-ratio imbalance but also by the economic roles these men were expected to play. When lifted by men transplanted into an urban-industrial society that valued them chiefly as raw manpower, the *giglio* took on new meaning as a form of festive resistance. Against the reality of hard and ill-paid wage labor supervised by other ethnic groups, rituals like the dancing of the *giglio* functioned as an alternative masculine world to that of everyday work. Analogous in some ways to labor unions, which offered a similar chance for social and economic brotherhood, religious festivals went beyond unions in offering a creative space for the refiguring of oppressive work conditions. As Robert Orsi has suggested, such festivals provided a welcome escape for men, through the opportunity for a display of energy and enthusiasm in self-fulfilling and voluntarily undertaken labor.[33]

More pointedly than other Italian *feste,* the dancing of the *giglio*—which in its afternoon-long drama of physical struggle stresses such essential requirements for unskilled labor as physical strength, obedience, and cooperation—turns blue-collar work into a source of satisfaction. The performance is remarkable for its replication of the grim reality of physical work in a capitalist economy. It follows a strict hierarchy in which the *capo*'s orders determine every move that the lifters make ("his word is law," as one participant has put it).[34] It is driven, literally, by the muscle power of the men moving the tower ("you'll see the men struggling," the same participant has said, describing what a spectator will witness at the performance), who lose their individuality as they are massed together under the *giglio*'s platform. The men thrust, heave, and stagger, taking tiny steps that move the *giglio* forward only a bit before they let it crash down again onto its supports. Again and again this effort is repeated over the course of the afternoon, as the men get ever more tired and have to work harder on each lift. But the joke on capitalism is that all this effort produces nothing but symbolic capital and profits nobody except for the men performing it. The performance erases the distinction between productive and nonproductive, profitable and unprofitable work. In the brief interval of the performance, the men under the tower become the owners of their labors and all its benefits accrue to them. If labor is "the tribute paid towards a necessary order," as Pierre Bourdieu claims, then the *giglio* offers tribute to a different order, one imagined as an alternative to normative economic structures.[35]

Today, however, the masculinist working-class solidarity that spawned the *giglio* performance in turn-of-the-century Brooklyn and gave it a particular set of meanings has been eroded. The work force has been reconfigured—becoming among other things more skilled and less male-dominated—in ways that make earlier cultural meanings of the *giglio* less persuasive. Although the *giglio*'s function as an antidote to work still has some relevance, the men who lift the *giglio* are now as likely to be insurance salesmen, doctors, social workers, and small-business owners as manual laborers working under oppressive conditions. Lifting the *giglio* may, in fact, for many men be their only acquaintance with hard labor. So if there continues to be solidarity among the lifters, it is not as uniformly blue-collar as it once was. And the rescripting of the terms of manual work offered by the *giglio* performance may no longer be as meaningful as it once was.

Just as important, the exclusion of women from the *giglio* performance no longer goes unquestioned. But despite pressure for change, women are still not allowed to participate, and their continued exclusion is often rationalized on the grounds that to admit women would be a betrayal of tradition. Such a rationalization, however, cannot help but point to the gender inequity that underpins the *giglio* performance. Especially for younger Italian-American women within the community, the masculinist bias of the *giglio* presents an identity problem, since it seems to link Italianness with masculinity in a way that effectively cuts them off not just from the performance but also from the ethnicity it performs. Unlike many other male ritual performances, the *giglio* does not even offer women supporting-cast or behind-the-scenes roles, since all the organizational work for the performance is carried out by men. For many women, then, the *giglio* is a vexed performance of their ethnicity, one that forces them into the position of onlookers rather than full-fledged participants and that denies them visible participation in their cultural heritage.[36] The image of communal harmony projected by the *giglio* can thus be accepted only by ignoring the women who are scripted out of the drama or relegated to the role of spectators.

Another predicament faced by the *giglio* performance arises from the way that what were once Italian enclaves have had their demographics reshaped. From the late 1950s to the early 1970s, many Italians in Williamsburg relocated to the suburbs; at the same time, members of other ethnic groups moved in. Since the early 1980s, Williamsburg has attracted artists and others driven out of Manhattan by high rents. Today, the neighborhood is multiethnic, and many of the Italian Americans who perform in and watch the dancing of the *giglio* no longer live there but travel from out of town for the festivities, becoming tourists at the site of their own ethnicity. At the same time, since the neighborhood's ethnic composition has shifted, the *giglio* is now brought into contact with new audiences who are not themselves Italian American.

In this changed context, the *giglio* continues to stand as a visible sign around which Italian-American identity can be constructed, even if only on a part-time basis. But it has become an ambiguous sign, one that must respond to cultural changes that question certain of the grounds on which it was founded, including male dominance, working-class solidarity, and ethnic exclusiveness. Likewise, although some of the spectators, particularly the Latinos who now make up a large segment of the neighborhood's population, share the Catholic heritage that underlies the performance, others do not. So a religious gap has opened up in the local community that once did not exist. What is unusual about the *giglio* performance is that it has been particularly effective at surviving in the face of these altered circumstances, proving resilient enough to respond to the demands of new audiences while still functioning for its participants within a changed cultural context. The reason for this success has to do in large part with the narrative the *giglio* enacts and with the structure of the performance. Both narrative and structure offer a way of accommodating the *giglio* to changed circumstances while also continuing to meet the needs of its participants.

While the narrative aspect of the *giglio* is muted, it nonetheless serves as a kind of deep structure for the performance. Only one character from the Paulinus story is impersonated—the Turk, who is played by a local man who is joined in his boat by other men dressed as his crew (Paulinus is present in the ritual only in inanimate form as a statue atop the *giglio*). The plot is condensed into the stop-and-go, delay-and-progression movement of the boat and tower and their final meeting in front of the church. There is no dialogue, only the songs and music performed by the band and singer. Sketchy though this narrative structure is, it is still sufficient to represent the story of Saint Paulinus and to slant it toward a particular interpretation. Although Bourdieu may be right in claiming that rituals find their *"raison d'être* in the conditions of existence and the dispositions of agents who cannot afford the luxury of logical speculation," the agents behind the Brooklyn *giglio* have managed to construct a dramatic logic within their ritual that realigns key elements of the legend in order to best face their conditions of existence.[37]

Giglio, Feast of Saint Paulinus, Brooklyn, New York, July 1996. Photo by the author.

Figured as a way of performing and displaying a distinct and supposedly traditional identity, one difficulty the *giglio* faces is that of marking its performers as excessively "other" and hence as intransigent threats to ideologies of national unity. Although the narrative undergirding the *giglio* performance is of course open to multiple readings, certain aspects of it are pitched toward assuaging fears of excessive otherness or of the ethnic strife and cultural intolerance that might develop from that otherness. The narrative revolves around the themes of invasion and return, destruction and preservation of community, and ethnic antagonism and reconciliation, in each case favoring ameliorative rather than destructive resolutions. The version of the legend most widely known to the Brooklyn participants and on which they understand their performance to be based begins by describing how marauding Saracens attacked Nola and tore apart its community by capturing the men of the town and taking them away to become slaves. In this scenario, ethnic fears and hatreds are given free expression as Saracens are cast in the role of hostile invaders, ethnic outsiders who destroy the (Italian) community. But, interestingly, the legend does not dwell on this initial moment of invasion and destruction. Reconciliation is instead brought about quickly and ethnic differences are smoothed as the Turk sets Paulinus free and the captured Nolani are returned to their town. Since the *giglio* performance enacts not the raid-and-capture part of the legend, but only the release-and-return, the resolution of ethnic antagonisms becomes the central message of the drama. This ameliorative message is vividly staged in the climatic moment when the boat full of Turks and the tower bearing Paulinus meet in front of the church and the *paranze* from both groups clasp hands. As an ensemble, legend and performance give expression to ethnic tensions but foreground a celebratory reconciliation of differences.

Both official church publicity and media accounts have been eager to emphasize the integrative aspect of this part of the narrative. An article in the *New York Times* for July 14, 1994, for instance, ran under the telling headline "Celebration of an Ancient Italian Feast Yields Lessons for Modern Brooklyn."[38] The article itself stresses the performance's ability to communicate ethnic tolerance and its demonstration of cultural integration, which the writer takes as "a testament to the community's willingness to go beyond past stereotypes and rally around common issues"—a phrasing that acknowledges the potential divisiveness of ethnicity but seeks to reformulate it as contributing to the commonweal.

The performance further underscores this message of reconciliation and cultural harmony through its structural emphasis on social cohesiveness. Packed four deep under the beams supporting the *giglio*'s platform, their heads almost resting on each other's shoulders, the men serving as lifters lose their individuality and meld into one mass, an effect that is heightened by their costumes of white pants or shorts, T-shirts with the *giglio* printed on the front, and white or red caps—costumes that make them look like "Boy Scouts gone to seed," in the words of one observer.[39] The lifting itself is highly ritualized. As the band plays the theme song "O' Giglio e Paradiso," the lifters take their places while the *capo* steps in front of them. When the *capo* raises his cane into the air, the lifters jerk upright, everyone cheers, and the tower is lifted. The *capo* then shouts "musica" and the band plays his chosen song while he directs the lifters in their steps. The *capo* is aided by lieutenants standing at the corners of the *giglio*, who relay his instructions to their team and help the *paranze* by pushing in the required direction of a turn. Each lift is carefully synchronized and depends on a strict hierarchy of orders carried out faithfully by the lifters. When the lifts are completed, the men and bystanders embrace and slap each other on the back in an exuberant show of affectionate bonding that offers a compelling and infectious image of group harmony. From the church's roof, a favored position for watching the performance, what the spectator sees at the end of each lift when the *giglio* is dropped back onto the ground is the tightly knit group of men who had been densely packed under the tower dispersing and threading out into the crowd of spectators where they are absorbed into and mesh with the thousands of onlookers.

At the same time, although the *giglio* performance is on one level about male power, that power takes on a benign look as physical strength is translated into devotion to tradition, to community, and to family. The various lifts are usually performed explicitly in honor of deceased friends and family, whose names are called out by the singer before each lift. As one participant has remarked about what it means to be a lifter: "For this moment I mean something, I'm worth something, I have contributed something to the sufferings of society, to the loneliness of people."[40] The performance thus encodes a symbolics of strength in which physical endurance and strength are leashed to piety and honor. The powerful male body is consolidated in the performance into a potentially frightening mass grouping, yet its potency is smoothly refigured as sign of community togetherness and mark of familial loyalty, a refiguration that has the effect of defusing its latent violence.

The processional format of the dancing of the *giglio* also offers an interpretation that insists on cultural inclusiveness. Street processions are often understood by anthropologists as mechanisms for marking out a group's territory, with the movement of the procession through the streets acting to reassert the group's claim to a specific place.[41] Through the processional route a geopolitics is thus constructed that works to define the community's borders. In the case of the dancing of the Brooklyn *giglio,* however, the geopolitics have as much to do with dispossession as with ownership of urban space. The *giglio* performance may be temporally drawn out, taking an entire afternoon to perform, but it is spatially hemmed in, confined to a relatively small space on two intersecting streets that form the perimeters of the church complex. Other parts of the festivities—most notably the *"capo* line of march"—penetrate deeper into the surrounding streets. But the dancing of the *giglio* takes place in a tightly defined space. Once again, multiple readings are possible. To some, this constricted performance space might suggest loss of neighborhood territory and hence of ethnic identity. But to others, it might imply that the Italian-American community knows its place and will not force itself on other ethnicities now resident in the neighborhood. In the latter reading, the spatial boundaries of the performance suggest a shy and diffident ethnicity that is aware of its own territory and hence might be easier for outsiders to accept.

Within this sharply delimited urban space, the performance itself proceeds in a markedly nonaggressive and noninvasive way. Although it celebrates raw masculine strength, the movement of the procession is structured around delay and anticipation, with the climax continually postponed. The performance is choppy, interrupted. Each lift moves about thirty feet and takes two or three minutes before the tower and boat are dropped. During the long intervals between lifts, spectators and performers alike mill about, talking, eating, and drinking. These long delays break down barriers between performers and audience while also deconstructing the performance itself. As the procession makes its way through the streets, the men joining into one mass during each lift and then dissolving away among the spectators in the intervals between lifts, a psychodrama of disintegration and reintegration is performed again and again. What might look like an intimidating display of a powerful and, for non-Italian spectators, possibly alienating identity becomes instead a tentative and continually interrupted mingling of insiders and outsiders that defuses possible ethnic tensions, which might be exacerbated by crowding thousands of people together within two blocks. (The performance is heavily policed, but the officers mingle with the crowd and serve chiefly to move spectators back to make room for the lifting.) In a manner that responds ingeniously, even if probably unconsciously, to the shifts and fragmentations in social and economic relations within and outside the community, the ritual exploits a structural hesitancy that avoids conflicts associated with an aggressively asserted ethnicity.

In addition to these narrative and structural features that help it negotiate fears about a strongly expressed ethnicity, the *giglio*'s allure also owes something to its ability to present itself as a "genuine" and "authentic" cultural tradition with deep roots in history. For many members of the Brooklyn community, the meaning of the *giglio* is its connection with the past—a specifically medieval past imagined as a repository of a people's history. The longevity of the performance is thus a matter of some importance: the 2002 feast program, for instance, proudly bills itself as the 115th annual feast of Our Lady of Mount Carmel and Saint Paulinus (despite the fact that the feast in Brooklyn appears to date to 1903). The emphasis is in fact everywhere on duration, continuity, and tradition linking past with present. The children's *giglio,* for example, which is a twenty-five-foot tall replica carried by boys in a separate performance, is described in the church's flyer as a way for the community's boys to "insure the future of this festival by carrying on this deep rooted tradition." The dancing of a children's *giglio* is, however, a fairly recent innovation found only in Brooklyn.[42] Similarly, continuity between Italy and the United States is emphasized. To mention just two examples, the theme song for the performance continues to be sung in Italian, even though few participants now speak the language, and the feast program gives directions for how to get to Brooklyn from Rome and Nola, suggesting that Italians make annual pilgrimages to participate in the Brooklyn performance, even though very few appear to have done so; the movement is in fact all in the opposite direction, with New World *giglio* tourists going back to watch the Nola performance, a route that reveals on which side of the Atlantic the cultural value lies. In these and other ways—such as the insistence that the performance represents a real historical event involving Paulinus or that it dates from the early Middle Ages—the *giglio* performance exhibits a nostalgia for historical roots and a longing for a cultural tradition whose reinventedness is studiously ignored.

Part of the reason for the refusal to contemplate the reinventedness of the *giglio* ritual has to do with the fact that tradition is often understood in terms of a simplified idea of transmission in which cultural ideas or values are handed down from one generation to the next across time. This seems to imply a conservative process in which values remain stable despite changed contexts; it is that stable value that in fact is often taken as the hallmark of tradition. But although it may challenge the notion of a stable link between past and present, change is always a part of the transmission of culture, and so is the possibility of discontinuity or rupture. Tradition, then, perhaps has less to do with the persistence of old forms and more to do with the ways in which elements are articulated or linked together. These elements do not have a fixed position, but can be reshuffled in whatever way fits the needs of present circumstances. But despite the practical flexibility of tradition, the yearning for a sense of connectedness to the past and a belief that such connectedness has to be unbroken in order to be genuine often leads to just the kind of insistence on fixed tradition, roots, and origins that informs attitudes toward the *giglio*.

The unconscious decision to suppress awareness of the *giglio* as the continually reinvented tradition that it is also says something about the demand for an authentic, not spurious or made-up, cultural heritage that can stand as the icon of a genuine and deep-rooted community. In the rhetoric of authenticity that currently shapes responses to cultural objects of all kinds, "real" cultural traditions are privileged over "fake" ones and preserved performances and artifacts over those that have been invented.[43] To realize the importance of the claim to an "authentic" cultural tradition that can be taken to constitute a genuine ethnic identity, one has only to look at recent debates over Native American tribal rights, which often hinge on whether or not individuals who are now deliberately re-creating an absent culture after a century or more of forced assimilation and attendant loss of original language, rituals, and self-governance can be said to possess an "Indian" identity distinct from that of their neighbors whom they often resemble in nearly every way.[44] Understood as a rallying point for ethnic identity, the *giglio* helps maintain the Brooklyn community, even as that community has become increasingly far flung. As one performer who still lives in the neighborhood has said: "Though a lot of people move out . . . they always come back. [In] July, they're always Brooklynites. They always come back."[45] For the *giglio* to act in this way as an identity marker for its community and for the *giglio* to attract outsiders, as it does, it must be perceived as a real tradition with a lengthy history that derives from Italian roots. To acknowledge itself as a reinvented tradition, one cobbled together out of bits and pieces of Italian and American culture, would diminish its ability to perform its cultural work of dramatizing a vital and genuine ethnicity.

Although this yearning for an authentic community tradition might appear to be at odds with the widespread marketing of ethnicity whereby ethnic differences are promoted as tourist attractions and cultural commodities, in the case of the *giglio* the two are interdependent. Certainly for many spectators the *giglio* performance is consumable on terms very similar to those that control the consumption of the "Italian specialties" sold in street booths at the performance. And the same may be true for at least some third- and fourth-generation Italian Americans in the community, who have become only "part-time consumers" of their own ethnicity.[46] In one sense, then, the *giglio* ritual is just another item to be added to the list of *zeppole, bracciole,* and spicy Italian fare sold at the festival. But part of the appeal of the *giglio* is, as the church's flyer puts it, that it gives everyone the chance not just to consume but also to "experience" an ages-old Italian ritual now available right here in New York. Spectators may be indulging in a kind of ethnic tourism, but they want that tourism to let them participate, not just gaze from a distance, and they want their experience to be real not fake. On both counts, the *giglio* obliges.

As this offer of participation in a "genuine" cultural experience suggests, the *giglio*'s stock in trade is its supposed authenticity and its participatory, experiential nature, both of which position it as an antidote to the social fragmentation, anomie, and cultural homogeneity of the contemporary United States. As one participant has put it: "Every culture has their tradition and their rituals that they have brought over by word of mouth and by action to keep their people alive. . . . Imagine the hundreds and hundreds of years where the world is moving all around you, the Renaissance happens, technology happens, but in this little corner of the world the people are still living out a story and a legend that is in their blood and in their system. And they don't only hear the story, but they actually live the story."[47] These words deftly capture the charm of the genuine tradition the *giglio* claims to offer, a tradition that continues to be not only recited but enacted and lived out.

It is tempting to see in the *giglio*'s promise of access to a living and authentic tradition at least a partial reason for the recent attention that the performance has attracted from academics and the media. Scholarly work on the *giglio* began in 1981 when two graduate students in folklore at the University of Pennsylvania were hired by a consortium of Brooklyn cultural institutions to survey the borough's folk life in a project funded by the National Endowment for the Arts and the National Endowment for the Humanities. The graduate students in turn hired Joseph Sciorra, an anthropology student and folklore enthusiast who lived in the community, to study the performance from the inside.[48] In 1989 the Brooklyn Historical Society mounted a special exhibit on the *giglio,* focusing regional attention on the performance, which it presented as a part of Brooklyn's history. In both of these endeavors, the *giglio* was understood as a mark of a vital ethnicity that nonetheless could be readily conscripted into a larger story about Brooklyn, and by extension the United

States, as an amalgam of ethnic groups. The newspapers and television stations that feature segments on the performance tend to see the *giglio* in a similar light, focusing on its "colorful" and rather quaint ethnic touches, but emphasizing cultural harmony as well. Far from shunning this outside attention, participants in the performance have welcomed it. The church has developed a press kit consisting of photos highlighting the performance and has willingly embraced a wider audience. As a consequence, the *giglio* performance has become a thoroughly media-savvy and self-conscious event, aware of the fascination it holds for outsiders.

The popularity of the *giglio* ritual hinges on its ability to balance the promise of participation in an authentic community tradition against demands that such participation be packaged in a palatable form. By avoiding expressions of ethnicity that might present Italian Americans as too strongly "other" and that might therefore engender discomfort about cultural differences and by emphasizing themes of reconciliation, the *giglio* performance accommodates itself to current ambivalences about ethnicity.[49] Perhaps tellingly in terms of the model of ethnic identity it projects, the *giglio* performance now also casts itself as a vehicle for the championing of the ethnic identities of all groups, as have other Italian festivals, such as the one sponsored by Our Lady of Pompeii Church in Soho, New York, which began in 1973 with a declaration by then-mayor John V. Lindsay to the effect that the festival would "reflect once more the unity of the many ethnic groups in our city as all peoples partake of this celebration."[50] In a similar vein, the leader of the *giglio* band has remarked: "When you come to our neighborhood during the time of the feast . . . you are going to find other people besides Italian people in the street. . . . People come and visit and want to see this phenomenon and want to be part of it. For that day they all become Italian in spirit, in flavor, and feeling."[51] This gesture of inclusiveness that would make everyone Italian for a day suggests how the *giglio* seeks to adapt the ethnicity it performs for general consumption. The *giglio*'s success lies precisely in its susceptibility to being taken as an instance of authentic yet sanitized ethnicity, able to be "experienced" in all its vitality but unlikely to offend anyone.

The perfect originary myth for that authentic yet inoffensive identity lies in the medieval past. In the *giglio* performance we can see the creative use of the premodern past to meet the needs of the present. By imaging itself as a cultural link to a medieval past, a time envisioned as existing before the divisiveness of modernity that can serve as an anchor not just for Italians but also for everyone, the *giglio* repositions itself to address concerns about the potential divisiveness of cultural difference. Balancing an insistence on continuity, tradition, and community with tentativeness, awareness of boundaries, and an offer of at least symbolic inclusiveness, the *giglio* ritual deftly avoids giving the impression that it might be a bit of gristle in the melting pot of America that refuses easy assimilation even now in what one scholar has described as the "twilight" of Italian ethnicity as the group's distinctiveness is waning.[52] From its first importing, up through the mid-century crisis that threatened its survival, and into the present, the *giglio* has shown adaptability in meshing the "old ways" with changing circumstances in the New World. Along the way, the *giglio* has managed to preserve a strong sense of cultural heritage for the benefit of the community while also accommodating itself to altered circumstances. The *giglio*'s creative resilience should be a reminder that traditions, even when genuine, aren't set in stone and that new ways can be creatively joined to old. The work of the medieval in this process of reinvention is to serve as a mooring point, as a sign of longevity, and as a source of value and stability beyond the vicissitudes of the present. In so doing, the medieval past provides a mechanism by means of which the Brooklyn *giglio* community can imagine that it possesses an ages-old tradition, one whose reach into the far past underscores its value and also assures it efficacy for the present.

CHAPTER 5

America's Passion Plays

Starting in the middle of the nineteenth century and continuing well into the twentieth, America—or at least a significant segment of it—experienced an infatuation with passion plays. By 1850, wealthy travelers were making their way to Oberammergau in Bavaria to soak up the atmosphere of a *Passionspiel* that had become a required stop on the European grand tour. As magazines published reports of their experiences, a wider public learned of a performance tradition that had largely disappeared elsewhere and developed an appetite for the genre. Although the first attempt to stage a passion play in America met with defeat, by the end of the nineteenth century passion plays had become a staple of the entertainment industry, particularly on the lecture and religious revival circuits. The enthusiasm for passion plays spawned some strange products performed by unexpected groups in unlikely venues. There were passion plays enacted by the *hermanos penitentes* in the Southwest; the 1901 performance in the Skwa village near Chilliwack, British Columbia, in which men from the tribe put on a passion play; the Hill Cumorah "Mormon" Passion Play in Palmyra, New York, performed annually by members of the Church of Jesus Christ of the Latter Day Saints; and even marionette passion plays, in which puppets enacted sacred roles.[1] There were hundreds of early passion-play films, as well as stereopticon lectures and recitations based on passion plays. And there were passion plays that developed into local tourist attractions, such as the Black Hills Passion Play and the Great Passion Play of Eureka Springs, Arkansas. Offering a glimpse of the sentiments frequently associated with such plays, the Great Passion Play's promotional material states that the play

> takes you back 2,000 years to the greatest story ever told, to the final days of Jesus Christ's walk on earth. . . . From the authentic re-creation of Jerusalem and the colorful spectacle of the market place to the soul-stirring crucifixion, to the electrifying scene of Christ's ascension, the cast of 250 and the state of the art lighting, sound effects and original music combine to bring you a professional and moving performance that holds the attention of all ages.[2]

This chapter examines three interlinked performances, which as a group map the history of the passion play in America: literary accounts of Oberammergau's

Passionspiel, for most Americans the iconic passion play; Salmi Morse's spectacular *Passion Play* of 1879, the first passion play staged—even if only briefly and amidst great controversy—in America; and the Black Hills Passion Play of Spearfish, South Dakota, the oldest and most famous of the tourist-attraction passion plays in the United States. The fad for passion plays inevitably raises questions about the place of religion in American public culture, not least because passion plays take as their subject one of the most highly charged events of Christianity, the Crucifixion and Resurrection of Jesus. Not surprisingly, passion plays have been lightning rods for religious controversy and have faced charges of anti-Semitism as well as blasphemy. Less obviously, the obsession with passion plays also raises questions about America's relations with its European past. In the case of the German-derived Black Hills Passion Play, which arrived in the United States during the build-up to World War II, the problem of the past was quietly solved, as we shall see, by bypassing the actual cultural and religious history of the play in favor of a detour into a generalized medieval past that was called forth in order to turn the performance into a self-proclaimed "American institution."

Because they reveal the difficulties of importing a problematic section of the medieval past—religious devotion manifested in dramatic enactments of the most sacred scenes of Christianity—into modern American culture, passion plays are of particular interest for a study of medieval drama in America. In an American context, passion plays, which were an accepted and even privileged part of medieval European culture, could be imported only after their thorny religiosity had been tamed. The three performances discussed in this chapter demonstrate the problems involved in importing passion plays and the strategies that with varying degrees of success were employed to overcome them. As Rainer Warning has remarked, religious drama is the genre that most forcefully demonstrates the alterity of the Middle Ages, so it should be no surprise that passion plays were difficult to import into an American context.[3] Paradoxically, however, as will become clear, invocation of that alterity is precisely what finally allowed passion plays to be smuggled in.

Although their precise origin remains in dispute, passion plays—that is, plays featuring the events surrounding the Crucifixion of Jesus—appear to have developed in medieval Europe out of the Latin liturgy and the ritual ceremonies of Easter week. While it is generally agreed that the Latin passion play did not derive directly from the Easter liturgy—Karl Young, in his monumental study of early church drama, claimed that the passion play arose from the poetic laments of the Virgin Mary over the Crucifixion and death of her son, while Sandro Sticca believes that it grew out of Gospel narratives and the newly Christocentric attitudes of twelfth-century Europe—the passion play is undoubtedly tied to Easter dramas such as the reenactments of the visits of the three Marys to Jesus' sepulcher.[4] In their earliest form in the tenth century, these reenactments were brief compositions, or tropes, designed, so extant texts suggest, to be sung in monastic churches as elaborations on the Easter service. These *Quem quaeritis* texts—so called because they focus on the question put to the three Marys by the angels guarding Jesus' tomb, "*Quem quaeritis in sepulchro?*" ("Whom do you seek in the sepulcher?")—in some instances probably featured only antiphonal singing without any dramatic action or impersonation, but in others included dialogue and costumes. In both cases, these elaborations remained an integral part of the liturgy and were performed in church as part of the service.

By the eleventh and twelfth centuries, however, full-blown liturgical plays were being recorded in separate playbooks rather than in the breviaries, ordinals, and other service books where the earliest *Quem quaeritis* enactments had first appeared, suggesting that during these centuries such performances were beginning to stand alone even if they were still performed as part of the church service. By the late twelfth or early thirteenth centuries, complex Easter plays designed to be performed outside of the liturgical service had been created, as plays from Montecassino and Benediktbeuern attest. These plays also began to mix lines in the vernacular languages with the Latin of the liturgy. In some cases, even if the parts were still played by clerics, as was the norm, these plays may have been performed outside churches, as was the case with the *Seinte Resureccion,* a fragmentary Anglo-Norman play on the Resurrection, which was apparently enacted outdoors during the summer.[5] Young notes that compared with the many medieval plays on the Resurrection, the number of plays dramatizing the Crucifixion is small; we know of no dramatizations of the Passion before the early thirteenth century and relatively few after that date that were sponsored by the church, perhaps because the ceremony of the Mass itself was felt to offer sufficient representation of the Passion.[6]

Of these Easter plays, the Benediktbeuern *Passion Play* (*Ludus de Passione*), the longer of two passion plays from the Carmina Burana manuscript, represents an especially sophisticated example that suggests the scope of such plays.[7] The Benediktbeuern play features a large cast that includes Pontius Pilate and his wife, Herod and his soldiers, the chief priests, a merchant and his wife, various disciples, Mary Magdalene, Hebrew boys, a Pharisee, and Jesus, among others. Its actions cover such biblical and apocryphal stories as the miracle of the blind man and Zacchaeus, Jesus' entry into Jerusalem, a lengthy exchange between Mary Magdalene and the merchant who sells her worldly adornments before she repents, the raising of Lazarus from the dead, the betrayal by Judas and the condemnation of Jesus, the Crucifixion, and the lamentation of the Virgin Mary. The parts are meant to be sung as well as spoken and mingle Latin with German. As these features show, the elaborate and action-filled Benediktbeuern play mined the rich dramatic possibilities that could be discovered in stories about the last days of Jesus' life—possibilities that found expression in other medieval plays and that would be exploited in the large-scale passion plays of subsequent centuries.

In its original European contexts, the medieval passion play was a theatrical form that easily accommodated religious and secular impulses, readily found performance venues within as well as outside of the church, and meshed with the cultural expectations of the people who sponsored, performed in, and watched it. In modern America, however, passion plays encountered trouble on every front. While most of the attempts to stage passion plays in America reveal the recalcitrance of this cultural material from the medieval past, the one success story—the Black Hills Passion Play—shows a strategic use of medievalness as a way of framing and making acceptable a potentially volatile cultural artifact. The three performances in this chapter show the pitfalls that were faced by the attempts at mounting American passion plays, as well as what it took to succeed.

The Oberammergau *Passionspiel*

The archetypal passion play for most nineteenth-century Americans was the one mounted every ten years in the small Bavarian town of Oberammergau. Although passion plays had survived in other places in Europe,[8] Oberammergau's became by far the most widely known, its fame spread by German intellectuals bent on appropriating it for nationalist purposes and by foreign tourists eager for an alternative to modern industrial culture. As the German actor-manager Eduard Devrient put it, using the language of *volkisch* nationalism, Oberammergau's "innocence" and "untroubled childhood joy" was appealing because it showed that "the old hoard of the German folk spirit is indestructible and inexhaustible."[9] The play's remote yet relatively accessible location—safe even for solitary female travelers—added to its appeal, as did romantic legends of its origins. According to these legends, the play began when the town vowed to present a passion play every ten years if spared from the plague that was ravaging Europe; its request granted, the town mounted the first performance in 1634.[10] More prosaically, that the play had over the years undergone a series of revisions making it acceptable to modern audiences and to Protestants also no doubt boosted its popularity.

The tendency toward quiet modification to suit changing tastes is evident as early as the oldest surviving manuscript of the play, which dates from 1662 and is a composite of medieval and later sources. The largest section of the play comes from a fifteenth-century playbook from a Benedictine monastery in Augsburg. Another significant chunk was copied from the 1566 *Passion and Resurrection of Christ* by Sebastian Wild of Augsburg, a student of Hans Sachs; Wild's play was based on a 1543 play by the English Protestant reformer Nicholas Grimald. Other parts of the play may have been lifted from an earlier Oberammergau Resurrection play or another Tyrolean Passion play.[11] In its mixing of high and low styles, its use of devils and personified abstractions (Death, Sin, Avarice), and its conclusion with the Harrowing of

Hell, this composite version of the play, which was performed with minor revisions for the next eighty years, bears many traces of the attributes of medieval religious drama.

Much to its advantage in terms of its survival, however, the medieval qualities of the Oberammergau *Passionspiel* were gradually tempered when, starting in the mid eighteenth century, the play underwent several major revisions. As James Shapiro recounts in his study of the play's history, the first revision came in 1750, when Ferdinand Rosner, a Benedictine monk from the nearby monastery of Ettal, doubled the length of the play (from 4,900 lines to 8,500) and significantly reshaped it in what Shapiro describes as a "Baroque, Jesuit-influenced, operatic style."[12] Rosner's changes included modifications in versification such as the introduction of alexandrines for the choruses; the insertion of tableaux vivants between acts; the addition of musical passages; and the expansion of various parts (such as for Veronica). After the play ran afoul of religious authorities in 1770, another Benedictine monk from Ettal, Magnus Knipfelberger, was entrusted with simplifying Rosner's text while also purging the play of its objectionable parts, which he accomplished by shortening it, confining Hell to musical interludes, and changing the title from the "new Passion" (*Nova Passion*) to the apparently more innocuous "The Old and New Testaments." Another significant revision came in 1811, when Otmar Weis, a monk still residing in the now closed Ettal Monastery, changed the old verse form into realistic prose, deleted elements that did not conform to biblical accounts (such as Veronica and blind Longinus, as well as all the devils and allegorical figures), and altered the title yet again (to "The Great Sacrifice on Golgotha"). The last major revision was made in 1850 by Joseph Daisenberger, one of Weis's students; Daisenberger trimmed long speeches and outdated language while enhancing character motivation and creating a tighter plot. He also made doctrinal changes that increased the play's appeal for Protestants.[13] Daisenberger's text, which remained in use until 1980, contained eighteen acts, sixty scenes, and twenty-four tableaux, and called for some five hundred performers; a single performance lasted eight hours, with a break around noon. This was the version of the play watched by nineteenth-century tourists: medieval in some ways, yet aware of and responsive to modern sensibilities.

But while the play text was being revised, the performance in other ways remained unaltered up until the third decade of the nineteenth century; that is to say, it stayed local and relatively small-scale. The play's small-town quality was a large part of its appeal for tourists, whose arrival, ironically, broadened the play's scope considerably. As far as we know, for most of its early history, the Oberammergau play had been staged in the village churchyard, but in 1830 a new open-air stage capable of holding 5,000 spectators was built on land sold in the dissolution of the Ettal Monastery.[14] What had been largely private performances now became known to the outside world. In 1760, 14,000 spectators, most of them from the surrounding area, came to see the two performances of the play, a record attendance reached again only in 1830 when 13,000 people watched ten performances on the new stage. By 1860, that number had shot up to 100,000, most of them from abroad, especially England, many attracted by the play's aura as an expression of the pure faith of innocent rustics (an aura the villagers took pains to protect). The number of performances also increased, from 4 in 1810 to 656 by 1910.[15] Revenues likewise multiplied. Before 1800, the town had lost money on every performance, but after 1850, the play became a commercial success, as "the pious villagers" turned their pageant into a spectacular theatrical monopoly.[16]

Following in the footsteps of their European counterparts, wealthy Americans soon discovered Oberammergau, and magazine articles and travel accounts featuring the Bavarian play began to proliferate. The numerous eyewitness reports published for British and American readers in such magazines as *Blackwood's, Macmillan's, The Century,* and *Colburn's New Monthly Magazine* still make good, if sometimes overly effusive, reading.[17] These reports, written by both men and women alike, typically mingle observations about local travel sites and customs, firsthand reportage on the performance, assertions of the passion play's uplifting benefits, and—when coming from writers with a scholarly bent—information about its medieval origins, usually identified as the urban biblical cycles that were performed throughout Europe and England in the fourteenth and fifteenth centuries. For at least some tourists, it seems, Oberammergau appealed to an historical imagination eager to find survivals of medieval folk customs that preserved the ethos of a simpler, more devout era.

The allure of Oberammergau is easily detected in the magazine reports filed by travelers making the cultural tour to the little Bavarian town. A few examples suffice to capture their flavor. In 1870, *Putnam's Monthly Magazine* published an account by Lucy Fountain, who along with a female companion had gone to see that year's performance.[18] Fountain describes how the "two lovelorn damsels" head off on their own to Oberammergau for an adventure. After touching on the novelties and difficulties of travel, including the challenge of dealing with feather beds, fleas, and beer-drinking locals, Fountain's narrative arrives in the village, where the two women almost immediately encounter "Joseph Mair" on the street, dressed for his part as Jesus. Fountain comments that "this untutored peasant must have been absorbed in the spirit of his part for months, so perfect did his whole appearance answer to the ideals of Titian and Rubens." When Fountain and her companion attend the performance, which she tells us involves a cast of five hundred and is watched by six thousand spectators, she is particularly struck by the realism of the play. Watching the procession that precedes the play, Fountain remarks that "the scene was intensely real as the multitude entered, strewing palm-branches and shouting hosannas." As the play itself begins, she explains that "there was nothing to recall one from the illusion of the piece. The dresses, so perfect and

The Crucifixion, Oberammergau Passion Play. *Harper's New Monthly Magazine* 42 (January 1871). Courtesy of the Special Collections Department, University of Iowa Libraries, Iowa City, Iowa.

so simple; the acting, so earnest, so natural, so devotional; the hundreds of people thronging the wide streets of that immense stage; the utter absorption of every one in the play, not even the merest supernumerary appearing to re-member for one moment that he was acting, and before an audience." Al-though Fountain complains about aspects of the production, including certain tedious and slow-moving sections, she stresses the transcendence of the whole experience, observing that "when one reflects that this marvel of beauty . . . is the production of untutored peasants in a remote village of Bavaria . . . the *Passionspiel* of Ober-Ammergau becomes indeed a Miracle-play."

In the following year, *Harper's New Monthly Magazine* published two ac-counts that echo the tenor of Fountain's essay. One of the accounts is primar-ily interested in the tourist experience; the other is concerned with the contents and history of the play. In the first account, entitled "A Passion-Play Pilgrim-age," M. D. Conway focuses on the adventures of travel much more than on the play proper.[19] Conway spends a number of pages discussing the journey to Oberammergau, commenting at length on local customs and the sights to be seen (especially the legendary ones) before the traveler reaches Oberammer-gau. Once in the village, Conway lodges with the Lang family, whose daughter played Mary Magdalene in that year's play. We are told about Conway's ac-commodations, particularly the feather beds that also seemed noteworthy to Fountain and that Conway finds uncomfortably hot on summer nights. Like

Fountain, Conway is struck by the way the passion play mixes sacred and profane and illustrates this intermingling by telling us about having heard someone say, "Last night I was drinking beer with Simon Petrus." The essay also shows an awareness of the theatrical history of the passion play, and Conway comments that Oberammergau has preserved the medieval "Miracle Play" when it has died out elsewhere. But Conway skips over a detailed analysis of that history, referring the reader to the "very careful account" of miracle plays in general and Oberammergau's passion in particular that had appeared in the January issue of *Harper's*.

That essay, published anonymously as "The Passion Play in Oberammergau, 1870," is both an eyewitness account of the performance and a detailed scholarly history of the passion play, at Oberammergau and elsewhere; it is accompanied by a number of engravings that help re-create for the reader the experience of watching the Oberammergau performance.[20] The first sentence sets the tone for what follows and reveals the author's tendency to read the history of the passion play in evolutionary terms: "The history of the religious drama is the history of the gradual development of Christianity out of the forms and customs of paganism." From that opening, the author moves to a discussion of the shift from pagan to Christian festivals and the development of the first "Mysteries, or Passion Plays," as outgrowths of the licentious and buffoonish *mimi*'s plays of the third century A.D., an origin that in the author's view explains "the peculiar character which these early Christian dramas exhibit." The essay goes on to note that the term *mystery* comes from "ministerium," which means ministry or function, and thus is equivalent to the Spanish *auto*. Citing scholarly work on the English mystery plays, the author gives a brief history of medieval drama, relating how church processions and representations starting in the time of Gregory the Great gradually developed into plays and tableaux vivants that were performed across Europe as well as in England (explicit mention is made of the Chester and Coventry biblical cycle plays).

The author next offers a brief account of the village of Oberammergau, its demographics, and the economic impact of the play. We are told that in 1870 the village had a population of around twelve hundred residents, most of them peasants employed as woodcarvers. At the center of the village stands a churchyard. Around it are cottages built of stone covered with plaster, each with a little garden of vegetables, fruit trees, and roses. "An atmosphere of general peace and good-will seems to pervade the place," the author claims, "and pursuing the even tenor of their way, the villagers come and go, making their faith their life." This being the character of the villagers, we can understand "with what a sense of reverence and pious care" they perform the play. Does filthy lucre taint this world of pious innocence? No. Although the play is a financial boon for the village, the profits are split equitably, with churches and charities getting a cut. The author guesses that the cost for the season, which runs from May to September, is about thirty-six thousand florins (which the author estimates as equivalent to eighteen thousand dollars), with each performance taking in about five thousand dollars. At the end of the season each actor receives a share of the profits, with Christ earning two hundred florins and each child six; the remainder of the money goes to the church and charities, we are informed. Commercialism, that bugbear of modernity, is thus, in this author's view, channeled into the acceptable guise of civic and religious benefits to all, while an appropriate hierarchy of remuneration is maintained.

After a lengthy description of the contents of the Oberammergau play and inclusion of translations of some of the speeches—strategies that seem aimed at making the performance accessible to readers—the writer moves to a consideration of the play's impact on both performers and spectators. Although the peasants, we are told, "show their childish interest" in the play by laughing at moments such as the Ascension, in which Christ really ascends thanks to "some theatrical contrivance," in general the author applauds the play as "a spectacle which must have a most humanizing effect on those who witness it." The emphasis in this account is emphatically on the moral effects of the play and the play's transformative powers. In an unexpected coda that reveals what are perhaps prevailing attitudes toward the play's history, the author spends the last few pages quoting an account by Anna Bushby that appeared in the September issue of *Colburn's New Monthly Magazine*. Mrs. Bushby offers a glimpse—unusual in tourists' accounts of Oberammergau—of the current historical context for the play. She comments, for instance, that the actors' roles must have been particularly difficult that year, since many of them had just learned that they had been drafted into the Prussian War. Bushby concludes:

> It was a marvelous spectacle altogether—one to which no description can do justice, and which was well worth a journey across half Europe to witness. It is impossible to speak too highly of the grace and dignity displayed by many of the actors, and their admirable delineation of the characters they personified, though they were quite self-taught.

While Bushby is remarkably alert to the pressures of present realities on the play, she nonetheless retreats into a reading in which the ennobling effects of the performance are seen to offer a palliative for history's woes. War cannot be avoided, but the play can in some way transcend it. For Bushby and presumably many of her readers, the play thus offers an escape from present history through retreat into what is imagined as a more benign past.[21]

That most early accounts were uncritical of Oberammergau's passion play, particularly of its anti-Jewish moments and of the cash nexus that grew up around it, suggests the strength of the desire to see Oberammergau in a specific light, as a relic of an earlier era of innocent Christian piety. Although there were some dissenting voices, most notably that of Richard Burton, who drew attention to both the anti-Semitism and the commercialism of the *Passionspiel*, they were for the most part drowned out under the general acclaim.[22]

As these magazines suggest, the way in which most Americans encountered the passion play was through a secondhand description, often accompanied by illustrations, of a tourist's experiences of the simulacrum of a medieval play that Oberammergau had carefully constructed. By consigning reproduction of the passion play to the medium of print, these accounts skirted the problems that live enactments might (in fact, would) face. In particular, the strident religiosity of the passion play could be tempered by the distancing effect of written publications aimed at middlebrow readers who could confront the play in the privacy of their own rooms. Importation via the representational form of print effectively tamed the passion play for American consumption.

To identify the historical logic at work in these literary representations we need only note their frequent reference to early English miracle and morality plays as points of comparison with the Oberammergau *Passionspiel*. The Reverend Malcolm MacColl's *The Ober-Ammergau Passion Play* (1871), for example, which was popular enough to go into four editions by 1871, includes "practical hints for the use of intending visitors" to Oberammergau as well as "remarks on the origin and development of miracle plays."[23] An essay on religious relics in London describes "miracle plays" as "the chief means by which the masses, without books, or ability to read if they had possessed them, were taught the histories of the Bible," and adds that although such plays have died out in most places, they linger "in some remote districts of France and Spain, and particularly at Oberammergau, Bavaria, where the Passion is dramatically represented every tenth year, and where it last year constituted the chief attraction on the Continent."[24] The reason for recounting the history of medieval plays, another writer asserts, is that "it is only by a knowledge of the early history of such dramas that we can understand the spirit in which they are given by these peasants of Ober-Ammergau."[25] This invocation of miracle plays as a way of contextualizing the Oberammergau passion shows the medieval past being used as a kind of containment strategy that helps to explain the performance and make sense of what might seem its odd or disturbing features. For many Americans, it seems, Oberammergau could be most easily enjoyed and understood if it were seen as a survival of medieval performance traditions.

While print proved an accommodating medium for the importing of the Oberammergau passion, so too did the educational talk. The Bavarian play in fact became a fixture on the lecture circuit, where it was often the subject of illustrated talks that used magic-lantern slides and, when they became available starting in 1897, films as illustrative accompaniments. As with literary accounts, lectures, which targeted the desires of middlebrow audiences for cultural self-improvement, effectively collared the potentially troubling aspects of Oberammergau and made the passion play palatable for Americans by transposing it into the acceptable (and secular) format of the educational spiel. One especially popular lecturer was John J. Lewis, who was billed as "the apostle of the passion play in America"; his specialty was a "Picture Play of Oberammergau" that was later reincarnated as a film version.[26] Hundreds of early passion-play films were also made, most of which unfortunately are now lost. The film pioneer Sigmund Lubin, for example, appeared in his own version of the Oberammergau passion play.[27] These films were typically shown as part of a larger entertainment, which usually featured magic-lantern slides, lectures, and musical accompaniment. A particular hit was Marie Mayer, who played Mary Magdalene in the Oberammergau Passion Play of 1910, and was billed in 1917 as the first actual participant from Oberammergau to appear in America.[28] (In 1900, an American producer tried to offer the main performers at Oberammergau five thousand dollars each to perform in a passion play in New York, but they turned him down, apparently out of fear of lessening the value of Oberammergau's performance.)[29] All of these entertainments suggest a craving for an imported Oberammergau play, albeit one reshaped to suit middle-class American needs and one in which the more troubling aspects of Oberammergau, including excess piety, the immediacy of dramatic enactment, and impersonation of divine figures, were kept under control.

That these were indeed troubling aspects of the passion play is made clear in a sensational photographic project late in the century. Apparently inspired by the Oberammergau play, which he had seen in 1890, the photographer Fred Holland Day produced some 250 negatives of the Passion, with himself in the role of the Jesus. To make the pictures, Day staged scenes depicting the Passion and Crucifixion in the rocky New England landscape around Willett Pond, Massachusetts, enlisting friends and neighbors to play supporting parts and using carefully chosen costumes and props—even going so far as to order wooden crosses from a Syrian carpenter and constructing a crown of real thorns. In the weeks before the production began, Day remained in seclusion while his hair grew long and denied himself food to the point of emaciation. The subsequent photographs of the Crucifixion show a gaunt and haggard Day "nailed" to a wooden cross in a convincing tableau of physical agony that was part play-acting, part reality. "The Seven Words," as Day's series was called, was controversial from the day it was first shown in the Philadelphia Photographic Salon of 1898, and critics in America, and later abroad, perhaps not surprisingly condemned Day's portrayal as blasphemous.[30] It was apparently fine for the villagers in Oberammergau to parade about costumed as Jesus and the apostles, but quite another matter for eccentric Americans to do the same.

Despite the Day fiasco, by the end of the nineteenth century, a passion for Oberammergau could be taken for granted, so much so that an 1891 advertisement for a new Kodak camera could tout its product by claiming its incomparable value for capturing shots of such attractions as Oberammergau.[31] If Oberammergau had become part of the cultural landscape of America, at least in its middlebrow reaches, the passion play was nonetheless still a suspect form, as the controversy over Day's photographs demonstrates, which risked charges of blasphemy and religious impropriety. This was especially the case when it came to staging the passion play, rather than representing it through cultural forms such as the magazine article or the lecture within which it could be safely demarcated and distanced from the immediacy of theatrical representation. To mount a passion play on the stage—where an actor would be required to impersonate the deity, where the audience would encompass a wider slice of society, and where the very nature of theatrical representation would invite charges of sacrilege—was a far more difficult undertaking, as Salmi Morse would discover.

Salmi Morse's Passion

In San Francisco during the Lenten season of 1879, Americans had the chance to watch a passion play on their own shores in what has to rate as one of the most spectacular theatrical events in the history of theater in the United States as well as one of the oddest. Although Old Testament stories had previously been written for the American stage—for example, Royall Tyler's *The Judgment of Solomon*[32]—and tableaux of biblical scenes performed by "living statue" troupes had been popular throughout the nineteenth century, as far as is known no American acting company had ever performed a biblical drama in which Jesus was impersonated until Salmi Morse's *The Passion: A Miracle Play in Ten Acts* appeared. Morse's play might now seem little more than a curious footnote to theatrical history, yet in its day and for years after it was a sensation. Newspapers in the United States and abroad chronicled its brief but fitful days on the stage in San Francisco and New York, as countless readers followed the controversy the play engendered.[33]

Morse's theatrical ventures came as a last enthusiasm in a peripatetic career full of self-invention and ambitions unfulfilled, which has been thoroughly described by Alan Nielsen in his detailed study of the rise and fall of Morse's play.[34] Although Salmi Morse (or Samuel Moss, as he was also known) claimed to be an Englishman from Norwich, he was actually born of Jewish parents in Germany in 1826. He arrived in California in 1848, lured as were so many others by the Gold Rush, after having run a clothing and dry goods store in New York City. After a three-year stay, he departed for Australia, where he operated a hotel in Melbourne during its gold rush; he then landed in Turkey and later England before returning to California in 1858, where he bought a ranch in Mendocino County. In 1865, Morse gave up ranching and moved back to San Francisco, and then on to Santo Domingo (now the Dominican Republic) with his wife, Harriet, where they were involved in a land-annexation scheme of some political notoriety. They remained in Santo Domingo for seven years before Morse came back to San Francisco, without Harriet. Through an acquaintance at the Park Hotel where he had lodgings, Morse came into contact with San Francisco's theater world and in 1877 put up the cash to produce his first theatrical venture, a futuristic play called *Anno Domini 1900*, which he had written himself.

Although *The Passion* was expressly not created in the mold of Oberammergau, which Morse considered to be anti-Semitic, it undoubtedly flourished in the context of the fad for the Bavarian passion play. While Morse claimed to have seen and been inspired by passion plays abroad—in Oberammergau as well as Jerusalem, Madrid, and Rondo, the latter reportedly the native city of Archbishop Joseph Alemany of San Francisco, who was an early supporter of Morse's play—the veracity of this account is uncertain, given Morse's tendency to embellish his past.[35] Based on what is known of Morse's whereabouts, Nielsen notes that Oberammergau is the only one of the four passion plays that Morse is likely to have seen and he could have done so on only two occasions, in 1830, when he would have been four years old, or in 1840, when he was fourteen. During the other years in which Oberammergau's play was performed, Morse was in San Francisco (1850), at his Mendocino ranch (1860), and in Santo Domingo (1871).[36] Given publicity about Oberammergau in the press, however, and the fact that the 1880 performance was approaching, it is also possible that Morse's wife's claim that she gave him the idea for the play from a newspaper article she read is true.[37]

Whatever the source of his inspiration, sometime in 1878 Morse wrote a "dramatized story of the evangelists," whose completion was noted by the drama critic George Barnes in his column in the *San Francisco Daily Morning Call*, on October 6, 1878. In a generally sympathetic tone, Barnes described the "bold experiment" Morse was undertaking by making "man's salvation the subject of a stage drama."[38] Perhaps in fear of being too bold, Morse had taken the precaution of seeking the approval of Archbishop Alemany, a seemingly shrewd tactic that, as Nielsen shows, would have the unintended consequence of turning Protestant ministers against the play. Morse had the play printed and also took the unusual step of having it copyrighted.[39] In January 1879, Morse was invited to read his play for Catholic officials and the public at St. Ignatius College. The response was apparently enthusiastic, despite the in retrospect ominous decision of the Protestant clergy not to attend; the *Daily Alta California* concluded a review of the reading with the statement that "Mr. Salmi Morse has succeeded in composing a Passion Play which heartily gained for him the warmest congratulations and applause of all present, and which will rank as a literary labor of importance."[40]

In its printed form, *The Passion* consists of ten acts comprised chiefly of long dialogues, which on the stage would be accompanied by pictures and tableaux recounting the major events at the end of Jesus' life. The first act of the play features Mary's presentation of the infant Jesus in the Temple, where he is hailed by Simeon as the Messiah. A messenger of Herod then appears, warning Mary and Joseph to flee with their child. Act 2 portrays the slaughter of the innocents ordered by Herod as Mary and Joseph hide from the Roman soldiers. In act 3, Salomé dances before Herod and demands the head of John the Baptist. Act 4 takes place at the Brook of Cedron, where Jesus delivers parables and chides Judas for his mercenary attitude (this scene sets the motive for Judas's subsequent betrayal). Acts 5 through 9 cover the biblical scenes from the Last Supper through the Crucifixion and the taking down of Jesus' body from the cross. The final act depicts the Resurrection and Ascension. Although there is little deviation from the standard biblical account, a notable invention and the only hint of Morse's natal religion is a scene in the sixth act in which Pilate and a Jewish elder named Eliezer debate the Roman occupation of Judea, and Pilate agrees to protect the Jewish Temple from defilement.

It is not completely clear how Morse's *Passion*, which he had apparently originally intended to present in narrative rather than dramatic form, made it to the stage. He surely must have been aware that a passion play faced some obvious liabilities as commercial entertainment, not least the fact that everyone knew the plot in advance (as Oscar Wilde quipped when told during an Oxford examination that he could stop translating a passage on the passion from New Testament: "Oh, do let me go on. I want to see how it ends"). Whatever Morse's original intent and whatever the obstacles to transforming the Passion into theater, it happened—and with help from some of the most illustrious names in the nineteenth-century theater business. As the editor and drama critic William Winter (1836–1909) tells it in his biography of the impresario David Belasco, who helped in the play's production, sometime in early 1879, the actor James O'Neill (father of the playwright) became interested in the play. Although O'Neill later claimed that he had to be persuaded to take the role, Winter asserts that the young actor, who at the age of thirty-two had yet to make a name for himself and so might have been eager for a major role, very much wanted the part of Jesus and persuaded the manager Thomas Maguire to produce the play, with financial backing from Edward Baldwin.[41] By February 1879, rehearsals were under way at the Grand Opera House, a large theater with seating for nearly four thousand spectators. Along with O'Neill as Jesus, the other major actors included Lewis Morrison as Pontius Pilate, Samuel W. Piercy as Herod, King Hedly as Judas, May Wilkes as Salomé, and Olive West as the Virgin Mary. Belasco has described how they scoured San Francisco for the rest of the cast, employing two hundred singers and four hundred men, women, and children in various roles in the ensembles.

As rehearsals progressed, Belasco observed that "every one seemed to be inspired," none more so than O'Neill, who became obsessed with his part, going so far as to give up smoking and other small indulgences, and walking the streets with a "holy" expression on his face. Belasco, too, became in his own words "a veritable monomaniac on the subject," never without a Bible under his arm; he even began, so Winter claims—although this is hard to believe of the energetic and worldly Belasco—to think of the monastic life as a vocation. Belasco frequented the Mercantile Library to study two of its paintings (the dance of Salomé and the Last Supper) for inspiration for the stage designs and developed a number of striking special effects. The extravaganza production included a flock of live sheep for the scene in which Joseph and Mary come down from the mountainside and a hundred mothers with infants in their arms for the massacre of the innocents scene. Extensive use was made of fabrics and stage lighting to generate the proper mood.

The play, billed as a series of "Lenten season" performances that would be "rendered with every circumstance of Solemnity and attention to historical facts,"[42] opened on Monday, March 3, 1879, in a swirl of controversy and last-minute attempts to halt the production. Even though the *San Francisco Chronicle* ran two long pieces about the play before its opening, one of which framed Morse's *Passion* within the context of medieval European drama in an apparent attempt to lessen its potential blasphemy by linking it to an "ancient" performance tradition, this historical overview did not help the play's chances for success.[43] On the day of the scheduled opening, Monday, March 3, 1879, two members of the San Francisco Board of Supervisors attempted to persuade Maguire to close the play. When he referred them to Morse, who refused their request, Supervisor James O. Rountree introduced a resolution making it a misdemeanor "to exhibit, or take any part in exhibiting, in any theater or any other place where money is charged for admission, any play, performance or representation displaying, or intended to display, the life and death of Jesus Christ" or "any other play illustrative of scriptural subjects or characters."[44] The city district attorney did not, however, carry out the injunction and the play opened as planned.

What spectators saw was, as Belasco's account reveals, a grand spectacle, but also a reverential one that attempted to meet critics' complaints about its potential blasphemy. In large part, the play did so by trying to present itself as anything but theater. The usual curtain was replaced by a painted drop depicting Calvary from afar, there was no preshow concert or curtain-raiser, the names of actors were omitted from the program, music adapted from Bach's *St. Matthew Passion* was used for the overture, and audiences were warned to refrain from applauding until the end. The performance also ended with the fourth act, which depicts the trial before Pilate, Maguire and Morse having apparently decided to omit the scenes of the Crucifixion and Resurrection in order to appease critics.

For at least some viewers, these tactics worked. A review in the *San Francisco Chronicle* described the performance as "a solemn tragedy presented with the utmost solemnity." Even if the lines were often "ungraceful," the costuming was sumptuous, the tableaux impressive, O'Neill's impersonation riveting, and the entire effect "realistic to the last degree." In the massacre of the innocents scene, the setting was, in the words of the *Chronicle* reviewer, "a wild gorge in the desolate mountains of Judea. The lights are subdued; amid the wailing of the orchestra the holy family descends; there are but few words exchanged; it is rather a living picture, vivid and by no means displeasing." In the fourth act, "the curtain rises on a scene of surpassing beauty. It is a touch of Eden—the umbrageous groves, the green pastures, the still waters, and in the foreground a group of silent figures. There is not a sound in all the house save the low moan of the music, every note of which seems to throb upon sympathetic strings."[45] According to Winter, Belasco recalled that when O'Neill came up from his dressing room and appeared on stage with a halo, women sank to their knees and prayed; when he was stripped and crowned with thorns, many fainted. Belasco claimed he had never "seen an audience as awed as by 'The Passion Play.' "[46]

Perhaps because it inappropriately evoked—or was thought to evoke—responses like these that seemed to smack of excessive religious fervor in the context of what was supposed to be a commercial entertainment, the play fell victim to attacks by a loose alliance of Protestant preachers, politicians, and the press, as Nielsen shows. Protestant clergy opposed the play for a number of reasons. One of them was that, as a stage play in which a mere mortal represented the deity and a commercial venture that charged admission, *The Passion* was blasphemous. The irony, of course, was that critics who defended the pious rituals of simple peasants at Oberammergau were quick to attack the blasphemy and commercialism of Morse's *Passion*, blind to the fact that the Bavarian peasants were reaping a greater profit from their production than were Maguire and Morse. The preachers' attack also focused on the secular and spectacular features of Morse's play as well as on its supposedly pernicious influence on the lower classes, whose religious passions they feared it would inflame. (Although Winter's report that "ignorant Irish" who saw the play "were so distempered that, on going forth, some of them, from time to time, assaulted peaceable Jews in the public streets," has been often repeated, Nielsen finds no historical evidence to support this claim of public disturbances.)[47] The preachers also attacked the play because they viewed it as a product of Catholicism, whose profits would go to support Roman Catholic institutions, overlooking the fact that it had been written by a Jew. Armed with these objections, the preachers attempted to mount public sentiment against the play and to influence the press to denounce it, a tactic that at least partially succeeded. On Friday, March 10, the board passed a slightly revised version of Rountree's ordinance and forwarded it to the mayor, who initially was rumored to be planning to veto it, in part it would later turn out, because he had seen *The Passion* and found it unobjectionable. Mayor Bryant ended up doing nothing, with the result that the ordinance by default became law, but only on March 21, 1879.[48]

Meanwhile, *The Passion* ran for ten performances, until March 11, 1879, when it closed to allow the leading actors to take up roles in *The Miner's Daughter,* starring Rose Eytinge. Although many accounts attribute the closing of Morse's play to the force of censorship, Nielsen argues that *The Passion* was originally planned for no more than a week's run and that its closing on March 11 was expected to be only temporary.[49] In any event, the play opened again, after *The Miner's Daughter* had finished its three-week run at the Baldwin, on April 15, Easter Tuesday, at the Grand Opera House. A more elaborate and longer version was promised, and the final acts were to be included. Reports in the local press by drama critics suggest that the performance was a success, with the last, religiously loaded, scenes being judged, in the words of one critic, "beautiful in design, admirable in color and grand in effect."[50] But aesthetics couldn't trump religion or politics and at the end of the performance, A. E. C. Bradford, a police officer who had watched the entire performance, walked backstage and arrested O'Neill for impersonating Jesus in violation of the newly passed city ordinance. Released on bail, O'Neill performed again on Wednesday, April 16, 1879 in *The Passion*. Officer Bradford was once more in the audience and this time, after the performance, arrested ten others (accounts vary as to whether or not Belasco was among them). While the legal wrangle unfolded, *The Passion* continued its performances, but, either because audiences had dwindled or because the inevitable was sensed, the end of its run was announced.[51] O'Neill and the other actors were subsequently fined for contempt of court—O'Neill to the tune of fifty dollars, the other actors five dollars each.[52] It has been estimated that Baldwin lost his entire $25,000 investment in the play.[53]

Nielsen argues that *The Passion* was doomed to failure from the start, and not just for religious reasons. With an overabundance of theatrical venues—the Opera House, the Baldwin, the Bush Street Theater, the California, Billy Emerson's Minstrels, the Tivoli Opera House, and many others—San Francisco supported an excess number of entertainments for a city its size.[54] A large theater like the Opera House, with its four thousand seats, would have been hard pressed to turn a profit under these circumstances, no matter what play it mounted. Additionally, Morse's play came at a time of social and economic stress for the city of San Francisco, which was in the midst of a depression that saw an influx of unemployed laborers who pushed the population to more than 230,000. A series of anti-Chinese rallies and riots by mostly Irish Catholic workers followed, which had the effect of pitting laborers against a largely Protestant merchant class.[55] In this turbulent socioeconomic climate and in a saturated entertainment market, a production like *The Passion* in Nielsen's view faced almost insurmountable odds.

While Nielsen's arguments are persuasive, the play's subsequent history suggests that it would be unwise to dismiss the role of religious controversy in its demise. After the play ended in San Francisco, Morse brought it to New York, where he and Maguire offered *The Passion* to the impresario Henry E. Abbey, who planned to produce it at Booth's Theater, which Abbey extensively renovated in order to make it an appropriately solemn venue for the play (during the run, the theater would be renamed Booth's Temple).[56] Abbey did his best to ensure that the play not inflame religious passions, trying as Morse and Maguire had also done to mask its appearance as a theatrical event and make sure its moral side was emphasized. New York's ministers, however, were besieged by the press for responses and for three months before the play's opening the controversy was whipped up. And this time the protest was not confined to Protestants but included every religious sect. New York's large number of newspapers also fueled the controversy, and their drama critics weighed in, including William Winter, who at that time was writing for the socially-minded *New York Tribune* and who panned the play on aesthetic not religious grounds as "one of the most tedious compositions that ever were written."[57] As Nielsen notes, the battle in the dailies was taken up by the theater's own newest trade journal, Harrison Grey Fiske's *New York Mirror,* which led the anti-*Passion* crusade.[58] The nineteen-year-old Fiske, seizing on *The Passion* as a chance to make a grand splash, attacked the play and its supporters while also lobbying the city to legislate against it.

Even in the face of these attacks, plans for the play continued. Auditions for the cast began on November 11, in order to find actors to supplement the leading roles played by O'Neill, the Morrisons, and other members of Baldwin's Stock Company who had been hired by Abbey for the New York production.[59] (The part of the Virgin Mary was apparently to be played, the *Dramatic News* reported, by "a young Hebrew girl" from New York, who was reputed to be a friend of Morse).[60] The large cast and crew proceeded with rehearsals and staging, but two weeks before the play was to open, New York City's aldermen passed a resolution to shut it down (interestingly, the only dissenting vote was from an alderman who had seen Oberammergau's *Passionspiel* that year).[61] At the same time, a group of prominent theater men, including the tragic-actor Edwin Booth, denounced the play. Four days later, in the Sunday papers on November 28, 1880, Abbey announced that he was withdrawing the play.[62]

Temporarily retreating from theatrical representation, Morse decided at this point to return to a safer medium, by offering a reading of his play, on December 3, 1880, on the Cooper-Union's lecture hall stage. The audience was small but according to press reports attentive and appreciative.[63] (Just one week later, John L. Stoddard would give a stereopticon presentation of the 1880 Oberammergau *Passionspiel* at Chickering Hall.) Despite this modest success, Morse vowed to stage *The Passion* in New York, no matter how long it took, and for a while had the support of O'Neill, whose career was foundering and who wished to return to his role as Jesus. One of Morse's backers, the costumer Albert J. Eaves, who had provided costumes for the 1880 *Passion* production, suggested that, since objections to *The Passion* were based on the fact that it was a stage spectacle, Morse should produce it in a nontheatrical space using an amateur cast. Morse agreed to do so, locating an old building on 23rd Street between Fifth and Sixth avenues, at one time a Protestant church and most recently a stable (did that connection with the biblical account register on Morse, one wonders?), for the purpose. By November 1882, *The Passion* had been cast (without O'Neill, whose career had begun to pick up), using unknown performers, and on December 23, Morse applied to the mayor for a permit to open his "Shrine of the Holy Passion," but his application was denied. Morse resubmitted his request to the new mayor, Franklin Edson, who also refused to grant him a license. Undeterred, on February 16, 1883, Morse presented the first four acts of *The Passion* as a "rehearsal," for an invited audience of around one hundred. A "full rehearsal," once again for invited guests, was announced for February 24, even though Morse had not yet secured a license. As the play began, police moved forward and arrested Morse, who in the subsequent trial was acquitted. Morse scheduled yet another dress rehearsal on March 30, 1883, reinviting those who had been in attendance in February. Although the amateur acting was criticized in the press, the staging met with favor, even without Belasco's guiding hand, as did the music. Encouraged by this success, Morse planned his first paying performance, but was blocked by an injunction brought by the Society for the Reformation of Juvenile Delinquents (a group that suggests the moralistic and paternalistic forces ranged against Morse's play).[64] Finally admitting defeat, on April 13, 1883, Morse announced that he would give up his attempts to stage *The Passion*. After Morse's death by drowning in the Hudson River on February 22, 1884, under mysterious circumstances, O'Neill tried three times to have *The Passion* revived, in Omaha, Nebraska, in 1889, and again in 1891 and 1896, but was blocked each time.[65]

Although the commercial stage, even when refashioned as "temple" or "shrine," proved unable to accommodate Morse's play, the new technology of moving pictures was more hospitable. A year after O'Neill's last attempt to stage the play, *The Passion* was filmed by Rich G. Hollaman, the proprietor of a wax-figure and lantern-slide museum called the Eden Musée.[66] Hollaman had seen the film of a passion play in Horitz, Austria, that had been produced by the theatrical managers Marc Klaw and Abe Erlanger and had aired in Philadelphia in 1897.[67] Observing the film's poor quality and being acquainted with Eaves, who still had the costumes and script of Morse's *Passion*, Hollaman decided to produce his own version. Along with the actor Frank Russell, Hollaman leased the roof of the Grand Central Palace in New York and filmed the *Passion* in December and January of 1897–98. In the nineteen-minute film, Russell played Jesus, Frank Gaylor was Judas, and Fred Strong was Pilate. Nielsen notes that the film perhaps provides a rough idea of what Morse and Abbey's production might have looked like, given that Henry Vincent, who was hired by Hollaman and Eaves to direct, might have been the same Vincent who served as stage manager for Abbey's proposed 1880 production.[68] Additionally, it is likely that Morse's script served as a basis for the spoken narration that accompanied the film screenings and turned the nineteen-minute film into a two-hour performance.[69] In Hollaman's film, then, Morse's play was finally performed using live actors impersonating biblical figures in a paying venture; the grand irony, of course, is that spectators had no idea that they were watching Morse's play, since the film with considerable astuteness about current attitudes was deliberately advertised as a version of the Oberammergau passion.

When the film opened at the Eden Musée on January 30, 1898, to positive reviews from the press, it was clear that Hollaman's strategy of presenting the film as a version of Oberammergau had been successful in positioning it less as a play than as an uplifting illustrated lecture about that well-known performance. The *New York Mail and Express* reported one month after the Musée opening that the "cinematographic pictures of *The Passion Play* are attracting thousands of people to the Eden Musee." During the early part of 1898 the film drew large audiences of clergymen and churchgoers and became a must-see for devout Christians. "I would advise all Christian people to go and take their friends whom they desire to see leading a Christian life," said one minister, "for here they will get a vivid portrayal of the life and sufferings of the world's Redeemer, and at the same time hear the story of the Gospel given in a most striking and convincing manner, which certainly must leave a lasting impression for good."[70] Hollaman and Eaves began selling copies of the film, at $580 apiece, and it was bought by the theater patrons and churchmen whose protests had been so strong against Morse's play. It was also purchased by traveling exhibitors like Lyman Howe, who planned to screen it in commercial venues.[71] Thus even though it had failed on the stage, Morse's *Passion* flourished in mufti—disguised as wholesome educational fare depicting an Old World religious drama—on the lecture and traveling exhibition circuits. There it helped create the context for another—and much more successful—attempt by an immigrant to mount an American passion play. This time, the stager of the Passion would be careful to link his play with the medieval past and to insist that he was not its creator but merely its importer.

The Black Hills Passion Play

The success of that immigrant's efforts is apparent in the longevity of the Black Hills Passion Play, which has been performed annually each summer in Spearfish, South Dakota, since 1939; it was also mounted each winter in Lake Wales, Florida, from 1953 to 1999, when it ceased after becoming embroiled in disputes over renovation of the amphitheater in which it was staged.[72] The production in South Dakota typically runs from early June to late August, with three weekly performances and has a supporting cast of some 250 players, including community performers as well as professionals. The play currently draws about 150,000 viewers per season.

The success of the Black Hills Passion Play says a good deal about the strategies required to import a passion play into America and also points to American ambivalence about such plays. What is particularly striking about the Black Hills play is that, with seeming effortlessness, it has avoided all the semiotic burdens that sank Morse's venture. That feat was in part accomplished by cannily invoking the play's medieval origins and using them as a smokescreen to conceal potentially unsettling aspects of the play long enough to transform it into "an American institution" that could flourish in a cultural space beyond history—and beyond reproof.

Like Morse's play, the Black Hills Passion Play is essentially the creation of one man, Josef Meier, who was born in 1904 in the town of Lünen, Westphalia, in northern Germany. Lünen, which was chartered in 1265, is today a city of about ninety thousand people in North Rhine-Westphalia, on the Datteln-Hamm Canal and the Lippe River, near Dortmund. It is a rail hub, a port, and a coal-mining and manufacturing center, where machinery, motor vehicles, and aluminum and glass items are produced. The seventeenth-century castle of Cappenburg lies nearby. According to James Wright, the play came to America when during the early 1930s a man from Pittsburgh named Fred Hardesty saw the Lünen play and asked Meier's father to perform it in the United States. Eventually, Josef Meier, who inherited the role of Jesus from his father, was induced to abandon his medical studies at the University of Münster and to bring the play to the United States.[73] Meier recruited ten principal players from the cast to accompany him and arrived in New York in 1932 with, as he has been quoted as saying, "an assortment of Biblical costumes, a brass chalice 300 years old, and a tattered text,"[74] a statement that shows Meier's not inconsiderable talent for modest myth-making.

Even in its earliest years, the play began to adapt itself to its new contexts, the cultural complexity of which was perhaps indicated by the site of the first performance of this German Christian play in the United States—a venue known as the Syria Mosque Theater in Pittsburgh in 1932. This performance used an English translation of the text prepared by Meier in Germany, with what linguistic fluency and awareness of American tastes we can only guess. Meier seems to have been a shrewd master of cultural positioning and after several years of touring, which gave him the chance to gauge American reactions to the play, in 1935 he rewrote the script, eliminating various scenes and concentrating on the last seven days of Jesus' life, striving for a simpler story of greater appeal to American audiences.[75] He also rewrote the speeches of the High Priests to eliminate the "hateful language" of the "old version" that he felt wasn't "close to the truth"—and thus attempted to strike passages that might seem anti-Jewish.[76] From 1932 to 1938, the production toured most of the major cities in the United States, with the exception of the seat of the professional theater, New York City, a bypassing that showed Meier as being shrewder about his audience than Morse had been.

During the touring years of the play, as Meier learned that community support was crucial to the success of his venture, that important structural feature took hold, as did a positioning of the play as heir to a long Old World performance tradition. Wherever he performed, Meier booked the play through civic sponsors and enlisted the backing of local church leaders. To muster clerical approval, he invited all of the clergymen in a town to attend at least one performance and then asked them to write letters of recommendation to church leaders in other towns, thus setting up a network of ecclesiastical support for the play.[77] Community involvement was also strengthened by tapping local citizens to play supporting roles in the production. These strategies had the fortunate effect for the play's future survival of aligning it with an Oberammergau-inspired style of simple folk piety rather than with the commercial theater. Oberammergau seems in fact to have lurked in the background, as an undated playbill for the play suggests. Advertising an upcoming four-night performance of "the original Passion Play of the Black Hills with Josef Meier World Famous Christus Portrayer," accompanied by the Lünen players, the playbill stresses the play's—and the entire genre's—German origins, boasting that "The Passion Play, in its origin, is essentially Teutonic." The playbill goes on to describe the play's beginnings in the twelfth-century church and its gradual move into the hands of the laity in the sixteenth and seventeenth centuries. Meier himself is billed as coming from a long line of players of biblical drama, a claim that shows what would become a consistent strategy of constructing Meier as the inheritor of a centuries-old performance tradition.[78]

Whether consciously or not, Meier's decision to locate the play in the Black Hills also linked the play with Oberammergau, by using a remote American site to replicate the desirable qualities of the small Bavarian village. Like Oberammergau, Spearfish was off the beaten track, but not so far off as to be inaccessible; it was scenic, and it was an appealing tourist destination that could offer the added value of other local attractions. All that ideological work could not, however, completely conceal the fact that the play was a thoroughly commercial enterprise and that business interests were what brought the play to South Dakota. The story of the move from touring production to regional spectacle is in essence a story of enthusiastic entrepreneurship. In 1938, businessman Guy Bell was seeking a tourist attraction for Spearfish and having heard of the Lünen play while it was touring in Sioux Falls, South Dakota, contacted Meier.[79] After negotiations, including a pledge that the Black Hills businessmen would build an outdoor amphitheater for his use, Meier brought the play to Spearfish for a brief run in 1938. In 1939 Meier's company settled in Spearfish and the play was renamed to signal its attachment to a specific place. That year, performances were mounted each Wednesday and Sunday evening from June 18 through September 13. Since 1939, the Passion Play has been performed every summer in Spearfish, except for a few years during the Second World War when gas rationing restricted travel. After settling in the Black Hills, Meier continued to take the play on tour during the winter months, to provide extra income, but in recognition of the power of place, the play even on tour was billed as the "Black Hills Passion Play."

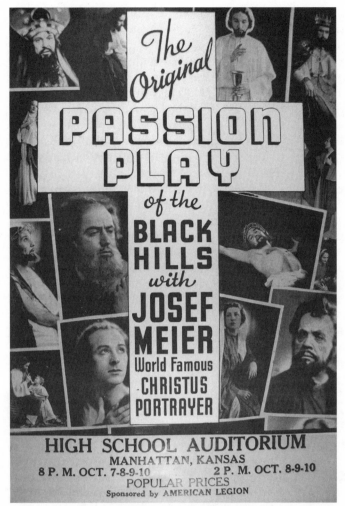

Playbill, The Original Black Hills Passion Play, date unknown. Courtesy of the Special Collections Department, University of Iowa Libraries, Iowa City, Iowa.

While the play reaped considerable symbolic benefits from its rural location, Meier had to work hard to attract paying audiences. Most of the publicity for the play was, and remains, regional, aimed at tourists from nearby states who might be inclined to watch a religious play while taking in the other local sights, with word of mouth and distribution of flyers and publicity folders being the chief marketing tools. (The Lake Wales performance depends less on tourists than on church groups in Florida and Georgia, and so has been marketed rather differently, primarily through letters to regional churches announcing group rates for the performances.) In Spearfish, cast members have been responsible for distributing the approximately one million flyers that are printed to advertise the play.[80]

This intersection of the Black Hills Passion Play with business interests is a constitutive yet potentially problematic feature of the performance. In this regard, it is important to note that the Black Hills play differs from a number of other passion plays that developed in the early 1900s in not being entirely church- and community-sponsored.[81] Like Morse's, Meier's passion play, despite its Old-World aura, was and is a commercial venture. Although the Black Hills play perhaps gives the residents of Spearfish an occasion for communal bonding and fellowship as publicity asserts, the bottom line is that the play is owned and managed by Meier, not by the town.[82] And Meier's central role in the play, as we shall see, has been crucial to its successful importing.

Before turning to that topic, we need to consider the relations of the Black Hills Passion Play with history—local, national, and transnational—which are complex. Because the play is a pure import, with no indigenous ties to the Dakotas—no link to a local German community with a tradition of religious plays, for instance, or to any local cultural institutions—it is perhaps not surprising that it is largely detached from the local history of the region. That history is marked by the well-known western themes of expansionism, battles with and displacement of Native Americans, and transformation of the environment. Gold had brought European-Americans to Spearfish, where in 1876 the first building was erected. In 1877, the Sioux Title put an end to Indian hostilities, and Spearfish began to grow. In the same year, the first store was opened along with a post office. These were followed by a sawmill, a blacksmith shop, a livery stable, and a law office. In 1883, the Spearfish Normal School was established; now known as Black Hills State University, the school is a major employer of Spearfish residents. By the time of the 1890 census, the population of Spearfish had grown to 671. In 1893, a railroad was built through Spearfish Canyon for the purpose of bringing ore from mines for processing, but it soon developed into a scenic attraction. At the end of the century, Spearfish became the site for a Federal Fish Hatchery, now known as the D. C. Booth Historic Fish Hatchery, which was completed in 1899 and has supplied millions of trout to streams and lakes in the Black Hills. A road through Spearfish Canyon was completed in 1930, spurring further growth and making it easier for Meier's future audiences to reach him.

Not much of this history has had a discernible impact on the passion play. Local history matters for the play only to the degree that it is convertible into scenic attractions that can lure tourists to the Black Hills and, once there, to the play as well. Recognizing the appeal of history as diversion for vacationers, the play's publicity material almost immediately began pitching the area's other tourist attractions, which include Mount Rushmore, the Badlands, the Homestake Gold Mine, Deadwood Gulch, Devils' Tower, and other sites associated with the "wild West," such as the cemetery where Calamity Jane, Wild Bill Hickok, and Preacher Smith are buried. Treating local history as entertainment was an efficient way of drawing visitors to the play; it also had the potentially negative effect of making the play itself just another tourist attraction, an effect that publicity for the play tries to mitigate through an emphasis on the play's devotional aspects.

Modern transatlantic history has been just as thoroughly ignored. A program from the 1939 season, for example, contains an oblique reference to "the unrest on the European continent," but that historical moment is mentioned only because it has provided Americans with "the opportunity of seeing the Luenen Passion Play in the United States"—a manifestation of the tendency to read foreign disaster as homeland advantage. Continuing in the same vein, the program manages to turn the events of Hitler's Germany into the story of flight to the promised land, telling us that "the players sought a place in America where they could continue to present, unmolested, the ancient story." "After much searching," the program continues, "they chose Spearfish, in South Dakota's Black Hills." This refashioning effectively reduces the entire socioeconomic buildup to the Second World War to the happy occasion that brought about the importing of the play. At the same time, the program evokes the notion of American as a harbor for the world's displaced, a land that could rescue the play's "ancient story" and give it a haven in the remote reaches of the American West. German prewar migration is thus presented as a lucky chance for the play, which is now safe and sound, and for Americans, too, who serendipitously have the opportunity to see an Old World drama on their own shores.

While exhibiting a general retreat from the historical events of the past two hundred years, the Black Hills play turned to a more distant past—as is suggested by the reference to "the ancient story" of the play—that is evoked not just as source but also as stable anchor for the production, in a move to position it outside of history, if by history we mean events that have determining effects and consequences. Looked at from this angle, the play is an extreme example of Hayden White's reminder that all histories—even performative ones, we might add—offer an incomplete representation of the "History" to which they aspire to offer access.[83] Invocation of the medieval origins of the play has been one means by which the play has claimed historical stability for itself while, not coincidentally, also removing itself from history and especially from that part of modern history that enfolds current controversies over the role of religion in public life. By emphasizing that the Lünen play dates to 1242, when it was performed by monks of the Cappenburg Monastery, Meier situated the play within a medieval performance tradition, thereby conjuring up many of the same themes that had proved so alluring for American enthusiasts of Oberammergau's play. The linking of the play to the secluded piety of medieval monks can be seen in the claim made by the 1939 program that Spearfish was chosen as the site for the play because it was "a quiet community far removed from industrial centers," an image of a bucolic preindustrial locale that recalls the appeal of Oberammergau, nestled in its remote valley. This out-of-the-way setting also offered a way for the Black Hills play to duck potential criticism of its religious themes by removing itself from the full gaze of public attention. Given that the play was marketed in large part through religious networks, those who found the play were predisposed to share its spiritual assumptions. Emphasis on the medievalness of the play was thus joined with the choice of location to situate the performance in a space that seems to escape or transcend the confines of real history.

These dehistoricizing operations are visible in the decades of publicity for the play, and particularly in the way that its self-presentation has evolved and been shaped for consumption by the American public. As brochures for the play show, the Black Hills play has faced anxieties about the relationship between its European past and American present, and about how to turn an "Old World" tradition into an "American institution."

These anxieties are immediately apparent in the eight-page brochure for the 1939 season, which is handsomely bound in a simulated mother-of-pearl cover with green lettering and a cut-out that opens onto the next page's portrait of Jesus on the cross.[84] The brochure is completely indecisive about whether to present the play as homegrown or as an import, an indecision that shows up on the cover, which bills the play as "The Original Black Hills Passion Play of America," and the first page, which calls it "The Original Lünen Passion Play of the Black Hills." The discourse of originality that is the one thing the cover and first page agree on is a constant feature of the play's publicity material and was perhaps in part inspired by a jockeying for position among competing American passion plays, such as the Holy Family Passion Play in Union City, New Jersey, which predates the Black Hills play and calls itself "America's Oberammergau" or the passion play in Bloomington, Illinois, which is billed as "the original American Passion Play" and as the "oldest continuously performed Passion Play in the United States."[85] No doubt realizing that its medieval European roots are what distinguish the Black Hills play from competitors, the 1939 brochure resolves the indecision over provenance by carefully positioning the play as the continuation of a long tradition of European passion plays. It does so by offering a history of the Lünen passion play, which is described as having begun with the enactment of the Resurrection on Easter morning in the chapel of the Cappenberg Monastery in Lünen and having developed by 1242 into a complete passion play that ran from Palm Sunday through Easter morning, initially in Latin but eventually in German, and that has continued into the present. In this history of the play's past, its European origins, broadly understood, are emphasized, while the assertion of the playbill for the touring production that "the Passion Play, in its origin, is essentially Teutonic," here goes unuttered. The specifically German roots of the play are thus quietly ignored in what can be seen as a first step in the Americanization process in which association with one nationality is replaced by a bland attachment to a generalized European Middle Ages.

The commercial aspects of the play also underwent a degree of strategic reshaping that implicitly drew on an Oberammergau-styled medievalism to present the play as the traditional ritual of devout amateurs. In line with this effort, the 1939 brochure emphasizes the subjugation of the performer to the role and to the tradition, noting that in the Lünen play the actors are trained for their parts from childhood, beginning by performing in group scenes or in the singing of hymns and later specializing in a particular role. While the brochure includes a list of dramatis personae accompanied by the names of the actors, each actor is presented as inseparable from the role and as fulfilling a sacred trust, a relationship that is signaled in each actor's pledge to conduct him- or herself onstage and off "as a worthy member of the Passion Players." Meier is so completely subsumed by his role that he is billed not as actor or director but as " 'Internationally Famous Christus Portrayer." The role is described as one for which he has been ordained from birth, since he hails from a family with a long tradition as "Biblical Dramatists." Kinship ties govern the other major roles and similarly conflate actor with part, with Clare Hume (Mrs. Josef Meier) as "Mary, 'the mother,' " and baby Johanna Meier as 'the Child.' " This central cast of Lünen Players and Meier family is, according to the 1939 brochure, joined by hundreds of local actors and chorus members, an arrangement that presents the play as nonprofessional and noncommercial. This antitheatrical vision of the play is intensified in the accompanying photographs, which describe the play as a devotional ritual. Pictures show the infant Johanna, Josef Meier in various poses as Jesus, Clare Hume costumed as the Virgin Mary, a view of the outdoor amphitheater with its row of "mansions" in front of which the various scenes of the play will take place, and selected scenes from the play (the Last Supper, Christ before Pilate, Christ carrying the cross, the Crucifixion).

While stressing the devotional aspects of the play, the 1939 brochure also makes an effort to market the play as part of a cluster of tourist attractions in the region, which it accomplishes by including a three-page spread of photographs of local sights. The effect of this inclusion is to present the play itself as a piece of scenic history, worth visiting for the same reasons someone might travel to Mount Rushmore. Devotional performance is thus linked to leisure-time entertainments, a connection that might seem jarring until we recall Oberammergau's similarly successful merging of the two.

By the 1950s, anxieties about the relationship between Old World and New have been largely resolved through a fetishizing of Meier himself, as a brochure from the early 1950s reveals. Contained within a sky-blue cover featuring a color picture of Meier dressed in white robes and kneeling amid a heap of rocks, with his hands clasped in prayer and an anguished expression on his face, the sixteen heavily illustrated pages of the brochure focus almost exclusively on Meier alone, in his role as Jesus and also, in a new twist, as paterfamilias.[86] Virtually every illustration in the brochure features him—with Judas, before the High Priests, at the Last Supper, and of course on the cross. The text accompanying these photos emphasizes Meier's importance to the production: he is the one who brought it to America, who oversaw the building of the Spearfish amphitheater, who orchestrates each year's staging, and whose rendition of Jesus is "an unforgettable event." Meier is saluted as the "Internationally Famous Christus Portrayer," capable of the ultimate theatrical illusion of convincing spectators that they are not watching a play but rather are physically "present at the time when the events described first took place." In this presentation, Meier seems to have become embodied history, which has been, to quote Bourdieu, "internalized as second nature and so forgotten as history" with the result that it becomes "the active presence of the whole past of which it is the product."[87]

As Meier is increasingly foregrounded in the 1950s brochure, the other members of the cast fade from view. The list of dramatis personae that appeared in the 1939 brochure is replaced by a list of characters sans names of actors. Even Clare Hume Meier is reduced to anonymity, and despite being featured in a full-page photo costumed as the Virgin Mary her name goes unmentioned. This refusal to name the actors, which represents a shift from the practice of the 1939 brochure, seems designed, as was the similar decision by Morse and Maguire in their passion play of 1879, to draw attention away from the act of impersonation and to emphasize instead the religiosity of these representations. Where the actor is unnamed, his role absorbs him, thus suggesting that he is not a hired hand, but rather someone whose very identity has been subsumed under his role. This absorption by the role extends to Meier as well: O'Neill might not have been able to get away with parading about San Francisco dressed as Jesus, but Meier has no trouble remaining "the Christus Portrayer" even while prosaically working at his desk, as the 1950s brochure pictures him doing.

The 1950s brochure takes further steps to convince spectators that the play is not a theatrical performance mounted by paid professionals, but rather a pious amateur ritual. As in 1939, the audience is asked to refrain from applauding, once more presumably to present the performance less as theater than as spiritual event. The brochure goes even further in stressing the religiosity of the performance by including a "Prologue," attributed to Meier, that asks "ye Children of God" to "Open your hearts, and receive with childlike / confidence His great message." The prologue ends "That which you will experience today, Oh People, / Treasure well within your hearts; / Let it be the Light to lead you— / Until your last day." By introducing the performance with a prayer, the brochure attempts to position the passion play as devotional practice rather than theater.

The relation of past to present, of Old World to New, about which the 1939 brochure was indecisive, is settled by the early 1950s. Now the play is billed as "The Original Black Hills Passion Play, Luenen Version," a phrasing that claims the play for America, but without abandoning the link to Europe. Once again, we are given a history of the play's European origins and its transplanting to America, an account lifted virtually unchanged from the text of the 1939 program. Now, however, the brochure proclaims that the play has developed into "an American institution," one that is solidly planted on these shores. What follows is an assimilationist success story in which we are told that, "because the American public has received the Play so enthusiastically and because of its very nature and character, it is safe to say that the Passion Play is now well established and accepted as an American institution." Assimilation is here seen as overwhelmingly positive. Not only has it not diminished the play's innate qualities (its "very nature and character") or caused the play to abandon its roots or reshape its identity, but the play itself now stands as an image of a united and conflict-free America that "offers to the American people a place of pilgrimage; a place where racial and denominational differences are without meaning; a place where beauty and power are revealed." What the brochure presents is a vision of the Black Hills Passion Play as a melting-pot mecca, where all people can be joined harmoniously together in a place beyond divisiveness.

It is perhaps not insignificant that this "American Institution" contains a shrine to the cult of the family. The final pages of the brochure zero in on the Meier family at home in Spearfish, and this time they are presented not in their religious roles, but as ordinary people. We see a portrait of Josef, a shot of Clare Hume Meier, three pictures of Johanna (who appears to be around six-years old), then "action shots" of their home life in the Black Hills ("Out for a family ride," "A friendly game of tennis," "Cultivating the corn," and so forth), all accompanied by a description of a typical day in Meier's life. In a masterstroke, the last page shows the Meier family at an outdoor barbecue and, at the bottom of the page, Meier wearing a cowboy hat, sitting astride a rearing white horse—an image that powerfully evokes Roy Rogers and a fifties-style pop cultural appropriation of the American West. These immigrants have arrived.

Taken in its entirety, the 1950s brochure reveals a performance perfectly calibrated to appeal to middle-class Americans interested in family, religion, and a melting-pot success story. The allure of the latter should not be overlooked. While the Black Hills Passion Play proclaims its origins in Europe, those origins are presented in a distinctly flavorless way. We are not offered a picture of a colorful ethnic past or one linked to a specific national tradition, but instead, through emphasis on Josef Meier's entrepreneurial spirit, hardwork, and idyllic family life, we are shown an up-by-the-bootstraps immigrant success story of the kind so dear to American mythology. Meier is described as "a man of varied interests and skills," one who is not only acclaimed as an actor but "has also scored signal success as a farmer, cowhand, rider, veterinarian, horticulturalist, carpenter, painter." The scenes of the Meiers at home evoke the material comforts of middle-class life—beautiful home, spacious gardens, comfortable mix of white-collar work and manual labor, with ample time for family-oriented leisure. Although the brochure, with a shrewd sense of class attitudes, is careful to present Meier as a humble man, whom visitors often mistake for a maintenance man, hints of comforts and connections beyond the middle-class intrude, as in the photo of "Mrs. Fausch teaching Johanna" that suggests that the family employs a governess or "a friendly game of tennis" between Clare and Josef that implies they have their own tennis court. And how many maintenance men rate "a visit by Senator Bushfield and Potato Creek Johnny"? That final photograph, with its combination of two pinnacles of American success—the political and the pop cultural—unequivocally reveals the Meiers' true status. In these photographs, the Black Hills Passion Play appears not just as a wholesome religious-entertainment experience for the family but as an enviable example of an American success story.

Twenty years later, the process of Americanization appears to be complete, as we can see in some striking new departures. The sixteen-page brochure for 1973, while otherwise retaining the salient features of twenty and forty years earlier, has dropped "the original" from its billing of play, suggesting that originary claims no longer have to be made to secure a place for the play.[88] Similarly, while Josef Meier is once again referred to as the "Internationally Famous Christus Portrayer," this time he is described not just as appearing "with" the play but instead as "presenting" it, a locution that reveals the overtly directorial role he always played but was, until now, never allowed to claim. That the brochure can finally present him not as the vessel of an ancient tradition, but as a profit-seeking theater professional speaks volumes about the play's newfound security.

Frank entrepreneurship is also the theme of a two-page spread describing the winter performances in Lake Wales that began in 1953. Meier, we are told, had long wished to produce his play outdoors during the winter and once again "it was a question of finding the rather rare combination of suitable climate and picturesque background," which Lake Wales offered. Now, on four evenings each week in the winter, "the lights dim slowly in the Amphitheater and the streets of Jerusalem come magically to life." Lest Meier look too much the greedy capitalist, the brochure is quick to underscore the community's full participation in the Lake Wales production, in language that echoes what Lucy Fountain tells us she encountered at Oberammergau:

> The little child you may have seen coming home from kindergarten in the afternoon, is now running with outstretched arms to meet Jesus. The pleasant young lady who waited on you during the afternoon in the store or restaurant in Lake Wales is shouting a joyful hosanna as Christ makes his triumphal entry into the city of Jerusalem on Palm Sunday. The merchant who stumbles down the steps,

driven from the Temple by an angered Christ, may have been the one you saw that morning helping his friend to build a house. The friendly man who helped you at the Post Office is now carrying a spear, determined that the captured Christ shall not break away from him. The pleasant man you asked for information about fishing is now bowing his head in prayer as he sits with the Master in the Upper Room; and in like manner, Lake Wales Citizens from all walks of life enthusiastically enter into the task of telling with emphasis this great story.

The effect of this passage is to conjure up the image of a community-sponsored play (even if it isn't quite that) in which ordinary people assume saintly roles much as the Bavarian villagers did. Such an image obviously goes a long way toward enveloping the Lake Wales performance in a similar aura of spontaneous piety as well.

To a marked degree, the self-presentation of the Black Hills Passion Play in the 1970s shows the fruits of the assimilationist efforts of earlier decades. The brochure ends with four pages devoted to the Meiers' return to Spearfish at the close of the Lake Wales performance season and in this section blends the touristic features of the 1939 program with the family-focus of the 1950s one. Mount Rushmore rates a large color photograph, while the Bad Lands and Palmer Gulch get smaller treatments. Interspersed among them are shots of the Meier family "enjoying the winter in the Black Hills" (with son-in-law also included) and posed with their horses. Other pictures show Meier with various pets and "preparing an outdoor supper." Perhaps the most revealing image, however, comes on the last page. It consists of a bluish-tinted black-and-white photograph showing Meier in profile wearing a Tyrolean hat, posed against what appears to be an indeterminate European city; next to the photograph is a "Prayer of Francis of Assisi" ("Lord, Make me an Instrument of Thy peace; / Where there is hatred, let me sow love"). Echoing the message of inclusiveness expressed in the 1950s brochure, this image also allows overt signs of Meier's German heritage to intrude. Does that Tyrolean hat bespeak the self-confidence of the thoroughly assimilated? If so, then it signals the same for a play so closely tied to its importer that, as his obituary said when he died in 1999, it was "essentially Meier. When you think of the Passion Play, you think of Josef Meier."[89]

The Black Hills Passion Play represents the culmination of more than a hundred years of interest in America in passion plays. That interest, however, as we have seen has often been ambivalent, particularly when it concerns the propriety of theatrical presentation of religious material by professional actors for individual profit. The Black Hills Passion Play has for the most part succeeded in ducking those concerns. It has done so by offering American audiences an imitation of a European passion play, one that preserves the aura of tradition but avoids any direct confrontation with real histories near or far. "Its great appeal," as current publicity claims, "is based on the spectacle which brings to audiences a sense of reality and of being present in history as the events took place, whether they view it as a moving spiritual experience, or as timeless theater recreating the classical art form of Medieval passion plays."[90] By evoking what is perceived as a timeless and universal story of Christian mythology, grounded less in an actual German history than in an indeterminate medieval past seen as channeling biblical history, and organized around the iconic figure of Josef Meier as "Christus portrayer," the Black Hills play has encouraged a proleptic version of history. All traditions are of course selective, choosing to leap over unsavory or undesirable moments of the past, but the Black Hills Passion Play seems particularly disengaged from its many pasts—the past of the Black Hills, of German immigration to America, of modern biblical dramas, and even of its own early touring years in America. Instead, by evoking its medieval origins, the Black Hills play manages to transform itself into a free-floating entity, depicting but not engaging with past events. Unmoored from real history, but remaining "faithful to the historical traditions of Medieval drama," as current publicity puts it, "the Play maintains a living link in the development of the Theater, and of representations of the Passion of Christ."[91] This living link is in essence a costume drama in which medieval origins legitimize and anchor the play, while also substituting for a more recent and potentially problematic past.

The Black Hills play continues the infatuation with community-based biblical drama exemplified by the Oberammergau fads of the nineteenth and early twentieth centuries. At the same time, by cultivating clerical and community support and by aligning itself with smaller-scale moral and educational venues rather than the commercial stage, it skirts the obstacles faced by Salmi Morse's *Passion*. American delight in the pious and naively charming villagers of Oberammergau has in the Black Hills Passion Play been reshaped into wholesome middlebrow family entertainment. All of this has been done beneath the radar of professional theater and its watchdog organizations, including the press, which no doubt has contributed to the success of the Black Hills play. There is, however, something ironic about the play's relationship to the past, in that the medievalness of the Black Hills play may in fact be less constructed than it at first glance seems. Astutely using regional networks, word of mouth, and community and clerical support, the Black Hills play in practice has reproduced many of the conditions of existence of medieval biblical drama. The Black Hills Passion Play thus perhaps lives its medievalness in much more structurally important ways than its vague and romanticized invocation of medieval origins, which bypass the messy and painful history of the present, would suggest.

What all of these attempts at importing passion plays reveal—from magazine articles and lectures on Oberammergau through Morse's *Passion* and on to the Black Hills play—is how hard it is to make explicitly religious performances acceptable in American contexts. Despite the enthusiasm for foreign passion plays like Oberammergau, actually replicating such dramas in the United States has in recent centuries been a difficult undertaking. Literary and educational-lecture reenactments worked because they skirted the central problems of passion plays: the immediacy of the experience (and its attendant emotional impact, as witnessed in the spectators who fell to their knees during O'Neill's performance as Jesus) and impersonation of divine figures (with its suggestion of blasphemy). But in so doing, they also gutted the plays of what made them plays. Morse's failed attempt to stage a passion play showed exactly the obstacles that perhaps unconsciously motivated the preference for the distancing and containing effects of print and lecture. Why Meier succeeded has less to do with a changed cultural climate—although it is true that by the start of the twentieth century religious plays had made a comeback on the stage (heralded by stagings of the medieval play *Everyman* in England and America)—than with a shrewd deployment of the right tactics. In retrospect, all of Meier's choices (venue, casting, publicity) seem inspired, particularly in their dexterous use of an idea of the medieval to create an American institution. If, then, the Black Hills Passion Play stands as an immigrant success story, it is thanks to a particularly inspired performative historiography and an adroit use of the medieval past.

CHAPTER 6

Medieval Plays and Medievalist Players

In 1672, the duke of Newcastle wrote to Charles II, urging him to revive the morris dance, the maypole, and "all the olde Holyedayes with their Mirth." The duke's enthusiasm for these rituals—which by the mid seventeenth century had come to be associated with proscribed Catholicism as well as lower-class rusticity—probably derived from the fact that the duke knew they were well-suited to Charles's ideological construction of England as a merry band of brothers and of his kingship as, in the words of Peter Stallybrass, "a source of *license* rather than of control."[1] This rather surprising proposal for the royalist co-optation of pastimes that a century earlier had fallen into disfavor stands as an early attempt at the deliberate resurrection of the performances of medieval England and as such makes an apt starting point for reflection on a much more recent instance of theatrical appropriation—modern academic reconstructions of medieval plays. In the last thirty years, reconstructions of medieval plays have become increasingly common forms of scholarly activity, as colleges, universities, and centers for medieval studies have sponsored reconstructed plays as a part of their intellectual endeavors, which have quite a lot to say about the current ideological work of medieval drama in academic and intellectual circles in America.

As John Marshall has observed, modern British revivals of medieval plays can be conveniently divided into three waves, each with a distinct agenda, but all sharing the same legacy.[2] The first wave, led by William Poel and Walter Nugent Monck in the early twentieth century, was inspired by antiquarian interest, especially in plays thought to form part of Shakespeare's "background." The earliest modern production of a medieval English play, Poel's staging of the fifteenth-century morality play *Everyman,* was mounted in London for the Elizabethan Stage Society in 1901 in the courtyard of the Charterhouse, a medieval monastery turned pensioners' home.[3] Undertaken as an antiquarian experiment, Poel's *Everyman* struck a chord with viewers that would be echoed by later successful revivals; in the words of the critic for the *St. James's Gazette:* "The whole thing was so moving, so human, so real . . . the essential human vitality of the whole thing was what most strongly appealed."[4] A commercial as well as critical success, *Everyman* went on tour in the provinces and was brought to the United States in 1902. Excited by Poel's efforts, Nugent Monck, who had played Fellowship in Poel's touring production, founded the English Drama Society in 1905 and began reviving other early plays, including an attempted performance in 1909 of the N-Town *Passion Play*, which ran afoul of British blasphemy laws and was shut down before it opened.[5]

These early, exploratory productions were followed by a second wave of revivals motivated chiefly by religious and nationalist interests, although the antiquarian impulse had by no means disappeared.[6] This second wave, associated with T. S. Eliot and Dorothy Sayers, famously culminated in the 1951 production of the York Corpus Christi plays, which were directed by E. Martin Browne as part of the Festival of Britain, a national celebration designed to mark the end of postwar austerity and to tap into what was perceived as the "moral capital" associated with England's cultural and spiritual past—a moral capital lamentably lacking, many felt, in 1951.[7] During the York plays' two-week run, more than 26,000 tickets were sold, for a profit of 2,400 pounds sterling; they were the only festival event to finish in the black (the festival as a whole lost 10,000 pounds).[8] In the wake of this astonishing success, revivals of the English cycle plays in their original sites of performance—Norwich, Chester, Coventry—were undertaken, fueled by local and national pride as well as by hopes of cornering a share of the tourist trade.

Since the 1970s, more overtly scholarly interests have come to dominate the production of medieval plays, as, in a third wave, revivals have moved into the hands of academics whose chief goal is accurate historical reconstruction of the original staging for purposes of scholarly inquiry. University-based performance groups such as Toronto's Poculi Ludique Societas, the Medieval Players affiliated with the universities of Cambridge and London, the Joculatores Lancastrienses, and numerous other college groups are today responsible for many performances of medieval plays. These historical reconstructions currently loom large in the teaching and study of medieval drama, with performances now routinely scheduled as part of courses, academic conferences, and symposia.[9] Attesting to the importance of these reconstructions within academia, large sections of specialist journals such as *Research Opportunities in Renaissance Drama* and *Medieval English Theatre* are devoted to reviews of such productions. Reconstructed performances also frequently show up in discussions of the teaching of medieval drama, in surveys of the field, and as the subject of analysis in books and journal articles. Given all this activity, the casual observer, as Marshall has cleverly remarked, "could be forgiven for thinking that more medieval drama has been produced in the twentieth century than in its own time."[10]

The implications of this third wave of revivals, especially as it has been manifested in the United States, deserve fuller examination. In a striking departure from the practice of almost all other branches of theater history, the bulk of scholarly work on the drama of medieval England is now being carried out primarily on two fronts—the archive and the stage.[11] Large-scale research projects such as the Records of Early English Drama, which seeks to publish all references to early dramatic activity found in British archives, and increasingly ubiquitous scholarly productions of medieval plays presently absorb significant resources of time, money, energy, and interest, squeezing to the margins other forms of intellectual inquiry and knowledge production, such as interpretation and criticism. One scholar's remark that medievalists now prefer to produce plays, "rather than endlessly and tediously reinterpreting them in the manner of the Shakespeare 'industry,' " perfectly describes the way that performance has come to be seen as a vital alternative to a largely exhausted program of criticism and interpretation.[12] Little debate, however, has taken place over what this rechanneling of resources means for the study of medieval theater, whether in terms of the relations of medieval drama scholarship with allied fields such as theater history, performance studies, and literary criticism, or in terms of its position within the larger, nonacademic culture of the United States.

This chapter considers the importing of English medieval plays into America by academics (since the story of academic reconstructions of medieval plays from continental Europe follows a somewhat different logic, I focus here only on English plays). This act of importing is a mode of historical and cultural inquiry with its own history, which developed in response to particular circumstances and shapes the way medieval drama—and more broadly the premodern past—is currently understood. My discussion of reconstructed plays, which construct a Middle Ages for intellectuals and academics rather than for popular audiences, begins with the so-called demise of medieval drama in England in the sixteenth century, since the "death" of medieval drama is the event that made possible all subsequent revivalist and reconstructionist efforts. I next examine the development of medieval drama studies as a discipline, since this disciplinary history goes a long way toward explaining the turn to reconstructions as a form of academic inquiry. Finally, I consider the assumptions, methods, and goals of academic reconstructions, especially those produced in the United States, in order to tease out the significance for literary and cultural history of this turn to "original staging." Two of the unspoken agendas of medieval revivals are particularly deserving of scrutiny: first, the empiricist method and positivist faith that guide many reconstructionist efforts and that view reconstructions as a route to knowledge and, second, the revivalist goal of appropriating for the present the values—celebratory and communal—imagined to inhere in the plays. Although seldom part of the agenda of modern performances of other plays from the past, these two features have become an almost inescapable aspect of the current project of reconstructing medieval English plays: John McKinnell, for example, claims that when he was asked to produce a medieval play as part of the 1982 celebration of the 150th anniversary of the founding of Durham University, he was explicitly instructed that it should be both "a spectacular celebration and an academic experiment."[13] As we shall see, this demand that reconstructed performances of medieval drama serve as both intellectual inquiry and celebratory spectacle has important, even if largely unexamined, implications for modern America's relations with a medieval English past.

Unlike revivals in England, American reconstructions of medieval English plays are not—indeed, given the American colonies' revolt against the crown, cannot be—explicitly linked to preservation and honoring of a national culture. The terms of the heritage industry that underpin so many scholarly and popular revivals of medieval plays in England do not neatly apply to American reconstructions. Instead, American reconstructions map a more or less coherent, even if at times self-contradictory, set of relations between former colony and mother country, and reflect ambivalence about England as a potential source of cultural identity for Americans. Revivals in the United States are for that reason implicitly tied to debates about what constitutes an American national culture, and particularly what role the English past plays, or should play, in it. To which America does this English heritage belong? To what uses should it be put? Where does it fit within a multicultural society? Even though revivals of medieval plays seldom explicitly ask these questions, they nonetheless tacitly struggle with them, as they recast the English medieval past through the act of modern performance.

America's relationship to England is, needless to say, complicated. In flight not only from religious persecution but also from what were perceived to be debased English institutions, early English settlers determinedly sought a break with custom. And after the Revolutionary War, which severed many remaining ties with England, the sense of American difference from English traditions was institutionalized in the new nation's political systems. Yet, despite these avowals of a clean break with the past, renewal through the return to origins is a perennial theme of the American cultural experience. Given these ambiguous relations, it is not surprising that the reconstruction of medieval English plays by American academics inevitably involves some unsettled accounts with England.

The Demise and Resurrection of Medieval English Drama

The central feature of the revival of medieval English plays is that it hinges on—indeed, was only possible because of—their history of nearly complete obliteration in the sixteenth century. Abandoned (or eradicated, depending on the view to which one subscribes) in the late sixteenth century, for the next three hundred years the drama of medieval England—its biblical cycles, saints' plays, moralities, and other popular forms—languished in obscurity, virtually unread, unperformed, and unknown, a situation that changed only in the late nineteenth century, as medieval drama gradually attracted the interest of amateur and professional historians of the theater.

The story of the demise of English medieval drama has been compellingly told by Harold Gardiner in his 1946 *Mysteries' End,* which chronicled the death of the so-called Corpus Christi cycles or mystery plays, the large-scale biblical enactments that have often been taken as the quintessential form of medieval drama. Gardiner describes the systematic shutting down of the mystery plays between 1569 and 1580 by religious and political authorities, a process that virtually destroyed what had been the most vital cultural form of the preceding two hundred years.[14] While surviving records hint at the large amounts of money and energy that, beginning in the mid fourteenth century, had been poured into the dramatic performances that formed a central part of the ceremonial and religious life of English communities, only five complete texts of the biblical cycles, along with a few fragments, have survived: the plays from York, Chester, and Cornwall; the Towneley cycle, which has often been associated with the town of Wakefield in Yorkshire; and the N-Town cycle, which appears to have been linked to East Anglia. If other cities had plays, their texts have disappeared, as did the performances themselves as the communal religious drama of medieval England fell from popularity into obscurity near the end of the sixteenth century.

As scholars more recent than Gardiner have shown, this dismantling—which may have been less systematic than Gardiner claimed—was the result of a variety of forces, not all of them religious, and included such phenomena as the material decline of provincial cities, the growing hegemony of print culture, a spreading linguistic uniformity, the expense of mounting the cycles, and London's rise to dominance.[15] As provincial cities became less prosperous, they found it harder to bear the considerable costs of mounting the plays and appear to have become less invested in the prestige plays had formerly brought them.[16] At the same time, the spread of printed books undermined the importance of the visual and oral cultures that had spawned and supported popular theatrical performances. And growing linguistic uniformity rendered plays composed in regional dialects ever more inaccessible. Additionally, centralization of power in London and in the monarchy had a strongly negative effect on traditional drama, which had prospered in cities and towns other than London; as Peter Womack notes, by the end of the sixteenth century, urban drama had been "swamped by the idea of a centralised national culture" as towns like Chester where the great cycles had once flourished, became "commercially, politically, linguistically and culturally *provincialised*" [his emphasis].[17] The demise of most urban plays by the 1580s makes clear London's acquisition of political and cultural hegemony as provincial towns saw their powers wane; this demise also registers the degree to which Protestantism had been successful in erasing nearly all vestiges of traditional religion, with obviously dire consequences for the performances built around it.

Yet another blow to medieval drama was widening suspicion of popular culture, which led to suppression of popular festivity in villages and towns.

Secular entertainments like maypoles, lords of misrule, Robin Hood ales, and charivaris, as well as religious rituals like veneration of saints, Corpus Christi processions, pilgrimages, and other cultic activities, were discouraged or actively squelched through legislation during the sixteenth century.[18] A series of governmental decrees evinced royal discomfort with the potential for disorder latent in public and popular theater, starting in the 1530s with a letter from Henry VIII to the justice of the peace in York, asking him to be on guard against "any papists who shall, in performing interludes which are founded on any portions of the Old or New Testament, say or make use of any language which may tend to excite those who are beholding the same to any breach of peace."[19] Increasingly firm lines were drawn between elite and popular social groups and between secular and religious performances, a segregating that worked against medieval performances, which had thrived by bringing together secular and sacred themes, high and low social groups.

As a consequence of these material, social, religious, and cultural changes, theater quite literally lost its place in English communities and was withdrawn from streets, inn- and churchyards, public greens, and even great halls, retreating from all of the public or semipublic venues in which it had been performed for the preceding two hundred years. In London, starting in 1576, playhouses were built in the suburbs outside the city proper, a choice of site whose spatial logic reveals Elizabethan and Jacobean ambivalence about the legitimacy of theater and its place in society.[20] The public performances that survived in London's streets were state-sanctioned spectacles that did not challenge official ideologies as more polysemous and socially diverse medieval urban performances typically had. By the end of the sixteenth century, then, as Kathleen Ashley has observed, the "festival culture of medieval society that had brought different social groups together and had blurred the distinctions between play, worship, and socioeconomic function was fatally disrupted, and its characteristic performances ceased or were transmuted within their new contexts."[21]

Where traditional drama endured it was usually in altered or hidden form. Protestant reformers, perhaps surprisingly, offered one vehicle for survival, as Huston Diehl has shown, proving unexpectedly eager to co-opt the theatrical practices they reviled, as they drew on traditional performances to advance their new religious and cultural agendas.[22] Similarly, as Robert Weimann has demonstrated, the commercial theater of Elizabethan and Jacobean England was heavily indebted to medieval theatrical traditions for everything from ranting Herodlike kings to quack doctors, as the rummaged repertoire of proscribed medieval plays found its way in distorted form onto the early modern commercial stage.[23] Religious plays continued to be performed in churches into the 1590s and some cycles survived in partial form in the provinces; even in London, religious drama could still be found, so William Prynne suggests in his remarks about a private performance of a passion play in London on Good Friday in 1605.[24] In addition, traditional performances like the morris dance and mummers' plays survived in out-of-the-way pockets in the provinces, out of range of official attention. Material from the urban biblical plays also found its way into puppet shows, where it lived on in new guise as the entertainment of children or rustics.[25]

Much of this shape shifting was driven by surveillance of the contents of plays, which grew as religious regulation acquired greater momentum. A system of censorship that would last well into the twentieth century gradually took hold, starting with the censorship committee set up by the Privy Council in 1581, which was charged with reading all play scripts in advance in order to "strike out or reform" anything that seemed to threaten "Divinity and State."[26] As a result, by Shakespeare's time, the wide-open, few-holds-barred theater of medieval urban communities had become, in John Elliott's words, "a circumscribed area in which all might not be said."[27] Censorship would prove a persistent obstacle to the revival of medieval plays in England, and although it would have a much lesser impact in the United States, even there anxieties about religious propriety would remain an impediment to the revivalist impulse.[28]

However great the cultural blow might have been when medieval English drama ceased to exist, this demise had the positive effect of flash-freezing an entire body of cultural material. Forgotten by history, it was ripe for revival, even if that revival was a long time coming.

Medieval English Drama Revived

Modern revivals of medieval English drama in Britain and America date to the early years of the twentieth century, but are rooted in the enthusiasms of the nineteenth century, especially the enthusiasms of medievalists who under the impulse of antiquarianism and romantic nationalism resurrected the traditional arts and crafts as a way of resisting the perceived evils of industrial capitalism. The first wave of twentieth-century revivals of medieval drama in Britain has been charted in separate studies by Robert Potter and John Elliott, who have recounted how, under the auspices of the Elizabethan Stage Society and the English Drama Society, William Poel and Walter Nugent Monck gave twentieth-century audiences their first taste of medieval theater, in productions of *Everyman,* the *Interlude of Youth,* and selections from the Chester cycle plays. As Elliott emphasizes, the religious content of medieval plays proved a sticking point for British revivalists, thanks to the censorship system that over the centuries had effectively siphoned all religious content out of the theater. Although challenges to censorship had been mounted—most notably by the Church and Stage Guild, which had been founded in 1879 by the Anglican priest Stewart Headlam, who like William Morris sought to provide the masses with spiritual enlightenment through the arts and theater, and by George Bernard Shaw, who in the 1880s and 1890s sought to add religion to the list of subjects available for stage representation—the censors' policies remained largely unchanged.[29] When Poel staged *Everyman* in 1901, luck was on his side, however, and the obscurity of medieval drama worked in his favor, since the censors, who knew nothing about the play, assumed that *Everyman* was a kind of Shakespearean drama and therefore unobjectionable. Poel's production was in some ways quite radical (a woman, for instance, played the lead role and God was impersonated), but in others thoroughly conservative (it was a bowdlerized version, with no references to the Crucifixion or to the sacramental nature of the priesthood, an important theme in the medieval play). In subsequent productions, the radical bits were toned down, and the part of God, which Poel had changed to "Adonai," became the Voice of Adonai and was moved offstage.[30] Poel's *Everyman* was a critical and financial success and in 1902 was restaged at St. George's Hall in London and at the Imperial Theatre, Westminster, on the occasion of Edward VII's coronation, which signaled *Everyman*'s entry into the pantheon of officially approved entertainments. The play continued to be staged by Poel up to his death in 1935, and by Philip Ben Greet, an actor-manager who had joined the 1902 production.

Nugent Monck, who got his start with Poel, tried to introduce more plays into the revivalist repertoire, but his efforts were hampered by proscriptions against the enactment of sacred scenes. Using his own group of professional actors, the English Drama Society, Nugent Monck staged three of the Chester Nativity plays in London and Chester in 1906 and also took a production of *The Interlude of Youth* on tour in the provinces.[31] He attempted to stage scenes from the N-Town *Passion Play* and planned to produce all twenty-five of the Chester cycle's plays in Chester over a three-day period at Whitsuntide in 1907, as David Mills has shown, but that effort failed, in part because of lack of support in Chester for such a large-scale effort, but also because of concerns about the propriety of staging religious drama.[32] Mills cites one of Nugent Monck's supporters in Chester, the Archdeacon Edward Barber of Chester Cathedral, who in an article entitled "The Chester Mystery Plays: Their Origin and Purpose" that appeared in the *London Guardian* on September 26, 1906, noted that if the plays were to be produced, they would need to "be acted under conditions which would not be contradictory to their religious spirit and character."[33] Precisely what those conditions might be is left unsaid, but the insistence that the plays' spiritual qualities be protected shows what a revivalist was up against in trying to stage a medieval play. A more obvious impediment was the censorship system that forbade the portrayal of religious themes on stage. Although in 1907 seventy-one writers lodged a formal complaint against the censorship system, it was not until 1912 that the rule against scriptural plays was relaxed and Old Testament and nonsacred New Testament characters were allowed on the English stage—and even then the ban on impersonating the deity remained in place.[34] Despite Poel's achievement with *Everyman,* success in reviving other medieval plays was by no means assured.

When we turn from England to the United States, we find a similar first wave of revivals being staged in the early years of the century. Initially, most of these first-wave plays were imported from England, with the result that American audiences were exposed to medieval drama chiefly through touring productions from abroad. The motives for importing these plays were at least partially altruistic, as the first American production of *Everyman* suggests. Just a year after it had presented *Everyman* in England, Poel's company was brought to America by the theater impresario Charles Frohman, under the direction of Ben Greet; *Everyman* opened in New York on October 13, 1902, in Mendelssohn Hall. Frohman apparently had seen the English production and had been greatly taken with it; he brought it to America not expecting to make money from it, he claimed, but so that Americans might see "this fine and worthy thing."[35] Part of the play's value for Frohman appears to have been its link to the "old Mystery Plays which first created the Theatre"; whether Frohman was cannily positioning the play so as to increase its chances of acceptance by American audiences or was actually expressing his own sentiments, his words point to the same evolutionary historicism that underwrote the nineteenth-century recuperation of medieval plays: medieval plays are valued primarily because they can be seen as the first step on the ladder leading to the glories of the modern stage.[36] For the performance, Frohman carefully arranged the stage in Mendelssohn Hall to evoke a church, with an altar and other ecclesiastical appurtenances,[37] but even so the play met with initial hostility from the press and was criticized as sacrilegious; the *New York World* called it "a thing of the Dark Ages," which seems to sum up the press response.[38] *Everyman* eventually became a success, however, and in the following seasons was performed in Boston, Philadelphia, Toledo, and other cities as far west as St. Louis. It returned to New York in 1904 and yet again in 1907.

The historical attitudes at work in these early revivals are especially evident in a performance of *Everyman* staged at the Children's Theatre in the Century Theatre Building in New York City, beginning on March 10, 1913. Edith Wynne-Matthison, a member of Greet's Woodland Players, starred as Everyman in the Lieber company's special-cast production, which was mounted under the direction of Greet on a stage designed to represent the cloister yard of Salamanca Cathedral in Spain. According to a copy of the program, the cathedral was a place "where the early passion plays were performed by the religious orders in the XV and XVI centuries," and thus presumably made a suitable setting for the English play. The program adds that the performance will include "sacred choral and instrumental music of the XIII century, religious processionals and no intermissions," all strategies designed to evoke the properly reverential mood and to disguise the fact that the play was being performed on the commercial stage.[39] Wynne-Matthison's portrayal of the character of Everyman echoed Poel's original choice to portray a female Everyman, a preference that would form part of a pre–World War I tradition of assigning that role to women.[40]

Ben Greet's Woodland Players, Redpath Chautauqua. Postcard, date unknown. Author's collection.

Recognizing that the religiosity of medieval plays presented obstacles for the commercial stage, Greet found alternate venues for his revivals. His Woodland Players had become famous in England for their open-air performances, and Greet continued to seek out places for outdoor performances in the United States, frequently at colleges. The assumed educational value of the plays made universities a natural venue as did the fact that, in a country lacking in ruins or other sites associated with a medieval past, college greens and the occasional Gothic-revival university building offered suitable stand-ins. These college performances often hitched medieval plays to the safer and better-known star of Shakespeare, a coupling that also had the effect of underscoring the notion that medieval plays were important chiefly as precursors to Shakespearean drama. In June 1903, Greet's company performed *As You Like It* and *Comedy of Errors* at Harvard under the auspices of a committee from the English department, which included the scholars G. L. Kitteridge and J. H. Gairdner.[41] During tours in 1904 and 1905, Greet staged open-air productions of *Hamlet* at Berkeley, then performed *Everyman* in San Francisco, and subsequently traveled up and down the West Coast. In Tacoma, Greet's company performed *The Star of Bethlehem,* a version of the *Second Shepherds' Pageant* from the Towneley cycle, which had been prepared by a professor at the University of California, Charles Mills Gayley. The play was intended to be a companion to *Everyman,* and Greet himself took the comic role of the shepherd Mak.[42]

Greet's players performed at other colleges, as well, including at the University of Michigan in Ann Arbor, in a January 1907 production of *Hamlet* in which students were among the actors, inaugurating a tradition of mixed amateur and professional casts still common for medieval revivals.[43] In another college-based production at the Harvard Stadium in 1909, Frohman staged *Joan of Arc* with Maud Adams in the title role. The elaborate pageant, which featured mechanized settings, a hidden orchestra, and live horses, was performed for over 15,000 spectators and netted $15,000, which Frohman donated to Harvard.[44] A Baylor University performance of *Everyman*, billed as the "most famous of all Morality Plays," featured Elsie Kearndon Kearns and George Carlton Somnes along with Greet's Woodland Players.[45] Although there is no direct lineage connecting these early university-sited revivals to the academic reconstructions that showed up in the 1970s, they are surely linked in spirit.

Given that medieval revivals stressed the educational value of medieval plays, it is not surprising that they regularly appeared on the Chautauqua circuit, particularly under the auspices of Frank Lea Short, a New York director associated with Charles and Daniel Frohman. A publicity brochure from the Chicago-based Redpath Lyceum Bureau, a booking agency for the Chautauqua circuit, claims as one of Short's "noteworthy achievements" that of directing "the first Elizabethan Revivals ever presented to the general public which were immediately imitated by Possart in Germany and by Ben Greet in England and America." Short was credited with the first public performance of *The Second Shepherds' Play* from "the Towneley series of Miracle plays" and "the Mystery Play of 'Mankynde'" (the loose application of terms to describe the genres of the plays—*Mankind* is usually not described by scholars as a mystery play, while the Towneley cycle is—perhaps hints at the limits of awareness of the scholarly history of medieval drama). The brochure also emphasizes that Short has the right pedagogical credentials since his companies had played at many universities and that this university training "makes him peculiarly fitted to select and produce plays for the Lyceum."[46]

Exactly what to make of these plays was not always clear to spectators and critics. On the one hand, there was the camp represented by James Russell Lowell, who in a piece called "The Old English Dramatists," written for *Harper's New Monthly Magazine* in 1892, insisted that "the English Miracle Plays are dull beyond what is permitted even by the most hardened charity."[47] On the other hand, there were sympathizers such as the writer of another *Harper's* article in 1896, who provided a detailed discussion and synopsis of the Towneley *Second Shepherds' Play*, along with lengthy quotations from the play and tips on how to read Middle English.[48] For this enthusiast, medieval plays were clearly a source of entertainment, even if of a decidedly bookish sort.

Contemporary newspaper accounts suggest that many viewers rated religiosity the chief value of revived medieval plays.[49] Writing in the *Christian Register* about the Park Theatre production of *Everyman*, the Reverend Edward Everett Hale responded to the play's intended religious impact while also registering its pedagogical and moralistic value:

> The performance of a miracle play by an English Company in our different cities suggests a great deal to those interested in religious education. The performance is dignified, serious, and fits the real purpose of those leaders of the people who contrived such performances in the "Dark Ages." But I doubt if any person who attended this revival just to learn "how they did things" five centuries ago does not come away with the serious question whether the play cannot teach us all what is good for us.[50]

For the Reverend Hale, the play is of interest to modern spectators insofar as it can instruct them about the past and, even better, teach them how to be good. This insistence on the didactic value of medieval revivals, in terms of both their ability to re-create history, by telling us "how they did things" five centuries ago, and their ability to spur moral improvement tended to replace discussion of the aesthetic quality and entertainment value of the plays. Moral and intellectual edification, not art or pleasure, were the standards by which medieval revivals were to be judged.

If we return to England and to the second wave of revivals, starting in the 1920s and running through the 1960s, we can see the same emphasis on the religious and moralistic appeal of medieval plays. Inspired in part by medieval revivals, the Religious Drama Society was founded in England with the express purpose of promoting Christian drama; while sponsoring new plays by Dorothy Sayers and T. S. Eliot, it also shared the ethos of the medieval revival. *Everyman* continued to be a popular play and was revived by Poel off and on, including for the opening of the Canterbury Festival of Music and Drama in 1929 where three years later T. S. Eliot's *Murder in the Cathedral* was performed.[51] Many of the plays of the Religious Drama Society were directed by E. Martin Browne who in the 1920s and 1930s had established himself as a well-known director of religious plays in his position as director of drama for the Diocese of Chichester, where he put on the Mary cycle from the N-Town plays, not for profit or antiquarian interest but rather, as Elliott claims, as "an act of worship."[52] To instill the proper spirit, Browne's rehearsals often started with prayers, Elliott notes, and Browne insisted on preserving the anonymity of his amateur actors, subordinating them to the roles they played.[53]

Browne's selection as the director of the York cycle for the 1951 Festival of Britain ensured that the emphasis on re-creating a religious experience that was intended to have salutary effects was transferred to that highly visible and influential production. In the 1951 production, Browne presented a bowdlerized form of the Passion sections of the York cycle, with the scourging scenes taking place offstage and the nailing of Jesus to the cross being masked by banners. Browne's staging used the model of the Valenciennes miracle plays of 1547, and arrayed a series of "mansions" against the Abbey's ruins. One effect of this choice of setting was to underscore the sanctity of the York plays, with the ruins of the Abbey conveying a sense both of a lost sacredness that the staging of the medieval play in part helped recuperate. As Sarah Beckwith has argued, drawing on Pierre Nora's notion of "places of memory" (*lieux de mé-moire*), this focus on ruins as the archaeological remains of a lost history embodies history as "simultaneous plenitude and catastrophe, so enacting our possession by the past and our dispossession of it."[54] While appearing to conjure up a memory of the past and seeming to offer the fantasy of a possible recuperation of history, ruins in fact insist on the pastness of the past and deconstruct recuperative narratives of a whole and organic history available for the present.

The desire to use medieval revivals as symbolic vehicles for reconstruction of the past appears with particular force in another production of *Everyman,* also staged in 1951, this time in London in the Festival Church, St. John's, Waterloo Road, where it was directed by Hallam Fordham using volunteer actors and actresses. In this production, the character of Everyman was played by Fordham himself, who was a broadcaster and advertising manager of Yardleys of London; the role of "Kindred" went to Diana Lewis, a civil servant; and "Cousin" was played by Gordon Bryant, an engineer.[55] The recuperative goal of revivals was made explicit in this performance, which earmarked contributions from each performance for restoration of damage from World War II bombing of churches in London.[56] Could there be a gesture that better encompasses the reconstructionist hopes attached to revivals? Not only did this production promise to restore a past damaged by modernity's attacks but it also aimed, quite literally, to save the church at the same time. Rescue of monuments was thus joined with reassertion of the value of institutional religion in a grand attempt at simultaneous symbolic, material, and functional renewal grounded in a return to the medieval.

Attesting to the success of Browne's Festival of Britain production, by the 1970s all four of the extant cycles had been performed in full or partial versions in England.[57] But even while the religiosity of medieval plays was construed as one of their assets, it continued to be a sore issue. At Chester, for example, there were run-ins with institutionalized religion; one in 1973, over a contemporary-style performance, led to the end of using professional actors. In 1987, the Church of England was nervous about the inclusion of *The Last Judgment* pageant (most church-sponsored cycles now end on the uplifting note of the Ascension and thus avoid that problem).[58] Clerical attentiveness of this sort is one sign of the ideological difficulties that medieval religious plays still faced in England. Although revivalists had attempted to forestall complaints through the use of such "reverential" tactics as amateur performers and noncommercial venues, those tactics could go only so far in overcoming perhaps inevitable clashes between theatrical representation and institutionalized religion.

In the United States, the second wave of revivals was much more muted, having an upswing of neither Catholic sentiment nor nationalist impulses to spur it, as had been the case in England. For the most part, the second wave in America consisted of a continuation of themes and performances from earlier in the century. Ben Greet's company, for example, continued to tour the United States, performing *Everyman* and a selection of Shakespeare's plays. Greet's tours often had the feel of revivals of the company's earlier productions: for instance, a publicity flyer for the performance of *Everyman* at the Brooklyn Academy of Music, on January 31, 1930, proclaimed the return of Greet and "his brilliant cast of English players" brought back "by insistent demand of leading universities and cities that had them last season and those that wanted them but were unable to secure them last season." (In the previous year, Greet's company had performed at Brown, Columbia, Penn, Michigan, Illinois, Indiana, Wisconsin, Missouri, and a number of cities coast to coast.) The flyer commends Greet's ability to create "an essential atmosphere of medieval reverence." "Nothing detracts from the play's significance," the flyer continues. "His only modification of the true Elizabethan manner is in the use of richer and more elaborate hangings than were employed in the Elizabethan days."[59] As the phrase "medieval reverence" suggests, the desired effect was both to re-create the past and to preserve the sanctified aura assumed to inhere in the medieval original.

Recitals and readings in the years after 1920, many of them on the Chautauqua circuit, also featured medieval plays, which suited the moral-educational bent of that performance venue. An advertisement from the Slayton Lyceum Bureau from around 1920 announced a reading of *Everyman*, "the popular Sixteenth Century English Morality Play," by Mabelle Carolyn Church. Another publicity flyer heralded the 1930–31 season of Professor Davis Edwards, "the best reader of poetry in America," whose repertoire included *Everyman,* which he aimed at church groups, educational assemblies, and civic organizations. A 1927 flyer promoted Sydney Thompson, a performer of medieval legends and tales; her work was billed as especially well suited to clubs, schools, and colleges.[60] Also in 1927, Diana Huebert, the dramatic dancer, performed in three Max Reinhardt spectacles: *A Midsummer's Night's Dream, Danton's Death,* and *Everyman.*[61] This invasion of the lecture circuit suggests how popular a handful of medieval dramas had become as entertainments designed to instruct and uplift. The impression left by this second wave of revivals in the United States is that during the middle years of the twentieth century, a few well-known medieval plays became entrenched in dramatic repertoires, but only on the fringes of the commercial theater. Using the model so successfully created by Poel, mid-century revivals toed the expected line and presented medieval drama as edifying and morally useful.

Medieval Drama as a Discipline and the Turn to Archives and "Original Stagings"

The third wave of revivals in both England and America began in the 1970s as scholars of medieval drama increasingly turned to reconstructed performances as a mode of intellectual inquiry. Although it bears the legacy of earlier twentieth-century revivals, this third wave was also engendered by the specific history of medieval drama scholarship as a discipline, since it is within that larger disciplinary field that academic reconstructions find their ideological home.

One thread of that history ties medieval drama studies to popular medievalism. Like folklore, a discipline it resembles and overlaps with, medieval drama as an academic specialization includes among its forebears not only academics but also eager amateurs whose interest in medieval performance was in many cases motivated by a search for alternatives to modern mass society.[62] Part of the history of medieval drama studies (like the larger field of medieval studies in general, whose historical and ideological construction has been astutely analyzed by Lee Patterson and Anne Middleton)[63] thus lies outside academia proper, in the enthusiasms of amateur antiquarians as well as in the political and aesthetic interests of dissidents and revivalists who turned to the medieval past as an antidote to industrialized mass culture.

Another thread of the history of medieval drama scholarship ties it to the development of literary studies as a modern discipline. One of the problems that medieval drama studies has faced is that it is in many ways at odds, as Clifford Flanigan has observed, with the paradigm of formalist analysis that has marked literary studies until quite recently, and that continues to exert considerable influence, despite literary scholarship's move toward cultural studies in the past decade.[64] The institution of literature as it is known to us today was invented in the nineteenth century under the influence of Kantian aesthetics and growing national consciousness. As Flanigan notes, medieval drama, indeed most of medieval literature with only a few conspicuous exceptions, is almost entirely incompatible with these outlooks. Medieval drama has little to do with nationalism in the modern sense, evincing instead what can now seem a baffling combination of highly localized political interests mingled with a diffuse pan-European ethos grounded in the tenets and practices of medieval Christianity. Moreover, medieval plays rarely exhibit those linguistic, authorial, or formal qualities that make them rewarding as objects of aesthetic appreciation: they are written in inaccessible dialects, seldom can be attributed to an individual author, are didactically religious in content and stylistically rough, and often do not even survive in complete scripts.

The problem of medieval drama's lack of fit with prevailing literary paradigms was compounded by the fact that until the mid nineteenth century little was known about medieval plays.[65] This state of affairs is not altogether surprising, given that when performances disappeared, the texts of medieval plays, including the urban religious cycles, dropped almost entirely out of circulation, surviving in the hands of private owners or unnoticed in libraries, not to appear again until the nineteenth century. Although evidence of medieval drama began to be unearthed in the late seventeenth century, in usually disapproving comments by historians of the stage like Richard Flecknoe, Thomas Rymer, James Wright, Bishop Thomas Percy, and Edmund Malone, the neoclassicism of the age was by and large not disposed to value medieval drama or to waste time on its study. The realities of this situation are suggested by the first anthology of early English drama, Robert Dodsley's *Old Plays,* published in 1744, which focused chiefly on Elizabethan and Jacobean plays. The only pre-Shakespearean drama Dodsley thought fit to include were six "early plays" chosen as examples of "the progress and improvement" of the English stage; despite the claim about their antiquity, not one of these plays dates to earlier than the mid sixteenth century.[66] Medieval drama fared somewhat better in 1774 in a posthumously published collection of early plays gathered by Thomas Hawkins, which appeared under the title *The Origin of the English Drama;* Hawkins's selection of early plays was broader than Dodsley's had been and included the Digby *Slaughter of the Innocents* as well as *Everyman.*[67] Later in the century, the beginnings of romanticism sparked a renewal of interest in the medieval past, although, as Flanigan observes, this benefited drama less than other forms of medieval literary production.[68]

Despite this smattering of interest, it was only in the late nineteenth century that medieval plays began to receive serious scholarly attention from academics working in the various national literatures, with the appearance of studies such as Alessandro d'Ancona's *Sacra Rappresentazioni* (1872), Louis Petit de Julleville's *Les mystères* (1880), Wilhelm Creizenach's *Geschichte des Neueren Dramas* (1893–1903), and continuing into the next century, Edmund Chambers's *The Mediaeval Stage* (1903), Gustave Cohen's *Histoire de la mise-en-scène dans le théâtre religieux français du moyen âge* (1906), and Karl Young's *The Drama of the Medieval Church* (1933)—studies that even now remain to some extent definitive, even as their methodologies and conclusions have come under scrutiny. When medieval drama studies finally arose as a discipline in the nineteenth century, it was under the influence of German source study and primarily as a subset of Shakespeare studies; from that latter perspective, medieval drama was thought to be significant not in its own right but only to the degree that it could be seen as a precursor to Shakespeare's greatness. Methodologically, medieval drama scholarship was grounded on a positivist historicism that assumed an evolutionary development of drama from "primitive" medieval performances to the theatrical genius of Shakespeare and beyond; this historicism was largely unsympathetic to medieval culture and was marked by strongly antireligious—and especially anti-Catholic—sentiments. For most scholars of English literature, medieval drama remained obdurate material: too overtly didactic, too "religious," too crude, and too amateurish for comfortable assimilation to literary-critical values.

To a large extent, recent archival- and performance-based work in medieval drama studies can be understood as a defensive reaction to the two threads—popular and academic—of this early development of the field. A preference for performing rather than interpreting medieval theatrical texts echoes the aims of revivalists and reformers by substituting real-world activity (the staging of a play before a potentially broad audience) for sterile and cloistered scholarship, thus promising experiential and social as well as intellectual results from the scholarly efforts involved. At the same time, this preference emphasizes medieval drama scholarship's difference from and superiority to its closest disciplinary neighbor, literary studies, by freeing it from what many scholars of medieval English drama often see as the useless literary-critical project of spinning out endless interpretations.

Although archival work and the mounting of reconstructed performances might at first glance seem contradictory endeavors, they in fact share many assumptions and have much the same goals. In a penetrating analysis of the large-scale archival project known as the Records of Early English Drama (REED) project, whose stated aim is to find and publish all extant references to early drama in England, Theresa Coletti has convincingly argued that the focus on records-editing evinced in the REED project is ideologically linked to the turn to reconstructed performances and that both are attempts "to overcome—now and for all time—the marginalization of medieval drama in early drama studies and the English literary canon."[69] The REED project, which was founded in 1975 and operates under the auspices of the University of Toronto and with financial support from the Canadian government, represents a long-term commitment by a team of more than fifty scholars to make available surviving dramatic records. REED's findings are published in large volumes, each of which is devoted to a specific geographic region of England, with a total of fifty such volumes projected; typical entries record such information as accounts of payments, items of costume, names of actors, prohibitions, and disputes. The focus of the REED project is thus not dramatic texts per se, but rather records that reveal details about the circumstances surrounding the original performance.

The historicism underlying both REED and reconstructed performances is one that in Coletti's words insists on "the local, contingent, materially specific aspects of early drama" and that views recovery of lost or forgotten originals as the central goal.[70] A continuation of the antiquarian activities of the nineteenth century, Coletti argues, REED's work builds on the research of such antiquarians as Robert Davies, Thomas Sharp, and James Orchard Halliwell-Phillips. The career of Halliwell-Phillips is particularly instructive for its similarities to REED; as Coletti shows, Halliwell-Phillips's exhaustive examination of local records from across England—his scrutiny of parish records, wills, and subsidy rolls—provides an early template for the REED researchers' activities. Like REED scholars, Halliwell-Phillips prided himself on seeking out local documents that had never before been "properly examined" and on presenting the fruits of his research "in the least presuming form" so as to offer the reader "an unprejudiced and complete view of every known fact" relating to Shakespearean drama.[71] In place of the errors of earlier scholars, Halliwell-Phillips promised, in words that echo the ideal of the REED project, "accuracy and authenticity."[72]

In 1977, the impulses behind the REED project found dramatic expression when the University of Toronto Center for Medieval Studies staged the York cycle on pageant wagons, in a production that intentionally followed as closely as possible the performance conditions described in the records.[73] Since then, the Center for Medieval Studies, along with the acting group known as the Poculi Ludique Societas (PLS), has staged a major dramatic production every few years, usually with assistance from scholars and their students in the United States; between 1977 and 1988, PLS produced all four of the extant English cycle plays. PLS, whose productions are largely amateur and academic, grew out of a seminar conducted by Professor John Leyerle; its first public production was a 1966 staging of *Rafe Royster Doyster* for the Medieval Academy of America meeting in Toronto. In the words of two of its members, PLS's productions combine "a concern for authenticity with a strong interest in theatricality"; the company "has worked on the assumption that many medieval and Tudor plays are still viable theater, and that preserving the aesthetic integrity of these works often means retaining certain of their original conditions of performance." To that end, *PLS* has sought to "recapture the communal nature of early drama" by copying original staging as much as is possible and by retaining the original language of the plays.[74]

If the turn to reconstructed performances can be said to share the same privileging of accuracy and origins as the REED project does, it also partakes of the phenomenon of salvage that structures humanities scholarship in general and medieval studies in particular.[75] Traditional humanistic scholarship has long placed its hopes in a hermeneutics of retrieval in which the present is characterized as a state of loss and scholarship becomes a means of nostalgic recuperation. This yearning for recovery and reconstitution has additional importance for medieval studies, given that, as Louise Fradenburg has argued, a pervasive sense of bereavement structures all desires for the medieval. As Fradenburg notes, since the medieval past has acquired its value by virtue of being lost to us, "critical and scholarly acts accordingly gain their legitimacy by making up for that loss, by recovering an impossible relation to the alterity of the West's own past."[76]

In the United States, this theme of loss and recovery has not found physical sites so obviously perfect as have been available for "original stagings" in England. Indeed, American reconstructions have generally been unable to draw on any evocation of place whatsoever, since the United States offers no medieval ruins and no locales—no churches, fields, or towns—that are obviously linked to the medieval past.[77] As early-twentieth-century revivalists realized, universities with their lawns and neo-Gothic buildings are generally the best remedy for an absence of the medieval past from the built environment of the United States. It should come as no surprise that third-wave academic revivals have followed the example of Ben Greet's players in using universities as the most common location for reconstructed performances. But if medieval drama can be said to occupy a specific place within the cultural geography of the United States, it is in the relatively unfixed but evocative space of the ivory tower, which stands to some degree outside American culture. Reconstructed plays are thus not attached to specific towns or regions of the United States— as is generally the case in England—but to an academia that is perceived as being—and in some ways is—detached from the larger culture. The alterity of medieval drama is thus much more strongly emphasized in America than in England, since in England reconstructed performances can be situated in the streets of existing towns like York, for example, where the medieval past is a visible part of the modern cityscape.

The economic situation of American academic reconstructions adds to the sense of detachment from the larger culture. Unlike the situation in Canada, there are no sources of major financial support for reviving medieval plays in the United States, which has limited the ambitions of reconstructionists. The only large-scale American academic revival of the cycles has been the mounting at the University of California at Irvine of a tripartite *Plaie Called Corpus Christi,* funded by the university at a cost of approximately $35,000 per year, and performed over three years.[78] Tellingly, the Irvine productions were not scholarly projects in the same sense that Toronto's are: they did not re-create the original language or the "original staging" of the plays and they did not pretend to be historically accurate or even to remain faithful to the medieval text. For example, Irvine's 1986 production, entitled *The Nativity,* pieced together texts from three of the cycles, conflating different forms of staging (processional pageant-wagon staging as at York and staging in the round, as some scholars have assumed might have been used for some of the N-Town plays) for an indoor performance in Irvine's Fine Arts Village Theatre. In another break with original staging, the performance was staged indoors, not out, and the action took place on a long, rectangular scaffold, with the audience seated on either side. Given these deviations from the goal of authenticity, it is worth noting that the Irvine production was put on under the auspices of the theater department, rather than by a medieval studies group, which suggests why it was freed from the quest for historical accuracy that is part of the disciplinary imperative of medieval scholarship.

Lacking major financial support, most American academic revivals have been carried out in small-scale, independent productions. One example is the production of the fifteenth-century play *Wisdom* that was mounted by Trinity College in Hartford, Connecticut, in 1984 using an all-student cast. Trinity's medievalesque campus offered a chapel, banqueting hall, and processional route for the play, all of which helped enhance the sense of an authentic reenactment. Staged as if it were an Abbot's banquet masque performed in the great hall of Bury St. Edmunds in 1474 for King Edward IV, the play was presented in a modernized version that nonetheless did not stray far from the sense and sound of the original East Midland's dialect. Signaling the seriousness of the project and its status as an intellectual endeavor, the performance was accompanied by a symposium of scholarly papers and discussion.[79]

While mounting their own reconstructions, American academics have also played a role in Toronto's productions of medieval plays, contributing to performances and serving as spectators. In 1992, when the University of Toronto hosted a festival to celebrate more than twenty-five years' worth of performances by the PLS, groups primarily from the United States were invited to bring their own productions of any play written before 1642 that was one hour or less in performance-length. Participants included groups from Ohio State University, the City College of New York, the University of Michigan, Ohio Wesleyan University, and the University of Kentucky, among others.[80] This team effort demonstrates the way that, while Toronto has maintained central control of REED and PLS-sponsored performances, many American academics have shared in those efforts, as have British scholars.

As this border hopping suggests, academic revivals in the United States have a complicated relationship with nationalism. To the extent that there is an umbrella agency sponsoring reconstructed performances within American academia it is not tied to the U.S. government, but resides in the professional societies to which scholars of medieval drama belong, such as the Medieval Academy and the Medieval and Renaissance Drama Society, which are transnational in nature and which in that regard share the broad pattern of the institutionalization of medieval studies in America. By the mid twentieth century, as Anne Middleton has shown, the project proposed by medieval studies was "a massive intellectual program of redefined solidarity with a deep European past," that stood as a sign of the "coming of age" of the United States as a world power "and hence as a producer of world-historical significance." By allying itself with an Old World past, American medieval studies staked its claim to an intellectual authority grounded on co-optation of a European history. That history, however, was only available as an object of study because, as Middleton observes, it could be viewed as "without immediate intersubjective and historical relations with the investigators"; in other words, by the mid twentieth century the European Middle Ages could be researched, even if no longer understood. At the same time, like the other "area studies" that developed in the years following the Second World War, medieval studies almost immediately withdrew from engagement with other disciplinary discourses and increasingly followed its own research agendas.[81] As a subset of medieval studies, academic reconstructions of English medieval drama in the United States share this history, which is played out in the characteristic assumptions, methods, and goals of those reconstructions.

The Work of Academic Reconstructions

Two central assumptions underwrite third-wave revivals: that a reconstructed performance offers a route to knowledge about the original performance and that it can recapture the values associated with that original. To a degree, these assumptions echo the aspirations of earlier revivalists, who saw their efforts as revealing information about the theatrical past and as bringing values from the past into the present. What is different is the insistence of academics that reconstruction is a scientific effort and that the values it transmits are socially ameliorative.

Unlike most other theater historians, medievalists routinely accept reconstructed performances as empirically sound ways of "testing hypotheses" about the original staging of medieval plays. This test-tube method, or what Peter Meredith calls "the does-it-work approach," has been eagerly embraced for everything from solving small "problems" of staging (such as how to tie the actors' hands and legs for the mock jousting scene in *Fulgens and Lucres*) to providing sweeping "proof" of early performance practices (such as that the Towneley cycle was performed in the round outside a parish church).[82] Reconstructions are commonly seen as laboratory experiments, valuable for what they can reveal about early performances and by extension the meanings of plays as well. It has become an article of faith that a reconstructed performance, especially when it builds on the findings of archival research, can provide answers to questions of performance practice that are otherwise insoluble.[83] The test-tube method thus is assumed to offer what looks like an empirically sound way of turning hypotheses about medieval drama into facts: thanks to reconstructions testing the pageant-wagon performance style on the streets of modern York, for instance, medievalists now feel able to speak with certainty about the way the York cycle was originally performed.

It is not hard to see why an emphasis on the empirical value of reconstructions would appeal to the academics under whose auspices most performances of medieval dramas now take place. For a field that faces a fundamental lack of raw data—only a handful of surviving texts of plays, almost no eyewitness accounts of performances, little information about playwrights or actors, and very few visual representations of theatrical events—the promise of more evidence is an immediate selling point. Additionally, given the increasingly technocratic culture of the university, expenditures of time and money can be more readily justified if the performance is understood to be a laboratory experiment, rather than mere art or entertainment. The REED project, which is supported by public funds from the governments of Canada and the United States, understanding the advantages of speaking the language of technocracy, has shrewdly adopted performance as the best method to communicate the results of its archival research and so to justify public support.[84] Public performances give REED researchers a tangible way of demonstrating how they have spent public funds. In addition, the empirical method is attractive to humanist scholars, who all too often face skepticism about the value of the arts, including the value of studying them. Linking their endeavors to the prestige-filled work of science enables medievalists to legitimize their efforts—to themselves as well as to outsiders.

However understandable the appeal of the empirical method might be, the kind of testing being done in reconstructions of medieval plays deserves a closer look. As currently practiced, reconstruction is not primarily an experiment aimed at enriching modern theatrical repertoires, making early drama accessible for modern audiences, or offering social or political challenges, although these goals do figure into individual performances on occasion. Instead, the often explicitly stated aim of revivalist productions is to present the most "authentic" production that can be mounted, one that replicates the original in every detail and is "as historically accurate as possible" in the words of the producer of Duquesne University's performance in 2000 of *The Second Shepherds' Play*.[85] The publicity for the 1985 Toronto production of the Towneley plays, for instance, boasted that the cycle would be presented "as it might have been performed in the West Riding of Yorkshire in the year 1475." This quest for "as it might have been" has imbued productions such as the York cycle at Leeds (1975), the *Castle of Perseverance* at Toronto (1979), and *Mary Magdalene* at Durham (1982), to name just a few. What all of these productions attempt is a reconstruction of the original staging, costuming, and acting—in other words, a replication of the past in full verisimilitude.

Reconstructed performances follow the logic of metonymy, a trope often used by medievalists and one that is closely allied with positivist history's search for data.[86] Metonymy, which operates by means of substitution, is the trope of contiguity. It asserts the connection of present and past and assumes that surviving artifacts and events can be made to conjure up the whole of past reality. A reconstructed performance that adheres to the standard of "original staging" thus holds out the promise of bridging the gap between past and present. The hope of metonymic history is to offer overwhelming evidence of the truth of the past and to circumvent the need for interpretation or a conceptual framework for analysis. Metonymic history sees itself as a form of objective representation in which events are represented "as they really were" and as they reveal themselves without the mediating interventions of a speaker or interpreter. Like other forms of positivism, the reconstructed performance conceals its strategies and deflects attention away from its interventionism and constructedness in favor of a perceived transparency and nonproblematic

"Creation to the Fifth Day." York Cycle Plays, Toronto, 1998. Photo by
Gloria J. Betcher. By permission of the photographer.

factuality. Even though every reconstruction is a "production"—something
that is made, and remade, with each performance—the reconstruction downplays the fact that it has been produced as a form of evidence, not—as its ad-
herents insist—found.

The positivist treatment of performance as experiment works on the one
hand to legitimate the work of medievalists, positioning them on a par with
that currently most privileged category of knowledge-workers—scientists—
and on the other hand to offer a certitude that seems to remove the need to interpret, critique, and judge, by focusing on a self-evident and incontrovertible
display of evidence and "proof."[87] Because reconstructed performances cannot
readily re-create the original politics, ideological functions, or socioeconomic
valences of the medieval play, those aspects are inevitably downplayed. Reconstructions necessarily isolate the play from its original context, since that
context is impossible to re-create; as a consequence, reconstructions are ex-
tractionist forms of scholarship that remove a cultural item from its deep em-
beddedness in social life. Even on those occasions when a reconstructed performance is credited with enriching knowledge of original staging practices ("I
understand why each guild would do only one pageant," commented one participant after a City College of New York staging of selections from the

Towneley plays),[88] that knowledge stops at the borders of what can be visually and aurally represented and cannot tell us very much about relations between staged actions and the culture within which those actions took place. No matter how accurate it may be, no reconstruction can reveal a performance's original meanings or functions for spectators, nor can it reweave a play's connections to its initial cultural milieu.

A second assumption about medieval reconstructions is that they offer the opportunity for communal celebration. They accomplish this in part by shunning commercialization and professionalism, as the revivalist projects of early-twentieth-century medievalists did before them. Especially in the United States, nearly all modern performances of medieval plays are the work of people who are not theater professionals.[89] Nonprofessional productions, while sometimes simply a matter of necessity, are generally preferred for their apparent ability to preserve the communal qualities believed to inhere in medieval plays. The call for a "People's Festival" at York in 1969, for instance, can be understood as a powerful expression of desire for a return to community-based, amateur performances that would recapture "the medieval tradition of community participation"—a reaction, in other words, against the professional and experimental 1960 and 1963 Brechtian-styled productions by the London directors David Giles and William Gaskill, respectively, that were financial successes but drew vociferous local protest against allowing irreverent outsiders to tamper with sanctified traditions.[90] In the United States, where there is virtually no commercial or touristic market for medieval drama, community participation has not required defense since the academic community is generally the only group interested in medieval plays. Even then, however, amateurism and community participation are championed as one of the chief virtues of reenactments.

Amateurism is so important because it symbolically severs connections with the modern, commercialized world—including the world of professional theater—and thus enables the audience to imagine itself sharing in the kind of communal celebration that is often associated, accurately or not, with medieval performances. The underlying logic is not simply escapist, but also oppositional. Michael Bristol has argued that Shakespeare scholarship in the United States has always been motivated by emancipatory possibilities that "encourage the desire of Shakespeare scholars as a loose collectivity to be counted as separate from and oppositional towards the imperatives of the market."[91] If anything, medieval drama scholarship embraces emancipatory possibilities even more intensely. In kinship with the anti-industrial spirit of nineteenth-century medievalism, medievalist spectators often hope that reconstructed performances will inspire a kind of communal festivity assumed to be in short supply in modern life. Martin Stevens, for example, commented on the "moments of festive fun, planned and unplanned" in the 1985 Toronto Towneley cycle that re-created for him "the atmosphere of performance as communal celebration and integration—the stray dog who angrily barked at Cain making his way through the crowd; the children sitting unselfconsciously on God's empty throne during the Passion in riveted attention to the bloody spectacle played below. . . . These were the small scenes that helped light the way toward the full appreciation of the experience as a whole."[92] Another spectator at the Towneley performance remarked: "I forgot where we were. I felt what it was like to be a medieval peasant."[93] Similarly, Joanne Gates praised the University of Massachusetts' 1983 production of the Digby *Mary Magdalene* for capturing the appropriate "medieval atmosphere," which was established "by colorful costumes, by the crumhorns, tambourines, shawms, and chapel bells, by fluttering angels' wings and entr'acte jugglers." Most important for creating the right mood, however, was the unscripted appearance of a stray dog sauntering across the King of Marseilles' scene "with a string of Gluttony's sausages dangling from its mouth."[94]

Productions stressing theatricality and artifice, in contrast, have elicited hostile reactions. When David Giles, directing the 1960 York plays, used such Brechtian alienation techniques as blocking the Abbey ruins (where the York plays have been staged since 1951) with scaffolding, crucifying Christ backwards so that his face was turned away from the audience, and having God enter not gloriously through the picturesque central arch of the Abbey but casually at audience level, spectators were outraged.[95] The Abbey ruins, a Christ conventionally crucified, an omnipotent and splendid God—these establish the appropriately awe-inspiring tone and are demanded as a necessary part of the production. The barking dog and the unselfconscious children—these act as authenticating spontaneous moments of festivity that position the performance not as artifice but as something quasi-natural and unscripted. When awe and spontaneity combine, they work to convince spectators that they are not just watching a play, but instead are engaged in a deeply meaningful shared experience. Other such moments of mingled awe and spontaneity—the plane that roars overhead just as Noah, not realizing it is God speaking to him, says he hears a sound from above, or the sun that breaks through the clouds at the exact moment Christ is raised up into heaven—form part of the folklore of reconstructed performances, signs of their transformational power.[96] This strong preference for the spontaneous, the natural, and the unplanned shows how alive the nineteenth-century construction of a realistic or naturalistic Middle Ages still is: the value of medieval plays is their engagement with everyday life and their rejection of the corrupting effects of artificiality.[97]

The transformational power of medieval reenactments is presumed to include the possibility of a liberatory social bonding that mimics what is often associated with the social functions of medieval plays in their original contexts. Medieval plays, especially the biblical cycle plays from England, are often seen as attempts at enhancing *communitas* by creating at least the illusion of shared interests among spectators. From this perspective, the social function of the plays is seen as having been aimed at lessening the differences that divided original audiences—urban groups that were disparate and often antagonistic, as well as acutely conscious of status and authority—by replacing divisiveness with social harmony based on mutual interests. Although this functionalist approach has in recent years been critiqued by Sheila Lindenbaum among others, it nonetheless exerts a powerful pull as a way to understand the social function of the cycle plays.[98] Modern academic audiences often seek a similar experience of social cohesiveness with both the actors and their fellow spectators. According to a reviewer of Cornell University's production of the York *Christ Led Up to Cavalry* at Toronto in 1977, "the single most extraordinary moment of the entire Toronto production" occurred when Jesus, about to be dragged away, "approached within arm's reach of the spectators" and "wordlessly searched the faces in the audience with an expression at once dazed and reproachful."[99] Bonding with fellow spectators often comes from the sharing of physical hardships, especially when watching reconstructions outdoors: enduring downpours, the press of the crowd, weary legs, hot sun, hunger, and thirst become ways of connecting with everyone else. Describing the experience of watching the Towneley plays at Toronto, Peter McDonald noted that the "sheer physical effort expended by the audience for fourteen hours over two days enables members of the audience to escape from the passive role forced upon us by modern theatre architecture, and allows us to feel genuinely part of the community that celebrates the play."[100]

Total *communitas,* enclosing every possible division, is the mark of a successful reconstruction that dissolves normal social distinctions; as one reviewer approvingly observed of spectators at PLS performances: "jockeying for space in a crowded ground, the Toronto audiences level the boundaries that separate the present from the past, the community at large from the students and scholars, and even the skilled performers from the less skilled."[101] Aware of the demand for social bonding, reconstructions often try to find ways of breaking down barriers between performers and spectators so as "to engage the audience directly" and "make them complicit" with the actions of characters in the play.[102] Having actors move among spectators or bringing spectators into the performance (for instance, by having devils drag them off to Hell in Judgment scenes) is thought to increase opportunities for the kind of blurring of lines between audience and actor assumed to have marked medieval plays. Lack of *communitas,* in contrast, is taken as a sign of failure as in one performance in which the audience refused to join in singing the closing *Te Deum,* thereby denying itself "the possibility of expressing fully that sense of community with other members of the audience and with the actors and production staff" and thus failing to reconstruct "an important historical fact about the way in which these plays might have related to their one-time audiences."[103] This complaint deftly illustrates how the desire to experience social solidarity can be made to seem consistent with the empirical method: since such solidarity (so it is often assumed) was an important part of the original performance, it has to be conjured up again in any reconstruction that has pretensions to being authentic. If a reconstruction does not achieve the feeling of social bonding, then it must not have done its historical work properly.

This insistence on *communitas* allows the academics who mount and attend medieval reconstructions to affirm solidarity with one another while also expressing opposition to the larger, commercial culture surrounding them. It also marks academic audiences as different from ordinary spectators who not only do not evaluate a performance in terms of its ability to create the feeling of unity but who also often are uncomfortable with that agenda. Reviews of reconstructed plays that are performed before both academic and non-academic audiences make this difference clear: academic audiences understand their expected role, play along with the performers, and are rewarded with a feeling of transformation, while non-academic audiences are less attuned to expectations, less accommodating, and unable to participate in the social bonding. What the different reactions of these groups of spectators suggests is that the strong desire of scholars to participate sympathetically in medieval *communitas* may in fact tell us more about academic alienation than about the medieval theater.

Given that academics form a relatively homogeneous group to begin with, particularly in their sense of themselves as standing apart from the larger culture, the desired effect of transformative bonding is not terribly hard to come by. There is also little in the plays themselves that would block that effect, since the content of most medieval plays, including their once shocking mingling of piety and profanity, is uncontested material for modern audiences. The one topic that does remain controversial—the plays' pervasive anti-Semitism—is almost always cut out, further erasing the possibility of dividing spectators along lines of religious sympathy. In fact, since the time of Poel's staging of *Everyman,* active bowdlerizing and censorship—such as omitting Fellowship's offer of a woman to Everyman and Knowledge's allegations about the illegitimate children of sinful priests, not allowing God and Christ to play speaking roles, muting the realism of the crucifixion scenes, and seldom performing violent plays like the *Massacre of the Innocents*—has whittled away potentially polarizing scenes.[104]

Some scholars of medieval drama have expressed uneasiness about the sidestepping tendencies of reconstructed performances. Edward Burns was distressed by the way that the 1985 National Theatre production of "The Mysteries" replaced "the sense of a confrontation with great events made disturbingly present" with a sentimentalized nostalgia for past community.[105] In a similar response, Darryll Grantley objected to director Bill Bryden's predilection for a false "folksy jollity" and "a 'merrie England' feel" that, in Grantley's view, reinforced dated stereotypes of medieval drama as "simpleminded drama performed by unsophisticated men."[106] Martin Stevens likewise has noted that most reconstructions of medieval drama in their search for historical accuracy fail to do what the production of *Everyman and Roach* by Geraldine Fitzgerald and Jonathan Ringkamp, which turned Everyman into a Brechtian rock-opera and played before half a million viewers on street corners in New York, did: "channel those plays into the current of our own time."[107] But that is something reconstructions cannot do; placing their faith in a hermeneutics of reconstitution, reenactments of medieval plays position performance as a form of nostalgic recuperation, by desire and necessity kept separate from contamination by modern life.

Modern academic reconstructions of medieval plays project a mode of literary and cultural history that is grounded in particular conceptions of the relation between past and present; this mode champions preservation, faithful reconstruction, and, quite often, reverential homage as key features of its project. In academic reconstructions, an emphasis on recapturing "original staging" ends up isolating these plays both from recent developments in theory and criticism and from contemporary culture. The academic impulse is to freeze the past, reify it, and protect it from the present, which prevents that past from being creatively reappropriated, as happens more readily with popular performances of plays with medieval roots. While in the matachines dance or Brooklyn's *giglio*, medieval performances are absorbed into new histories, academic reconstructions cling to the idea of a past that can, with the right amount of work and research, be restored in all its fullness. That belief is a powerful one. Bristol has argued that the field of Shakespeare studies involves an "erotic submission" to Shakespeare's authority.[108] In the case of medieval drama studies, the authority of the bard is replaced by the authority of authenticity, as the rallying cry of "back to the original" offers its own erotics of submission to a fixed and inviolable past. The continuing appeal of reconstructed performances is that they promise access to a medieval past whose supposed values, while long departed, remain alluring.

The Future of Imported Rituals

The imported rituals described in the previous chapters have been caught in the midst of their histories: their beginnings can only be guessed at; their future is unknowable. But it is impossible not to want to consider what will become of them in the years that lie ahead. Will they continue to serve as anchors for their communities as they have done thus far? Or will they reach the end of their usefulness—be seen as more trouble than they are worth—and gradually fade away or, under the effects of a more drastic upheaval of some sort (massive gentrification of a neighborhood perhaps, the building of a new highway, or another large-scale construction project), be abruptly abandoned?

Because all of these performances are tied to specific communities, their fate is contingent on what happens to those communities in the coming years. Although there can be strength in marginalization, in being located in out-of-the-way places where not many people bother to look, a strength that these performances have to greater or lesser degrees relied on in order to take hold, thrive, and endure, there is also fragility for anything positioned beyond the mainstream of modern mass culture and out of sync with its voracious engine of progress and innovation. It would not take much by way of economic or demographic change to damage these communities irremediably: deaths, dispersals, slow decline, outside intrusions would all take their toll on the rituals that are one of their constitutive features.

These questions about the fate of the performances featured in this book are not, I believe, mere indulgence in anticipatory nostalgia, since they arise out of the workings of ritual and its relation with temporality. Ritual tends to halt the flow of history. That is, if we think of history as a diachronic story with a beginning, middle, and end, then ritual, with its continual return to the same thing over and over again, breaks with that teleological narrative. This is not to say that ritual is ahistorical, but rather that for ritual performances the past is always present and always ready to be carried forward into an already present future. That collapsing of time into a vastly expanded present is one of the things that makes ritual so efficacious: ritual-time offers the assurance of a permanence of meaning that can escape change—that great enemy of communities everywhere.

While it would be naïve to assume that communities are unable to absorb new members, adapt to encroachment, or renew themselves by reshuffling their constituent features, it seems evident that neighborhood social groups need a certain degree of continuity and coherence in order to survive, particularly within the anticommunitarian context of modern America. At the same time, the ritual performances in this book argue for the malleability of tradition and resilience of cultural forms, especially those that are as hybrid as these imported performances. I hope that this book has managed to suggest that in studying the transmission of a cultural artifact, we need to pay attention not only to the route of transmission but also, and more important, to the artifact's reinscription in new social contexts—a reinscription that always results in changes in its signification. The performing of any imported ritual makes its own demands, forms its own expectations, and creates its own significance within its new surroundings.

Within a contemporary America that has witnessed what Fredric Jameson calls a "weakening of historicity," imported rituals offer an alternative to prevailing attitudes toward the past.[1] As Jameson notes, the characteristic relationship of postmoderm America with earlier eras is that of historical amnesia, which renders us incapable of remembering the past or preserving a tradition that might offset the inexorable pull of the present. The postmodern flattening of history and emptying of its contents have given us in the realm of popular culture a new historicity that conjures up the past through objects, costumes, and styles that by being seamlessly blended with the present destroy temporal boundaries and put the historical past forever out of reach. Imported rituals evade that amnesia, by continually re-performing a past that is repeatedly incorporated in meaningful ways into the present.

The European Middle Ages as an historical construct also bear a peculiar relationship toward past and present. As a set of subjective attitudes toward the past, the Middle Ages have historically been defined in terms of the present. Created by early modern humanists to define what they thought they were not, but which in many ways they still were, the Middle Ages have, since their inception as a cultural construct, been thoroughly ideological: the Middle Ages are a historical period tied to a social myth.[2] That myth has to do with concerns about the present that have positioned the past as a place of refuge and reassurance. This positioning requires a simultaneous distance from and nearness to the past; the past has to be different enough from the present to provide solace and yet similar enough to be meaningful.

Although the term *medieval* can be used in a pejorative way in popular discourse to describe primitive, violent, or retrograde behavior, in the United States the medieval past is usually an aspect of affirmative culture and as such is imagined as the vaguely defined repository of all things culturally beneficent: closely knit communities based on shared ideals and labor, an aesthetically rich yet simple and pious culture, an economic order in which hard work leads not just to wealth but to happiness. To invoke this affirmative notion of the medieval is to conjure up a preindustrial golden age, free of the worst woes of capitalism and modernity. In its role as a positive cultural value, the idea of the medieval past thus has emancipatory force as a refusal of the present. In its emancipatory role, the medieval is soundly on the side of social goodness: it promises renewal and redemption as an antidote to the present.

This ideal of social goodness is reinforced in performances that link themselves to the Middle Ages, given the ambivalent relationship of theatrical performance with the larger political economy. The world of the commercial theater both is and is not part of the market system. That is, the theater is a form of commodity exchange in the sense that plays are staged for paying audiences with the hope of making a profit. Yet theater's symbolic exchanges—the ideas and meanings that circulate during a performance—are not completely reducible to the real-world market. This double-allegiance to and away from the market is even stronger in community-based ritual performances, where there are usually no fees for watching and where no profits beyond the symbolic accrue to participants. When ideas about the medieval past are allied with such performances, their quotient of social goodness rises exponentially.

Although the "medievalness" of the performances discussed in this book registers in diverse and by no means uniform ways on participants and observers, its presence always hovers around the edges of these imported rituals. What especially matters is that all of these performances can be taken, if we are so inclined, as repositories of an old tradition, one that is often understood to have roots in the "Old World." Hence medievalness in these performances often comes to stand as an all-purpose sign for tradition, European heritage, and an ethnic (or community) identity tied to that heritage. The medievalness of these ritual performances also often implies the opposite of "modernity": it is the *locus* of values—communal, noncommercial, self-sacrificing, familial— that seem to have no place in the modern world. Medievalism thus represents the conflated ideas of a "deep Europe" and a "deep past"—inchoately defined but deeply felt understandings of identity grounded in premodern history.

In *On Living in an Old Country,* a collection of essays on the politics of heritage, Patrick Wright discusses the "prole quarter" in Orwell's novel *Nineteen Eighty-Four.* As presented by Orwell, the prole quarter, distinct from history in its archival sense and from history as memory, is a working-class area, where what remains of the past are its relics and debris. Hard-pressed and degenerate, the inmates of the prole quarter are not so much individuals as, in Wright's words, "swarming disregarded masses." But the prole quarter is also "an amalgam where received ideas, clichés and remembered experience are mixed up together. The cultural deprivation they [i.e., the proles] suffer also provides for lives emptier of sanctioned meaning." For Orwell, redemptive moments in the prole quarter are always associated with survivals from a better past, and for Orwell the old is not just residual, but rather alive as traces that offer meaning and value, precisely because the prole quarter is not fully policed. Other survivals are also possible in this state of fortunate neglect. "Oldspeak" survives, there is "beautiful rubbish" in the wreckage of history, and although there are no stately homes or museums that might enshrine the past the attention is "nonetheless preservationist" even though "it focuses on bric a brac." Wright notes that when Winston Smith engages an old prole in conversation, what he hears is not "historically formulated testimony to Post-Revolutionary truth, but instead a mess of particularistic recollection and detail. He remembers better beer in the old days, and savours words, meanings, occasions rather than the generalised meanings of any philosophy of history." Tied in this way to the recollection of the "old days," prole memory seems to militate against properly historical consciousness; but for Orwell, this failure to abstract is a mark of strength. Prole memory is characterized by the fact that its recollections are filtered through a threatened but traditionally formed consciousness of everyday life: it is floating, legendary, always anthropocentric, and at times apocalyptic.[3] While I would by no means characterize all of the communities that sponsor imported rituals as inheritors of an uncomplicated populist view of history, the historicism of their imported rituals to some degree resembles Wright's description of Orwell's prole memory. Not rigorous philosophies of history, but filtered recollections, imported rituals offer a kind of historical consciousness that like prole memory is filtered through everyday life.

Unlike formal histories, popular performative historiography puts a premium on the experiential and the local rather than the global and the abstract. Performative historiography also follows its own historical logic based on assertion of tradition rather than reconstruction of a sequence of ideas and events. The past that performative histories narrate is a fluid one, shaped by the needs of the present. Those needs include the longing for a public identity that can make a community and its history visible. A recognizable relationship with the past thus becomes a necessary component of community self-assertion and preservation. Although the separation of memory and history into two separate camps in modern discourse may obscure their interrelations, performative historiography intersects in important ways with "unofficial knowledge" of the sort preserved in memory.[4] And memory and history are less at odds than modern theory would imagine. For one thing, memory is not a passive receptacle or storage system, unreflexive and unaware. What it strives symptomatically to forget is as important as what it remembers—memory is therefore not the antithesis of but instead is dialectically related to historical thought, as Raphael Samuel suggests.[5] Memory is also historically conditioned, changing color and shape according to the emergencies of the moment. While memory has no developmental sense of time—which in the realm of popular recollection is often mythologized as "the good old days" or "once upon a time"—it is inherently revisionist and never more varied than when it appears to stay the same. Thus while the popular memory at work in performative histories may not follow the same logic as that of written historiography, we should not dismiss its representation of the past or its insistence on that past's continued utility for the present.

The performances in this book demonstrate how Americans use history to understand who they are, where they live, and how they fit in with the larger, national culture that surrounds them. The local quality of these performances, their rootedness in one place, is also part of their appeal in a society of people on the move. Not only can imported rituals connect Americans to the cultural identities that they imagine as inhering in a premodern past, but they can also anchor people in a particular place that acquires added value for being the home of a traditional performance. The performance becomes a visible sign of the identity of the community and a marker of the geographic space it inhabits.

Seen from a broader perspective, the imported rituals that I have discussed here are important as barometers of changing social and economic relations, which are revealed again and again in struggles over popular or marginal culture, including performances like these. As Stuart Hall notes, at the outset of the industrial revolution in the nineteenth century, capitalism had a stake in the culture of the poor and working classes because the creation of a new social order underpinned by capital required the "reeducation" of its labor pool, which was in part accomplished by transforming popular traditions of all kinds.[6] This economic and social heritage of popular culture suggests that while it is often linked to a conservative tradition, in the modern world popular culture also involves struggle and resistance in the face of destruction of particular ways of life and their replacement with something new. The local performances of the communities in this book always risk being replaced by mass culture. The danger to ritual performances, then, is that in the universe of cultural exchange, not only is there appropriation, but also expropriation.

But it would be wrong to envision the communities that perform these rituals as discrete subcultures in possession of a separate and authentic culture made up of genuine traditions, if only because subcultures inevitably share the values of mainstream culture. It is worth recalling as well that the people involved in popular culture are also consumers of the products of the modern cultural industry—thus we find, for example, the band in Brooklyn's Saint Paulinus feast playing the theme from *Rocky* and other Hollywood films alongside the "traditional" *giglio* song. We may tend to think of commercial culture and authentic culture as completely opposite, but they aren't. They intersect. Any definition of one therefore has to include the other, since they are mutual constructs defined by their relationship. At the same time, cultural forms migrate in ways that make them not permanently subcultural or mass cultural, traditional or invented, or the inalienable possession of one group or another. Given all this flux, in the end perhaps what matters is less the "essential nature" of any imported ritual than "the state of play in cultural relations" that characterizes every exchange and struggle over cultural forms.[7]

While we might be inclined to worry about the future of the imported rituals discussed in this book, that "state of play" suggests such concerns may be misplaced. To date, the history of medieval drama in America has been one of disguise and transformation, in which resilience, creative poaching, and wily smuggling have helped shape hybrid cultures that can bridge past and present, Old World and New, while meeting the needs of communities forged under often harsh circumstances. Perhaps we can assume that this work of performative history will continue—at least until the material and ideological contradictions that spur the demand for its ameliorative efforts have been resolved.

Notes

Introduction

1. Richard Hakluyt, *The Principal Navigations, Voyages, Traffiques, and Discoveries of the English Nation*, 8:47. For a discussion of Gilbert's cargo and the use of drama in the English colonies, see my "Medieval America."

2. Despite their problematic resonances, I use the terms *New* and *Old World*, in part because the relationship between newness and oldness is central to the performances I discuss.

3. Christopher Bigsby and Don B. Wilmeth, introduction to *Beginnings to 1870*, 1:1–19; the quotations are from 1:1.

4. For these and other early performances in colonial America, see *Cambridge History of American Theater*, 1:20–22.

5. See *The Jesuit Relations and Allied Documents*, 28:250, 37:94, 36:148, and 63:301, respectively, for these performances.

6. For a general survey of these performances, see Peter G. Buckley, "Paratheatricals and Popular Stage Entertainment."

7. *The Jesuit Relations*, 18:82–87 and 14:264–66.

8. Ibid., 61:114–19. For the Jesuit use of native imagery and symbols, see John Steckey, "The Warrior and the Lineage."

9. Martin W. Walsh, "Christmastide Performance in Native New France."

10. Tzvetan Todorov, *The Conquest of America*, 80, and Stephen Greenblatt, *Marvelous Possessions*, 12–13.

11. Roger Thompson, *Mobility and Migration*, 12.

12. Joseph Roach, *Cities of the Dead*, especially 1–6.

13. Raymond Williams, *Marxism and Literature*, 115.

14. See the discussion by John Clarke et al., "Subcultures, Cultures and Class," 4.

15. For one influential account, see Homi K. Bhabha, *The Location of Culture*, especially 2–7.

16. The term *ritual* has proven notoriously hard to define, in part because, as Ronald Grimes notes, ritual studies is a "field upon which multiple viewpoints are focused," not a single method; see his *Beginnings in Ritual Studies*, xxvi. For a good introduction to the history of ritual studies, see Catherine Bell, *Ritual*. Bell states that there is "no clear and widely shared explanation of what constitutes ritual" (x), and notes that although the most clear-cut example of ritual involves "communal ceremonies closely connected to formally institutionalized religions or clearly invoking divine beings" (164), in recent years phenomena that do not involve religion—such as etiquette, sports, and political rallies—have been treated as rituals.

17. Richard Schechner, *Between Theater and Anthropology*, 96.

18. The work of E. P. Thompson and Natalie Zemon Davis has been seminal in pointing to the historical uses of ritual, particularly by marginalized social groups; see especially Davis's "The Rites of Violence," and Thompson's " 'Rough Music.' "

19. Jack Goody, "Against 'Ritual,' " in *Secular Ritual*, 33.

20. For a discussion of dominant, residual, and emergent cultures, see Raymond Williams, *Problems in Materialism and Culture*, especially 40.

21. Umberto Eco, "Dreaming of the Middle Ages," 63.

22. The participant's words were quoted in an article by Liz Spayd, "A Foray Into Days of Yore," *Washington Post,* October 5, 1992.

23. Eco, "Dreaming of the Middle Ages," 64–65.

24. The scholarship on modern medievalism is extensive; for a few representative studies, see Kathleen Biddick, *The Shock of Medievalism;* R. Howard Bloch and Stephen G. Nichols, *Medievalism and the Modernist Temper;* Allen Frantzen, *Desire for Origins;* John Ganim, "Native Studies"; *Medievalism in American Culture;* and the essays in the journal *Studies in Medievalism.*

25. Eugene Vance, "The Modernity of the Middle Ages in the Future"; quotation is from 140.

26. Roach, *Cities of the Dead,* 5.

27. For a concise summary of appropriation theory, especially as it applies to medieval studies, see the introduction by Kathleen M. Ashley and Véronique Plesch to their special issue of the *Journal of Medieval and Early Modern Studies* devoted to medieval appropriation.

28. See Bhabha, *Location of Culture,* and James C. Scott, *Domination and the Arts of Resistance.*

29. Ernest Gellner, *Nations and Nationalism;* the quotation is from 57. For nationalism in the American theater, see Jeffrey D. Mason and J. Ellen Gainor, eds., *Performing America.*

30. The phrase is from Bhabha, *Location of Culture,* 6.

1. Performing Conquest

1. Jean Baudrillard, *America,* 1–2.

2. Sylvia Rodríguez, *The Matachines Dance,* 2.

3. For this information on the Pueblos, see Ramón Gutiérrez, *When Jesus Came, the Corn Mothers Went Away,* xxiii, 3–36.

4. For the information in this and the following paragraph, I am indebted to David J. Weber's excellent history of the Spanish colonization of New Mexico in his *The Spanish Frontier in North America,* 80–133, and to Marc Simmons, "History of Pueblo-Spanish Relations to 1821," 178–93.

5. The impersonation of Fray Marco and Estevanico at Jémez is recounted in Joe S. Sando, *Pueblo Indians,* 43–46.

6. For the impersonation of Coronado, see ibid., 46, and Max Harris, "The Arrival of the Europeans," 153–55.

7. For these details about the expedition, see *Don Juan de Oñate,* 4–9, 390.

8. Ibid., 48, 321.

9. Ibid., 323.

10. Gaspar Pérez de Villagrá, *Historia de la Nueva Mexico,* 150. For the history of the *moros y cristianos* in Spain, see Max Harris, "Muhammed and the Virgin."

11. Harris, "Arrival," 145–46.

12. *Don Juan de Oñate,* 318–19, 322, and 394–96.

13. For Cortés's request, see John H. Elliott, *Spain and Its World, 1500–1700: Selected Essays,* 38.

14. Robert Potter, "Abraham and Human Sacrifice." Historians have shown that indigenous practices were fundamental to the functioning of Spanish institutions; see Charles Gibson, *The Aztecs Under Spanish Rule* and *Tlaxcala in the Sixteenth Century,* as well as Rebecca Horn, *Postconquest Coyoacan.* Horn notes that, in Mesoamerica, Spaniards came into contact with complex cultures and built their own colonial societies using an appropriated infrastructure and reshaping local practices into their own (1). Fernando Cervantes, *The Devil in the New World,* 42–43, argues that the enthusiastic response of the Aztecs to missionary theater had to do both with the prudence of the conquered and with a Mesoamerican tendency to incorporate alien deities into its pantheon.

15. Toribio de Motolinía, *Historia de los indios de la Nueva España,* 20; an English translation is available in *History of the Indians of New Spain.*

16. See Diego Durán, *Historia de las Indias,* 1:193 and 1:63. For an analysis of the perfor-

mance, see Adam Versényi, "Getting Under the Aztec Skin." Versényi argues that when the slave impersonates the god and when audience members wear his skin after he has been killed and flayed, actor, character, and audience all blend together (218–19). Fernando Horcasitas, *El teatro náhuatl*, believes this was a full-fledged drama with song, music, and dialogue (42).

17. For a discussion of this evangelical drama, see Othón Arróniz, *Teatro de evangelización en Nueva España*; Richard C. Trextler, "We Think, They Act," has analyzed the Spaniards' understanding of the functions of these performances. For Franciscans and drama in Spain, see Ronald E. Surtz, "The 'Franciscan Connection' in the Early Castilian Theater."

18. The performance is described by Motolinía, *Historia de los indios*, 202–13, who might have been its author. The performance has been discussed by Max Harris, "Disguised Reconciliations," and *The Dialogical Theater*, 82–92; also see Versenyi, "Getting Under," 224–25.

19. Marilyn Ekdahl Ravicz, *Early Colonial Religious Drama in Mexico*.

20. John Rainolds, *The Overthrow of Stage Plays*, sig. X3.

21. On the distrust and even demonization of Indian cultures, see Cervantes, *The Devil in the New World*, 25–39.

22. In 1530, the Franciscan archbishop of Mexico, Fray Juan de Zumárraga, began inquisitorial proceedings against Indians, a measure of the extent to which Christian conversion had failed to stamp out idolatry that was perhaps inspired by such incidents as the one in the Yucatán in 1610 in which two Mayan Indians declared themselves pope and bishop and ordained their own native clergy to assist them in the Mass; see the discussion in Richard E. Greenleaf, *Zumárrága and the Mexican Inquisition*, 68–74, and in Nancy M. Farriss, *Maya Society under Colonial Rule*, 318. The climax of inquisitorial fervor in Mexico came in 1562 in the Yucatán, where 158 Indians died in interrogations, 18 disappeared and many more were permanently crippled; see the discussion by Inga Clendinnen, *Ambivalent Conquests*, 76–77.

23. For a chronology of suppression of theatrical activities in New Spain, see Maria Sten, *Vida y muerte del teatro Náhuatl*, 210–12.

24. See the discussion of this censorship in Robert Potter, "The Illegal Immigration of Medieval Drama to California." Potter observes that lack of church sanction allowed a freer development of certain features of the plays, such as the distinctive role of the Devil as an antagonist in the *Los Pastores* plays (143–44).

25. John Clarke et al., *Resistance through Rituals*, 12.

26. See George M. Foster, *Culture and Conquest*, especially chapter 2 in which he argues that "conquest culture" represents only a small part of the totality of traits that make up the donor culture, and chapter 17, in which he argues that a conquest culture is formed in a relatively short span of time after which the intermingled traits of the indigenous and donor cultures become fixed or "crystallized" and resist further change; according to Foster, this is what happened in Mexico after the sixteenth century.

27. See William A. Christian, Jr., *Local Religion in Sixteenth-Century Spain*, especially 175–80.

28. The attack and Spanish response are described in *Don Juan de Oñate*, 427ff.

29. For New Mexico as a mission outpost, see Lansing B. Bloom, "Spain's Investment in New Mexico under the Hapsburgs," 9–10, as well as *Fray Alonso de Benavides' Revised Memorial of 1634*, 76–77.

30. Brotherhoods and confraternities, a feature of medieval European economic and cultural activity, were also found among other groups in New Spain besides the Pueblos. In Mexico, for example, many blacks belonged to *cofradías*, mutual aid societies that also sponsored festivities and were sometimes thought of as "nations" ruled by elected kings and queens. They were also places where resistance could be planned. In 1537 *cofradías* plotted rebellion in Mexico City, and in the failed rebellions of 1608, 1611, and 1612, the first step was the election of a king and queen by the conspirators; see Colin A. Palmer, *Slaves of the White God*, 54–55, 136–39, and David M. Davidson, "Negro Slave Control and Resistance in Colonial Mexico," 237. Rodríguez, *Matachines Dance*, 56, notes the connection between matachines and *hermanos* groups.

31. For Franciscan beliefs and spiritual practices, see John L. Phelan, *The Millennial Kingdom of the Franciscans in the New World*, especially 44–54.

32. Frances V. Scholes, *Troublous Times in New Mexico,* 15–17, 64–66. See Christopher Vecsey, *On the Padres' Trail,* 128–30, for the friars' reorganization of Pueblo ritual along Christian lines.

33. Gutiérrez, *When Jesus Came,* 74.

34. See Enrique D. Dussel, *A History of the Church in Latin America,* 64–70. For Pueblo rituals, see Alfonso Ortiz, "Ritual Drama and the Pueblo World View." Weber, *Spanish Frontier in North America,* 107–17, discusses techniques of conversion, noting similarities between Pueblo and Catholic religions and native manipulation of missions, including the way that some Pueblos may have incorporated Franciscans and Jesus into their cosmography as kachinas (i.e., representatives of mythological beings).

35. For a discussion of Nahua and Spanish *autos* that includes a reassessment of the evidence for them, see Charlotte Stern, "Reassessing the Nahua Autos."

36. Gutiérrez, *When Jesus Came,* 85–89.

37. Ibid., 114, 130–36.

38. Bernal Díaz del Castillo, *Historia verdadera de la conquista de la Nueva España,* 1:326. Harris, "Arrival," 157, argues for the hybrid nature of the dance. Mary Austin, "Folk Plays of the Southwest," 603, claims that the matachines is the earliest form of the Guadalupe drama linked to the miraculous appearance of Mexico's Virgin of Guadalupe. Gertrude P. Kurath, "The Origin of the Pueblo Indian Matachines," hypothesizes that the dance came from the Arabic *muddawajjihin* ("those who put on a face" or "those who face each other"), who were masked, wore motley costumes with ribbons and bells, made passes at each other with swords, and danced in pairs, often buffoonishly. John Forrest, *Morris and Matachin,* links the *matachines* with the morris dance. John E. Englekirk, "The Source and Dating of New Mexican Spanish Folk Plays," is skeptical of connections between the matachines and Spanish *moros y cristianos* (239–40), and, indeed, of any claims for Spanish origins of New Mexican folk plays, tracing the earliest texts to nineteenth-century Mexico. On dances of the conquest, see Mercedes Díaz Roig, "La Danza de la Conquista"; for *las plumas,* see Jeffrey H. Cohen, "*Danza de la Pluma*"; for *los santiagos,* see Harris, *Dialogical Theater,* 95–107.

39. A discussion of an elaborate *moros y cristianos* performance in 1463 in the Castilian city of Jaén, which ended in a theatrical baptism, can be found in Teofilo F. Ruíz, "Elite and Popular Culture in Late Fifteenth-Century Castilian Festivals," 296–318. For modern *moros y cristianos* performances, see Harris, "Muhammed and the Virgin." For a history of early Spanish theater, see N. D. Shergold, *A History of the Spanish Stage from Medieval Times until the End of the Seventeenth Century,* and Charlotte Stern, *The Medieval Theater in Castile.*

40. Anthony Pagden, *Lords of All the World,* 74, notes that "the struggle against Islam offered a descriptive language which allowed the generally shabby ventures in America to be vested with a seemingly eschatological significance." For a reading of the complicated role of the Moors in the ideological construction of the Spanish Empire, see Barbara Fuchs, *Mimesis and Empire.*

41. Although the matachines dance centers on the upper Río Grande, it is also performed in other parts of the Southwest. For an analysis of a matachines dance in a Texas border community, see Norma E. Cantú, "*Los Matachines* de la Santa Cruz de la Ladrillera."

42. Edward P. Dozier, *The Pueblo Indians of North America,* 187, speculates that the dance was transmitted to the Pueblos via Mexican Indians who accompanied the Spanish settlers.

43. Montezuma is often associated with the Pueblo hero Poseyemu, and the people of Jémez believe that Montezuma will return to deliver his people from the Spaniards; see Richard J. Parmentier, "The Pueblo Mythological Triangle," 619. Max Harris, "Moctezuma's Daughter," 153–54, argues that the Montezuma of the dances is not just the conquest version, but a more general "boundary figure" of Aztec cyclical history. Malinche or Malintzin was the Indian name given to Cortés indigenous translator and "mistress" (called Doña Marina by the Spaniards); it is usually assumed that the Malinche of the dances refers to this figure, but Harris suggests she may represent a form of the Virgin Mary (hence the white communion dress) and a female divinity of Nahua, a figure linked in the dances not with Cortés but Montezuma (150–51). Harris also notes

the similarity with the Molly/Marian of English morris and mummings, which he argues implies common roots in a continental European male-female dance character, which traveled both to England and Mexico (172).

44. Flavia W. Champe, *The Matachines Dance of the Upper Rio Grande,* 4–5; for an illustration of the Aztec headdress, see Bernardino de Sahagún, *Florentine Codex,* bk. 8, pt. 9, 83–84.

45. See Sandra Messenger Cypress, *La Malinche in Mexican Literature.* The stories of Sandra Cisneros ("Never Marry a Mexican" and "Woman Hollering Creek") and the plays of Elena Garro also explore the image of Malinche in terms of gender identity.

46. On Pueblo clowns, see "Teaching the Mudheads How to Copulate," in *American Indian Myths and Legends,* 279–80.

47. For a detailed description of the dance's choreography, see Champe, *Matachines,* 82.

48. Ibid., 17. Champe's book also includes recordings of the music played at San Ildefonso Pueblo.

49. Harris, *Dialogical Theater.*

50. Champe, *Matachines,* 91.

51. Ibid., 93.

52. For the second and third examples, see ibid., 33 and 96.

53. Joe S. Sando, *Nee Hemish,* 221.

54. The description in this section is based on the performances I attended on December 12, 1999, as well as on other published descriptions of the two Jémez dances.

55. The first Franciscan missionary to the Jémez was Alonzo de Lugo who arrived with Oñate in 1598 and probably built the first mission church, the San José Mission Church, on whose site there is now a state monument. The next missionary was Gerónimo de Zárate Salmerón, who arrived in 1621 and baptized 6,566 of the Jémez, built a convent and a chapel, and wrote a theological treatise in the Hemish language and, after returning to New Spain, an account of Spanish explorations, entitled *Relaciones: An Account of Things Seen and Learned by Father Jerónimo de Zárate Salmerón from the year 1538 to year 1626.*

56. Glancing across the temporarily empty plaza during the break in the 1999 performance, I noticed a former student of mine, a teacher at Jémez's high school. As we waited for the start of the second performance, he told me about a recent cultural exchange trip to China on which he and other teachers had just taken some of their students, a story that suddenly complicated my sense of cultural tourism.

57. In the 1970 dance described by Champe, the Indian Malinche was a woman dressed in white buckskin leggings and moccasins with a white wool mantle with green, red, and black designs fastened on her right shoulder; see Champe, *Matachines,* 90.

58. In the 1999 dance, somewhat incongruously, he carried an American flag.

59. The understanding of ritual as a liminal experience that temporarily removes participants from ordinary life and then reintegrates them with it has been developed by Victor Turner, especially in *The Ritual Process.*

60. In 1999, I was told that the women in the family with whom I had lunch had spent the past week preparing the food, including a hundred loaves of bread and an array of dishes to serve their anticipated guests.

61. For the Santa Fe Railway's promotion of the Southwest as a tourist attraction, see Marta Weigle, "From Desert to Disney World."

62. For discussions of the origins and revival of *Los Pastores,* see John E. Englekirk, "The Source and Dating of New Mexican Spanish Folk Plays"; María Herrera-Sobek, "The Mexican/Chicano *Pastorela*"; T. M. Pearce, "The New Mexican 'Shepherds Play'"; Juan B. Rael, "New Light on the Origins of Los Pastores"; and Stanley L. Robe, "The Relationship of Los Pastores to Other Spanish-American Folk Drama."

63. For information on the revival of *Mexicano* arts and crafts in New Mexico, see Charles L. Briggs, *The Wood Carvers of Córdova, New Mexico,* and Ann Vedder, "History of the Spanish Colonial Arts Society, Inc."

64. Rodríguez, *Matachines Dance,* 47. See also her "Defended Boundaries, Precarious Elites."

2. Selective Histories

1. *Albany Centinel,* June 1803; reprinted in the New York *Daily Advertiser* of June 29, 1803. The *Advertiser's* introduction says that the festival was "formerly universally celebrated, and still in the recollection of our ancient inhabitants, but which a change of manners has entirely abolished in this city," i.e., New York City. The text of the letter has been reproduced in Shane White's "Pinkster in Albany, 1803: A Contemporary Description."

2. Gabriel Furman, a nineteenth-century historian of Long Island, asserts that Pinkster had from the time of the first settlement been a Dutch holiday, which was then celebrated by both blacks and Dutch whites, and that by the start of the nineteenth century had become an entirely black festival; by the 1870s, Furman adds, it had "sunk lamentably low, and without any apparent reason"; see his *Antiquities of Long Island,* 266–67. Jeptha R. Simms, in chapter 5 of his *History of Schoharie County* (1845) notes that Easter and Pinkster are "days also noted in the annals of the Dutch." The former is celebrated mostly by children with colored eggs, the latter by "the colored population," who "are seen with smiling faces on that day, clad in their best apparel, going to visit their friends—often bearing flowers called by them Pinkster-bloomies."

3. Mary Louise Pratt, *Imperial Eyes,* 6–7.

4. For these two readings of Pinkster's function for whites, see Geneviève Fabre, "Pinkster Festival, 1776–1811," 13–18, and Shane White, " 'It Was a Proud Day,' " especially 25.

5. Joseph Roach, *Cities of the Dead,* 6.

6. For the establishment of the fur trade, see George L. Smith, *Religion and Trade in New Netherland,* 1–20, and Kevin McBride, "The Source and Mother of the Fur Trade."

7. David Hackett, *The Rude Hand of Innovation,* 13–14.

8. Ibid., 13.

9. Ibid., 15–16.

10. Donna Merwick, *Possessing Albany, 1630–1710,* 120–21.

11. Pehr Kalm, *The American of 1750,* 343.

12. For this and other information on the early demographics of Albany, see Hackett, *Rude Hand,* 15.

13. The 10 percent estimate comes from Hackett, *Rude Hand,* 180, n. 30. For slavery among the Dutch in New Netherland, see Edgar McManus, *A History of Negro Slavery in New York,* and Joyce D. Goodfriend, "Burghers and Blacks." Angola and the Gold Coast were early sources for the Dutch slave trade, but between 1630 and 1654 when the Dutch occupied some parts of Brazil there appears to have been shipment of some slaves from Brazil to New Netherland, which helps explain the similarity between Brazilian festivities and Pinkster; see David Steven Cohen, "In Search of Carolus Africanus Rex," 151.

14. David Steven Cohen, *The Dutch-American Farm,* 145.

15. Cohen, "In Search," 151–53.

16. George Howell and Jonathan Tenney, "Slavery in Albany."

17. Hackett, *Rude Hand,* 18–19. For the history of the Dutch Reformed church, see Gerald F. DeJong, *The Dutch Reformed Church in the American Colonies,* and Randall H. Balmer, *A Perfect Babel of Confusion.*

18. For information on liturgical celebrations in Albany, see Merwick, *Possessing Albany,* 74–76.

19. Elizabeth L. Gebhard, writing in 1909 about life in an old Dutch parsonage in upstate New York, said that "there was a great rivalry among the colored people as to which could throw the Paas-cakes the highest and still successfully catch them"; see *The Parsonage Between Two Manors;* cited in Cohen, *Dutch-American Farm,* 224–25.

20. Alice Morse Earle, *Colonial Days in Old New York,* 200–201. James Fenimore Cooper, *Satanstoe, or the Littlepage Manuscripts,* 95, calls wild honeysuckle "Pinkster Blossoms." Shane White, "Pinkster: Afro-Dutch Syncretism in New York City and the Hudson Valley," claims that Pinkster was celebrated like the English Boxing Day, when servants were given the day off after Christmas (68).

21. See Charles Read Baskervill, "Dramatic Aspects of Medieval Folk Festivals in England," 30.

22. See Elsa Strietman, "The Low Countries," 242, and Meg Twycross, "The Flemish Ommegang and Its Pageant Cars." For stagings of low-country plays, for which there is much visual evidence, see Wim M. H. Hummelen, "Illustrations of Stage Performances in the Work of Crispijn Passe the Elder."

23. Merwick, *Possessing Albany*, 75.

24. See White, "Pinkster: Afro-Dutch Syncretization," 72, for the suggestion of Anglocentric bias leading to neglect of colonial Pinkster.

25. Paul Gilroy, *The Black Atlantic*.

26. Alexander Coventry, *Recollections and Diary*.

27. William Dunlap, "Diary of William Dunlap," 161; cited in White, "Pinkster: Afro-Dutch Syncretization," 73.

28. Olive Gilbert, *Narrative of Sojourner Truth*, 43–44.

29. Hackett, *Rude Hand*, 46–8.

30. Ibid., 39.

31. Ibid., 58–59.

32. A description of the Fourth of July celebration was published in the *Albany Gazette*, July 5, 1799.

33. A "conspiracy" was alleged to have taken place in 1741 in New York City when an Irish indentured servant, Mary Burton, told investigators of a plot between her white master, John Hughson, and African Americans to overthrow the government; Hughson, she said, would be made king and a black man named Caesar, governor. Her claims about the planned kingship and governorship interestingly echo the practices of African-American Pinkster, as well as of other coronation rituals in the north; see Edgar A. Toppin, *A Biographical History of Blacks in America since 1528*, 47.

34. Lorenzo J. Greene, *The Negro in Colonial New England*, 154, notes that blacks in the Northeast were often accused of arson.

35. John Clarke et al., "Subcultures, Cultures and Class," 12.

36. As White, "Pinkster: Afro-Dutch Syncretization," 74, n.1 observes, this account is contradicted by James Eights, in his "Pinkster Festivities in Albany Sixty Years Ago," in *Collections on the History of Albany*. Writing in 1867 about scenes recollected from his youth, Eights stated that none of the black nobility, including the king, appeared on Monday.

37. "A Pinkster Ode for the Year 1803: Most Respectfully Dedicated to Carolus Africanus Rex." The title page identifies the author as "Absalom Aimwell"; the copy of the "Ode" in the manuscript collection of the New York State Library in Albany is identified as having been owned by Andrew Adgate, who is recorded as having died in 1793, ten years before the publication of the poem. For an account of the "Ode," see Geraldine R. Pleat and Agnes N. Underwood, "Pinkster Ode, Albany, 1803," 31–45.

38. Eights, "Pinkster Festivities," 325.

39. *New York Evening Post*, May 21, 1804; cited in White, "Pinkster: Afro-Dutch Syncretization," 73. The publicity blurb announced that the pantomime had already been received with "unbounded applause" at Covent Garden.

40. Fabre, "Pinkster," 20. Also see the discussion of minstrelsy's effects on black festivals in White, " 'It Was a Proud Day,' " 26–28.

41. Fabre, "Pinkster," 20, argues that Pinkster let whites ignore daily degradations of slavery by focusing on a privileged moment when Africans were "free."

42. Fabre, "Pinkster," 17, describes the author of the "Ode" as "both principal actor (an Afric insider) and distant observer."

43. Melvin Wade, " 'Shining in Borrowed Plumage' "; the quotation is from 213.

44. Furman, *Antiquities*, 266, describes slaves from Long Island coming in skiffs over to New York City to sell sassafras to make money for Pinkster.

45. Cooper, *Satanstoe*, 65.

46. Fabre, "Pinkster," 25–26.

47. For the locations of black festivities in New England, see William Piersen, *Black Yankees*, 121.

48. For the procession route, see "A Glimpse of an Old Dutch Town." According to this account, the procession started from " 'young massa's house' " (82 State Street).

49. Fabre, "Pinkster," 23.

50. See the "View of Saint Mary's Church," in the Manuscript Collection of the New York State Library (Prints 1732+).

51. Eights, "Pinkster," 325. The identification of Douw is in "A Glimpse of an Old Dutch Town," 526.

52. Fabre, "Pinkster," 18; White, " 'It Was a Proud Day,' " 25. "A Glimpse of an Old Dutch Town," 526, describes how Charles's master and fellow servants teased him for being a coward for having taken fright while accompanying his master to join the army at Saratoga. The same account records a moment of triumph for Charles, however, when he wins a horse race on ice before an assembled crowd of Indians, white men, and blacks (536).

53. "Albany Fifty Years Ago," 453.

54. Gilroy, *The Black Atlantic*, 16.

55. For Charles's fluency in Dutch, see "A Glimpse of an Old Dutch Town," 526, which describes a moment when, while accompanying his master to join the army at Saratoga, Charles mistook a clump of reddish sumac for the red feathers of the enemy and called out "Heer, ik zag een vyand" ("Master, I saw the enemy"). Fabre, "Pinkster," 18, observes that his costume "further demonstrated the blending and syncretization of cultural memories and the range of effects that a ceremonial garb worn by an African slave could create: from humour to parody, from irony to seriousness." Another description of the Pinkster king's costume says it consisted of a cast-off military coat decked with colored ribbons; see Mary Gay Humphreys, *Catherine Schuyler*, 38–39.

56. Cooper, *Satanstoe*, 65–79; for Cooper's use of Pinkster, see the "Historical Introduction," xvii. Also see James H. Pickering, "Fenimore Cooper and Pinkster."

57. Note that Eights, "Pinkster," 325, suggests something rather different, explaining that the different days of the festival were apportioned hierarchically: respectable crowd on the second day, upper class on the third, humbler on the fourth and fifth, and poorest on the last day.

58. Fabre, "Pinkster," 17.

59. Jane De Forest Shelton, "The New England Negro: A Remnant." Greene, *Negro*, 255, similarly argues that black election day rituals derived from white models.

60. See Hubert H. S. Aimes, "African Institutions in America," and Melville J. Herskovits, *The Myth of the Negro Past*. For more recent versions of this position, see Sterling Stuckey, *Slave Culture*, and A. J. Williams Myers, "Pinkster Carnival."

61. For example, paw paw, a popular gambling game played with cowry shells that is often mentioned as part of the festival's sports is thought by Gilroy, *Black Yankees*, 103, to stem from African divination techniques. For a discussion of the ritualistic and theatrical features of traditional African drama, see John Conteh-Morgan, "African Traditional Drama and Issues in Theater and Performance Criticism."

62. Sam Kinser, *Carnival, American Style*, 42–43; Kinser is here following Roger Bastide, *African Civilisations in the New World*, 7–10.

63. Aimes, "African Institutions," 15.

64. For Cuba, see the description by J. G. Wurdemann, *Notes on Cuba*, 83–84, 113–14; Wurdemann was an American doctor who visited Cuba four times in the 1830s. For Brazil and Peru, see Bastide, *African Civilisations*, 182. For black royalty in the Virgin Islands in the 1860s, see Thurlow Weed, *Letters from Europe and the West Indies*.

65. See Aimes, "African Institutions," 20–32, and Piersen, *Black Yankees*, 125–27. For descriptions of these celebrations, see Leon Beauvallet, *Rachel in New World*, 363, and Wurdemann, *Notes on Cuba*, 83.

66. These coronation rituals seem to be reflected in *La Batalla de los salvajes*, which preceded a performance about the conquest of Rhodes in Mexico City in 1539, a performance that featured more than fifty "negros y negras" on horseback led by a king and queen. The *cofradías* also spawned the first slave rebellion in Mexico in 1537; see the discussion in Max Harris, "Disguised Reconciliations," 21–22.

67. William Johnson, *The Autobiography of Dr. William Henry Johnson*, 60, asserts that

Pinkster was "in Africa a religious day, partly pagan and partly Christian, like our Christmas Day. Many of the old colored people, then in Albany, were born in Africa, and would dance their wild dances and sing in their native language." Johnson was born in 1833 in Alexandria, Virginia, but by 1851 was in Albany working for the underground railroad and later enjoyed a prominent political career. Frederika Bremer, a Swedish woman who observed similar festivities in Cuba in 1851, learned that there, too, festival kings had been born into the African royalty; see her *The Homes of the New World,* 2:306–8.

68. Henry Bull, "Memoir of Rhode Island."

69. Aimes, "African Institutions," 18.

70. Wade, " 'Shining,' " 213.

71. For a concise overview of summer revels in England, see Ronald Hutton, *The Rise and Fall of Merry England,* 27–38.

72. Cf. Edgar's coronation at Whitsun in 973, and a Whitsun feast given by William the Conqueror in 1085–86 at which a son was knighted; cited in Baskervill, "Dramatic Aspects," 50.

73. See Usk, *The Chronicle of Adam Usk, 1377–1421,* 94–97.

74. Baskervill, "Dramatic Aspects," 82–83. For a general description of festivals of misrule in medieval England, see Hutton, *Rise and Fall of Merry England,* 8–42 and 218–30.

75. This point has been made by White, "Pinkster: Afro-Dutch Syncretization," 70. Kinser, *Carnival,* 53, argues that carnival can be understood as "governed not by the logic of inversion but by that of ambivalence: surface/depth, past/present, reality/fantasy" in a totalizing, both-and rather than either-or fashion.

76. Greene, *Negro,* 128–38.

77. Cited in James D. Phillips, *Salem in the Eighteenth Century,* 272.

78. For the Hartford example, see J. Hammond Trumbull, ed., *The Memorial History of Hartford County, Connecticut,* 1:189; for Newport, see George C. Mason, *Re-Union of the Sons and Daughters of Newport, Rhode Island,* 156–57; both are cited in Piersen, *Black Yankees,* 139.

79. Wade, " 'Shining,' " 226, makes this point, as does Joseph P. Reidy, " 'Negro Election Day' and Black Community Life in New England."

80. These commercial features are mentioned by Eights, "Pinkster," 324, 327, and by Cooper, *Satanstoe,* 73, who describes a lion rumored to have been brought by Africans from Africa for the festival, but that turns out to belong to a showman.

81. Hackett, *Rude Hand,* 99.

82. Eights, "Pinkster," 323–27.

83. White, "Pinkster: Afro-Dutch Syncretization," 71.

84. Hackett, *Rude Hand,* 89–90.

85. *Freedom's Journal,* August 1, 1828.

86. See Reidy, " 'Negro Election Day,' " 113–14, for a discussion of changing black attitudes toward parades.

87. "A Glimpse of an Old Dutch Town," 526.

88. Richard Schechner, *Between Theater and Anthropology,* especially 79.

89. Another Dutch and African-American reenactment takes place at the Lefferts Homestead Children's Historic House Museum in Prospect Park, one of the few surviving Dutch colonial farmhouses in Brooklyn, which today is operated by the Prospect Park Alliance as a children's museum.

3. Philadelphia's Mummers and the Anglo-Saxon Revival

1. Eric Hobsbawm, "Introduction: Inventing Traditions."

2. *Philadelphia Public Ledger,* December 27, 1845; cited in Susan G. Davis, *Parades and Power,* 106.

3. Davis, *Parades and Power,* 105; also see Alfred Shoemaker, *Christmas in Pennsylvania,* 21, 73–85, and Richard Bauman, "Belsnickling in a Nova Scotia Island Community."

4. For the connection of German holiday festivities with English mumming, see Thomas Pettitt,

"English Folk Drama and the Early German *Fastnachtspiele*." Newfoundland, where mumming still flourishes and where Christmas maskers sometimes called themselves *belsnickles,* indicates the potential for the two traditions to mesh.

5. For the first example, see Richard Pennyworth Pyle's *Diary* (1686); cited in *Andrea Rothberg, "Philadelphia Mummery,"* 24. For the second, see the "Diary of Christopher Marshall," Pennsylvania Historical Society, MSS. Vol. F; cited in Charles E. Welch, Jr., " 'Common Nuisances,' " 95. John A. Fulton is reported as saying that his mother, who was born in 1752, as a young girl in Boston saw mummers perform what seems to have been a hero-combat play; see W. W. Newell, "Christmas Maskings in Boston," 178.

6. Cited in an article by Francis Burke Brandt, *Philadelphia Public Ledger,* November 20, 1930.

7. See Historical Society of Pennsylvania, *Collections,* 258. Charles E. Welch, Jr., *Oh! Dem Golden Slippers,* 21–22, takes these as evidence of early mumming, but Davis, *Parades and Power,* 208, n.76, finds less continuity for Philadelphia mumming in the historic record.

8. Samuel Breck, *Recollections,* 35–36.

9. See, for instance, Alan Brody, *The English Mummers and their Plays;* E. K. Chambers, *The English Folk-Play;* Henry H. Glassie, *All Silver and No Brass;* and Reginald J. E. Tiddy, *The Mummers' Play.*

10. This is a composite description. Herbert Halpert has distinguished four types of mummings: informal house-visits; informal outdoor processions, which sometimes turn violent; formal outdoor processions, which occasionally include morris dancing; and formal indoor plays—usually of the hero-combat type; see his "A Typology of Mumming."

11. See the Croxton *Play of the Sacrament,* and Tiddy, *Mummers' Play,* 148–56. For a discussion of one surviving mummers' play and its possible origins, see Karen Read, "The Symondsbury Mumming Play, and the People Who Uphold It." Read argues that the Symondsbury Christmas mumming is representative of earlier mummings in its use of the hero-combat and death-resurrection motifs. Thomas Pettitt, "English Folk Drama in the Eighteenth Century," similarly argues that the Revesby play was built from traditional pre-Reformation performances known to the local performers; Pettitt also notes that pre-Reformation plays often survive in truncated form as drolls and jigs performed as part of seasonal custom (24–25). Elsewhere Pettitt asserts that the mummers' plays of the eighteenth and nineteenth centuries derived from the interludes of the fifteenth and sixteenth centuries; see his "Tudor Interludes and the Winter Revels."

12. For such regulations, see Robert Ricart, *The Maire of Bristow Is Kalendar,* 86–86; *Records of Early English Drama: Chester,* 56; and *Memorials of London and London Life,* 658, 669.

13. Ronald Hutton, *The Rise and Fall of Merry England,* 8–12.

14. Henry Machyn, *The Diary of Henry Machyn,* 12–14. In an entry for the year 1561, Machyn describes how on December 27 a lord of misrule rode through London along with a hundred horsemen; they rode to the Temple where there were revels of misrule, including singing and playing (273–74).

15. For discussions of these different mummings, see Roger D. Abrahams, " 'Pull Out Your Purse and Pay' "; Robert Dirks, "Slaves' Holiday," who suggests that John Canoe figures combine English mumming with African dances; Marie Campbell, "Survivals of Old Folk Drama in the Kentucky Mountains"; and Max E. White, "Sernatin.' "

16. Thomas Pettitt, " 'Here Comes I, Jack Straw.' "

17. Davis, *Parades and Power,* 133–34, 156.

18. Ibid., 77–96.

19. Ibid., 97–98. For a discussion linking blackface minstrelsy and mumming with earlier European rituals, see Dale Cockrell, "Callithumpians, Mummers, Maskers and Minstrels."

20. Davis, *Parades and Power,* 109–10.

21. Davis's book is based on exhaustive research of Philadelphia newspapers from 1830–1860, and I have for the most part not retraced her footsteps. I have, however, picked up where she left off, searching the three major Philadelphia newspapers, the *Inquirer,* the *Evening Bulletin,* and the *Public Ledger,* from 1840–1901; complaints about violence at New Year's taper off after 1870, although disorderly conduct, particularly noise, is still noted from time to time.

22. All cited in Davis, *Parades and Power,* 105.

23. Similar incidents of disorder on Christmas and New Year's are reported in the *Public Ledger,* January 2, 1855 (false alarms of fire, arrests of disorderly parties, fines for drunkenness, reports of a disturbance in a tavern, fighting, and discharging of guns); the *Inquirer,* December 25, 1860 (arrests for crushing ladies' bonnets, drunkenness, and disorderly conduct); and the *Public Ledger,* January 1, 1867 ("turbulence and rowdyism," including tin-horns, pistols, and gunshots). Reports for the other years in the 1860s suggest that other ways of celebrating the holiday, combined with greater policing, have cut down on the disorder.

24. Davis, *Parades and Power,* 107.

25. *Public Ledger,* January 2, 1850; cited in Davis, *Parades and Power,* 107–8.

26. See Diane Lindstrom, *Economic Development in the Philadelphia Region,* 24–54, and Bruce Laurie, *Working People of Philadelphia.*

27. See Michael Feldberg, "The Crowd in Philadelphia History," and Elizabeth Geffen, "Violence in Philadelphia in the 1840s and 1850s."

28. See Davis, *Parades and Power,* 27–30.

29. See Davis, " 'Making Night Hideous.' " The description of Southwark as demonic appears in the *Public Ledger,* January 3, 1854; cited in Davis, *Parades and Power,* 186, n.27.

30. For a discussion linking the Luddites to the tradition of mumming, see Norman Simms, "Ned Ludd's Mummers Play." In Philadelphia, most assaults on authority took the form of attacks on the watch; see the *Public Ledger,* January 1, 1839; December 27, 1845; and December 28, 1846; all cited in Davis, 209, n. 93. G. M. Story similarly reports how the mummers of Newfoundland in the early 1900s were involved in local feuds and antigovernment riots in port cities; see his "Mummers in Newfoundland History."

31. Davis, *Parades and Power,* 107.

32. Howard O. Sprogel, *The Philadelphia Police,* 89–113.

33. Welch, " 'Common Nuisances,' " 98–99, finds no records of convictions or arrests for masquerading under this law.

34. *Inquirer,* January 1, 1861.

35. *Inquirer,* December 24, 1864, and *Public Ledger,* Monday, December 26, 1864.

36. *Inquirer,* December 25, 1872.

37. Ibid., December 25, 1878.

38. Davis, " 'Making Night Hideous,' " 185–99.

39. Lindstrom, *Economic Development,* 24–54. The earliest club, according to local memory, was the Chain Gang, formed about 1846 in south Philadelphia; see Welch, " 'Common Nuisance,' " 103.

40. Articles in Philadelphia's newspapers in the 1870s attest to the moving of holiday entertainments inside, describing celebrations in churches, benevolent societies, private halls, and theaters; see the *Inquirer,* December 24, 1872; *Public Ledger,* December 27, 1875; and *Inquirer,* January 1, 1879.

41. For all of these performances, see Davis, *Parades and Power,* 170.

42. *Evening Bulletin,* January 1, 1884.

43. *Public Ledger,* January 1, 1886.

44. *Inquirer,* January 2, 1889. Less organized parading also apparently was still occurring; see the *Public Ledger,* December 25, 1885, which comments that although there was none of the loud revelry that once was a feature of Christmas eve, there were still revelers, "but they marched around quietly and as they were in small parties and indifferently organized, they did not attract much attention."

45. *Public Ledger,* January 1, 1889.

46. Reported in the *Inquirer,* January 1, 1893. The *Inquirer* printed the names and addresses of the fifty-six clubs and noted that "many valuable prizes have been offered for the best-appearing clubs in various sections of the city, and all the organizations have spent much time and money in the preparation of elaborate costumes and unique ideas."

47. *Philadelphia Times,* December 31, 1893.

48. *Inquirer,* January 1, 1893.

49. Ibid., January 3, 1893.

50. *Call-Philadelphia,* December 30, 1893.

51. *Public Ledger,* January 1, 1897.

52. *Inquirer,* December 27, 1899.

53. Ibid., December 1, 1900, reported the city council's idea of one large parade of all clubs in the center city in conscious emulation of New Orleans' Mardi Gras as a scheme for welcoming the twentieth century. The *Inquirer,* December 4, 1900, quotes city council chairman Jacob J. Seeds, who comments that the city originally wanted the parade on New Year's Eve at night, but the clubs insisted on the morning of New Year's Day. The *Inquirer,* Thursday, December 13, 1900, noted that the clubs were demanding prize money.

54. *Public Ledger,* January 2, 1901.

55. *Philadelphia Record,* January 3, 1901.

56. Hobsbawm, "Introduction," 1–14.

57. Maurice F. Egan, "A Day in the Ma'sh."

58. Sam Warner, *The Private City,* 94–95.

59. Caroline Golab, "The Immigrant and the City," 203. Golab notes that one reason for the relatively small number of immigrants was that Philadelphia's economy had fewer openings for large numbers of unskilled laborers; textiles, printing and publishing, machine shop and hardware manufacture, and leather production were the city's largest industries.

60. *Inquirer,* January 23, 1888.

61. Ibid., January 8, 1893.

62. "From Greece, Russia, Bulgaria, Turkey, from Southern Italy and from countries of that kind we get immigrants that are a menace," reported the *Public Ledger,* January 4, 1903.

63. For a history of the settlement schools, see Allen F. Davis, *Spearheads for Reform.* The first settlement school was established in England in 1884, but the system quickly spread to the United States. According to David E. Whisnant, *All That Is Native and Fine,* 22, by 1891 there were six social settlements in the United States; six years later there were seventy-four, with more than one hundred by 1900 and more than four hundred by 1910.

64. "The Hull-House Labor Museum," 60.

65. Bruno Roselli, "An Arkansas Epic," 385.

66. See David Glassberg, *American Historical Pageantry,* 4 and 35; Glassberg notes the frequent use of medieval traditions such as maypoles and morris dancers in this reformist effort.

67. One writer who resisted these tendencies was Allen Eaton, *Immigrant Gifts to American Life,* who argued against the cult of "Americanism" of folk art enthusiasts like Holger Cahill.

68. See Whisnant, *All That Is Native,* esp. 11.

69. For demands that Italian immigrants "Americanize," see Salvatore Mondello, *The Italian Immigrant in Urban America,* 220ff. Both the Italian-American Civic League of New York and the Society for Italian Immigrants were also interested in Americanization.

70. Hudson-Fulton Celebration Commission, New York, *The Fourth Annual Report of the Hudson-Fulton Celebration Commission,* 1:5–7, 1:292–303. For other studies of performance and nationalism in America, see David Waldstreicher, *In the Midst of Perpetual Fetes,* and Len Travers, *Celebrating the Fourth.*

71. "London—Plantagenet."

72. The examples in this paragraph are all cited by Shoemaker, *Christmas in Pennsylvania,* 22–23.

73. Quoted in ibid., 23.

74. The discussion of mumming in this section is based on observations I made at the 1997 parade, as well as on visits and interviews conducted with participants during 1996 and 1997.

75. Lucas and Connor were quoted in an article by William Robbins, "For Philadelphia, A Day of Spectacle"; Speziale's remarks appeared in Michael deCourcy Hinds, "Philadelphia Journal."

76. In 1981, a federal district judge in Philadelphia ruled that two new string bands had the right to join the parade, forcing the Mummers and Shooters Association to allow them in even though the mummers wanted only twenty-three string bands; see "Judge Allows 2 Bands to Join New Year Parade," *New York Times,* November 8, 1981.

77. See the discussion of the economics of mumming in Rothberg, "Philadelphia Mummery." Rothberg was the first director of the Mummers' Museum.

78. According to Jack Cohen, the current director of the museum, in 1998 the city budgeted $50,000 for the museum, which covered salaries; the museum cost $1.5 million to build.

79. From a personal interview, October 1996.

4. Reinventing Tradition

1. Program for the 108th Annual Feast (July 5–16, 1995), printed by Our Lady of Mount Carmel Church, 1995.

2. For a discussion of the medieval Italian saint play, see Kathleen C. Falvey, "The Italian Saint Play."

3. Eric Hobsbawm, "Introduction: Inventing Traditions." For a discussion of the term *tradition* as it has been used by folklorists, see Simon Bronner, *American Folklore Studies.*

4. Hobsbawm, "Introduction," 12.

5. The quotation is from a participant, speaking in Jeff Porter, *The Men Who Dance the Giglio.*

6. For a general overview of the subject of white ethnicity, see the essays in Joseph Ryan, ed., *White Ethnics.*

7. An "unofficial" dancing of the *giglio* took place in the 1970s in an attempt to recapture some of the revelry—including drinking—that marks the Nola performance and that church sponsorship had suppressed from the official version of the feast in Brooklyn; it was not continued in the next year (information from a personal interview with participants and their family members, October 14–15, 1995).

8. Ambrogio Leone, *Nola: la terra natìa,* 3.6.

9. Gianstefano Remondini, *Della Nolana Ecclesiastica Storia,* 1.1.27. The passage reads: "Si sparse appena per la città di Nola la giocondissima novella del ritorno dall'africana schiavitù" when on June 21 there is a solemn procession "nella quale portano alcuni Artefici certi Mai, o Gigli, come volgarmente son detti, se son certe macchine in forma di globi, di piramidi, di navi, o simil altre cose, tutte adorne d'innumerevoli garofani, tra quali è situata la particolare insegna di ciascheduna di quelle arti, che le fanno."

10. Franco Manganelli, cited in I. Sheldon Posen and Joseph Sciorra, "The *Giglio.*"

11. Francesco de Bourcard, ed., *Usi e costumi di Napoli e contorni.*

12. "The Giglio Festa."

13. See the postcards from the end of the nineteenth century through 1970 collected in *Gigli in Cartolina* and *La Festa Antica.* Giuseppe Giusti, "Omaggio a S. Paolino 1997," provides accounts from 1837, 1894, and 1898, all of which describe a *festa* very like the present one.

14. At the 1997 festival, aside from a contingent of festival pilgrims from Brooklyn come to see the parent version—several of them on repeat visits—the only foreigners I noticed were some German tourists.

15. See the account by Gregory the Great, *Dialogues,* 3.1-3. There were three bishops of Nola named Paulinus. The first, born ca. A.D. 354, studied with the poet Ausonius, was converted, became known for charity and public works, and was canonized in 431. The Vandal raid described by Gregory, which has found its way into the breviary as the lesson for the festival of the first bishop Paulinus, occurred later, during the time of the third Bishop Paulinus between 513 and 535; see Sabine Baring-Gould, *The Lives of the Saints,* 6:304–6.

16. *Brooklyn in Transition,* 28–29.

17. Joseph Sciorra, " 'O' Giglio e Paradiso.' "

18. The figures are from Ira Rosenwaike, *Population History of New York City,* 70, and *Brooklyn in Transition,* 8 and 37.

19. Dominic Candeloro, "Italian-Americans."

20. Philip S. Foner, *History of the Labor Movement in the United States,* 3:256.

21. Edward A. Ross, "Racial Consequences of Immigration," 444; quoted in Salvatore Mondello, *The Italian Immigrant in Urban America,* 66–67.

22. Mondello, *Italian Immigrant,* 66–72.

23. "To Keep Out Southern Italians," *The World's Work* 28 (August 1914): 378–79; quoted in Mondello, *Italian Immigrant,* 142.

24. See, for example, "The Italian Problem," and John Zarrilli, "A Suggestion for the Solution of the Italian Problem."

25. Rosenwaike, *Population History,* 83.

26. John Foster Carr, *Guide for Immigrant Italians in the United States of America,* 16 and 71.

27. See Candeloro, "Italian-Americans," 182–83. Candeloro views street festivals as offering a kind of symbolic ethnicity that keeps alive the folk religion brought by the immigrants to America.

28. For early descriptions of Italian *feste* from the perspective of outsiders, see Ada Eliot, "Two Italian Festivals," and Antonio Mangano, "Italian Tent Work in Brooklyn." Mangano pointedly comments on the drunkenness and violence reputedly associated with Italian festivals, while also suggesting that *feste* are a waste of money and an inappropriate way of expressing piety.

29. The information in this paragraph comes from personal interviews with participants and from Posen and Sciorra, "The *Giglio*." For fuller descriptions of the history of the Brooklyn giglio performance, see I. Sheldon Posen and Joseph Sciorra, "Brooklyn's Dancing Tower," and Joseph Sciorra, "Religious Processions in Italian Williamsburg."

30. Monsignor David L. Cassato, formerly of Our Lady of Mount Carmel Church has said of the performance: "It's the blood of the neighborhood"; quoted in Garry Pierre-Pierre, "Museum of the Giglio."

31. Remarks made in personal interviews on October 14–15, 1995. In other interviews, both men and women repeated the claim that the *giglio* held the community together, insulating it against out-migration to the suburbs and providing a measure of stability that otherwise would not be available.

32. Silvano M. Tomasi, *Piety and Power,* 21.

33. Robert A. Orsi, *The Madonna of 115th Street,* 198–201.

34. A participant, speaking in *The Men Who Dance the Giglio.*

35. Pierre Bourdieu, *The Logic of Practice,* 117.

36. A clever response to this predicament of female exclusion from the festival was devised by one woman, who in the year when her husband was chosen as *capo,* wore the costume of a female Saint Paulinus when she opened her front door to greet the men who had come in procession to pick up her husband; see *The Men Who Dance the Giglio.*

37. Bourdieu, *The Logic of Practice,* 87.

38. David Gonzalez, "Celebration of an Ancient Italian Feast Yields Lessons for Modern Brooklyn."

39. Guy Trebay, "The Giglio," 80.

40. A participant, speaking in *The Men Who Dance the Giglio.*

41. See, for instance, the analysis of a Good Friday procession of the Virgin of Sorrows in Brooklyn by Kay F. Turner, "The Virgin of Sorrows Procession."

42. Posen and Sciorra, "Brooklyn's Dancing Tower," 34.

43. See Miles Orvell, *The Real Thing;* Orvell argues that the valorizing of authenticity was part of modernism and came about as the response of an industrial consumer culture that sought to return, through art, to a sense of the real, while affirming individual and community (155).

44. See the discussion of this dilemma as it touched on the Massachusetts Mashpee tribe in the 1970s in James Clifford, "Identity in Mashpee." The difficulty faced by the Mashpees was that they did not obviously form a "tribe": they spoke English; they were chiefly Baptists; they had intermarried with blacks and whites; they were "businessmen, schoolteachers, fishermen, domestic workers, small contractors" (278).

45. A participant, speaking in *The Men Who Dance the Giglio.*

46. This claim, made by Candeloro, "Italian-Americans," 187, who argues that suburbanization has turned old Italian enclaves into ethnic theme parks, is less true for Williamsburg than for many other old Italian neighborhoods.

47. A participant, speaking in *The Men Who Dance the Giglio.*

48. This information comes from I. Sheldon Posen and Daniel Franklin Ward, "Watts Towers and the Giglio Tradition," 144.

49. For a discussion of some of these ambivalences, see Stuart Hall, "New Ethnicities," 29.

50. Denise Mangieri DiCarlo, "The Interplay of Ritual for Italians in Multicultural Society," 112.

51. The band's leader, speaking in *The Men Who Dance the Giglio.*

52. Richard D. Alba, "The Twilight of Ethnicity among Americans of European Descent," 152.

5. America's Passion Plays

1. For a photograph of the Skwa Village Passion Play, see the Albert Henry Barnes Collection, no. 542, University of Washington Libraries, Seattle; for the Penitente passion plays, see Marta Weigle, *Brothers of Light, Brothers of Blood,* especially 31; the Hill Cumorah play has been performed since 1937 as a celebration of Mormon history; for marionette passion plays performed by Martin and Olga Stevens, see playbills in the Redpath Chautauqua Collection, Special Collections, University of Iowa Libraries, Iowa City.

2. The quotation comes from the Great Passion Play website, http://www.greatpassionplay .com. The Eureka Springs play was conceived in 1964 by the Reverend Gerald L. K. Smith, a one-time follower of Huey Long; in 1956, Smith was denounced by Richard Nixon as "a race-baiting merchandiser of hate"; see Saul S. Friedman, *The Oberammergau Passion Play,* 159, citing Arnold Forster and Benjamin Epstein, *The New Anti-Semitism,* 20.

3. Rainer Warning, "On the Alterity of Medieval Religious Drama," especially 266.

4. Karl Young, *Drama of the Medieval Church,* 1:493, and Sandro Sticca, *The Latin Passion Play,* 173.

5. For a useful overview of scholarship on the Latin liturgical plays, see C. Clifford Flanigan, "Medieval Latin Music-Drama." The chapter by Alan E. Knight in the same collection succinctly describes the *Seinte Resureccion* and later French passion plays; see his "France," 151–68.

6. Young, *Drama of the Medieval Church,* 1:492.

7. Munich, Staatsbibliothek, MS Lat. 4660, Carmina Burana, fol. 107r-12v; it has been edited by Young, *Drama of the Medieval Church,* 1:518–33, and David Bevington, *Medieval Drama,* 202–23. Reconstructed songs and music from the play have been recorded on *The Greater Passion Play from Carmina Burana.*

8. For studies of German Easter plays, see Rolf Bergmann, *Studien zur Entstehung und Geschichte der deutschen Passionsspiele des 13. und 14. Jahrhunderts;* Dorothea Freise, *Geistliche Spiele in der Stadt des ausgehenden Mittelalters;* and Rolf Steinbach, *Die deutschen Oster- und Passionsspiele.*

9. Quoted in James S. Shapiro, *Oberammergau,* 118.

10. Modern scholarship disputes this legend, and some argue that the play may have first been performed three hundred years earlier; see Friedman, *Oberammergau Passion Play,* 24–26.

11. See Hermine von Hillern Diemer, *Oberammergau and Its Passion Play,* 32.

12. Shapiro, *Oberammergau,* 61.

13. For these changes, see ibid., 68–73.

14. A new theater was constructed in 1890 and remodeled in 1930 and 1950; see Friedman, *Oberammergau,* 148.

15. For these statistics, see Shapiro, *Oberammergau,* 112, and Friedman, *Oberammergau,* 148.

16. The *New York World* reported that revenues in 1890 were $170,000; see Montrose J. Moses, trans., *The Passion Play of Oberammergau,* lxiii. The quotation is from Richard F. Burton, *A Glance at the "Passion-play,"* 75. For a discussion of the Victorian fascination with Oberammergau, see John R. Elliott, Jr., *Playing God,* 25–41.

17. These accounts are too numerous to list, but for typical examples, see Alexander Craig

Sellar, "The Passion-Play in the Highlands of Bavaria"; Arthur Penrhyn Stanley, "The Ammergau Mystery; or Sacred Drama of 1860"; Winold Reiss, "Oberammergau Players"; and Anna S. Bushby, "The Passion Play at Oberammergau in Bavaria." Bushby's account is quoted in the anonymous article discussed below, which was published in *Harper's New Monthly Magazine* in 1871.

18. Lucy Fountain, "Passion Play at Ober-Ammergau."

19. M. D. Conway, "A Passion-Play Pilgrimage."

20. "The Passion Play in Oberammergau, 1870." Another scholarly account comes in the early years of the next decade, in H. H., "The Passion Play at Oberammergau." This essay, once again an eyewitness account, compares Oberammergau to other miracle plays, including Chester's (914), about which the writer appears to know quite a bit.

21. In tandem with magazine accounts, books devoted to Oberammergau also proliferated from 1870. One of the earliest was Henry Blackburn's *Art in the Mountains: Story of the Passion Play*, which a reviewer declared "does not contain a great deal that is new," thus suggesting how widespread knowledge of Oberammergau already was; see the review in *The Atlantic Monthly* 27 (March 1871): 397–98.

22. Burton, *A Glance at the "Passion-play"*, especially 75. For another critique, see William Allen Garber, *The Passion Play Graft*.

23. Malcolm MacColl, *The Ober-Ammergau Passion Play*.

24. "Religious Relics in London," 897–98.

25. "The Last Representation of the Ober-Ammergau Play—in the Summer of 1880," 795.

26. Playbill from the Redpath Chautauqua Collection, Special Collections, University of Iowa Libraries, Iowa City. Another lecture, meant to accompany fifty stereopticon views of the 1900 performance of the Oberammergau play, survives in the Library of Congress; see *The Passion Play at Oberammergau, 1900*.

27. See Sigmund Lubin, "The Passion Play." For a concise overview of early passion-play films, see Musser's *The Emergence of Cinema*, 208–18.

28. Playbill, Redpath Chautauqua Collection, Special Collections, University of Iowa Libraries, Iowa City.

29. For the spurning of the producer's offer, see Janet H. M. Swift, *The Passion Play of Oberammergau*, 90.

30. For Day's defense of the photographer's right to portray sacred subjects, see his "Sacred Art and the Camera," 97–99.

31. "Harper's Magazine Advertiser," B021.

32. See Royall Tyler, *Four Plays by Royall Tyler*. There is no evidence that Tyler's biblical plays were actually performed.

33. Attesting to the play's entry into popular cultural history, Ambrose Bierce's *Devil's Dictionary* defines "Calvary" as "an eminence on Mission Street, where James O'Neill died for the sins of Salmi Morse"; see Ambrose Bierce, *The Enlarged Devil's Dictionary*, 33.

34. See Alan Nielsen, *The Great Victorian Sacrilege*, 29–49, for a thorough recounting of Morse's life.

35. "Letter from Salmi Morse, to the Public of San Francisco," *The Illustrated Wasp*, May 15, 1880; quoted in Nielsen, *Great Victorian Sacrilege*, 52.

36. Nielsen, *Great Victorian Sacrilege*, 52. Nielsen is primarily interested in the issues of censorship surrounding Morse's play and in Morse's attempt to invoke the First Amendment to protect the free speech of the stage.

37. From an interview with Harriet Morse; quoted in Nielsen, *Great Victorian Sacrilege*, 53.

38. *San Francisco Daily Morning Call*, October 6, 1878; quoted in Nielsen, *Great Victorian Sacrilege*, 49.

39. Nielsen, *Great Victorian Sacrilege*, 50–52.

40. *Daily Alta California*, January 23, 1879; quoted in Nielsen, *Great Victorian Sacrilege*, 56.

41. For this and other information about the production, much of it derived firsthand from David Belasco, see William Winter, *The Life of David Belasco*, 2:114–25. It is not entirely clear

why O'Neill accepted the role. In at least one account, O'Neill claimed that he was reluctant to do so; see Ada Patterson, "James O'Neill—the Actor and the Man," ix.

42. Programme for *The Passion,* 1879; quoted in Nielsen, *Great Victorian Sacrilege,* 93.

43. See "The Passion Play," and "Footlights," *San Francisco Chronicle,* March 2, 1879.

44. "The Supervisors Discuss It," *San Francisco Chronicle,* March 4, 1879.

45. "The Passion Play," *San Francisco Chronicle,* March 7, 1879.

46. Winter, *Life of David Belasco,* 2:124.

47. Ibid., 2:117.

48. Nielsen, *Great Victorian Sacrilege,* 77–87, 100.

49. Ibid., 101–2.

50. Albert Sutliffe, "Amusement Notes," *San Francisco Chronicle,* April 22, 1879.

51. Nielsen, *Great Victorian Sacrilege,* 107, 109.

52. Winter, *The Life of David Belasco,* 2:117–8.

53. Nielsen, *Great Victorian Sacrilege,* 112.

54. Ibid., 113–14. The definitive history of the theater in San Francisco is Edmond M. Gagey, *The San Francisco Stage.*

55. Nielsen, *Great Victorian Sacrilege,* 70–71.

56. Ibid., 138.

57. "The Drama," *Tribune,* October 18, 1880; reworked in Winter's *Life of Belasco,* 116–17.

58. Nielsen, *Great Victorian Sacrilege,* 146–71.

59. Ibid., 156–57.

60. "The Stage," *San Francisco Examiner,* December 12, 1880, and *Dramatic News,* December 4, 1880; both cited in Nielsen, *Great Victorian Sacrilege,* 158.

61. Nielsen, *Great Victorian Sacrilege,* 159–60.

62. "Mr. Abbey's Decision," *New York Times,* November 28, 1880.

63. "The Passion Play Read," *New York Times,* December 4, 1880.

64. See Nielsen, *Great Victorian Sacrilege,* 174–202, for the preceding information on the play's legal battles.

65. See Doris Alexander, *The Tempering of Eugene O'Neill,* 56, for O'Neill's attempts to revive the play. According to some reports, Morse's death was a suicide; but other evidence suggests that he was murdered by Thomas McGivney, a liquor retailer and backer of one of Morse's ventures who had become obsessed with Mary C. Blackburn, a young actress with whom Morse had become romantically involved and to whom he left the rights to *The Passion;* see Winter, *Life of David Belasco,* 2:122, who believed that it was a suicide, and Nielsen, *Great Victorian Sacrilege,* 215–17, who presents the evidence against McGivney.

66. The story of Hollaman's film was first told by film historian Terry Ramsaye in *A Million and One Nights: A History of the Motion Picture Through 1925* (1926; reprint, New York: Touchstone Books, 1986), 366–78. According to Ramsaye, the film was found in Huntsville, Alabama, in 1965, by Charles Nicks, whose wife's grandfather, Charles E. Huston, a Pennsylvania showman, had bought a copy and toured with it until 1905. Copies of the film are now in the George Eastman House Film Archives, Museum of Modern Art Film Study Center, New York. The film contains scenes not found in Morse's play; it also includes an opening sequence of a Bavarian village, perhaps added to the Passion (at a later date) from the Klaw-Erlanger film.

67. The Klaw-Erlanger and Lumière brothers' film of the Horvitz passion play is available on video from http://www.headfilm.ch/index/thema-9.html.

68. Nielsen, *Great Victorian Sacrilege,* 277, n. 33.

69. See Charles Musser, "The Eden Musée in 1898," 96, for a discussion of the techniques of early film at the Eden Musée. Some catalogs provided text for incorporation into the showman's presentation. The catalog for Lubin's *Passion Play* includes a model lecture that illustrates this common practice; see http://edison.rutgers.edu/mopix/resource.htm.

70. Reverend H. M. Warren, *Moving Picture World* (February 1908): 132; quoted in Charles Musser, *High-Class Moving Pictures,* 75.

71. Ibid., 71–79, for a discussion of Howe's screening of the *Passion Play.* Colonel Henry H.

Hadley, who was a Protestant evangelist, also bought a copy and used it in his touring revival shows.

72. After closing at the Lake Wales Amphitheater in 1998, the Passion Play was performed for one year at Carpenter's Home Church in Lakeland, Florida, before leaving the state for good.

73. Reported by James Camp Wright, "Development of the Black Hills Passion Play in Spearfish, South Dakota and Lake Wales, Florida," 21.

74. Josef Meier, quoted by Aubrey B. Haines, "A Passion Play Comes to America," *Pen* 43 (1968): 4; cited in Wright, "Development of the Black Hills Passion Play," 21.

75. Wright, "Development of the Black Hills Passion Play," 21.

76. Josef Meier, quoted in Arnold Nicholson, "America's Passion Play," *The Saturday Evening Post* (April 24, 1943): 16–17, 42–44.

77. Wright, "Development of the Black Hills Passion Play," 23, based on information from Nicholson, "America's Passion Play."

78. See "The Original Passion Play of the Black Hills," Redpath Chautauqua Collection, Special Collections, University of Iowa Libraries, Iowa City.

79. Wright, "Development of the Black Hills Passion Play," 3.

80. For information on the marketing of the play in its two locations, see Wright, "Development of the Black Hills Passion Play," 166–71.

81. The passion play of Zion, Illinois, for example, was founded by the Reverend Jabez Taylor in 1935; the passion play of Kearney, Nebraska, was first staged in 1936 by a local Presbyterian minister; and the Holy Family Passion Play of Union City, New Jersey, was begun in 1915 by the Reverend Joseph N. Grieft, a native of Luxembourg. For information about these plays, see http://www.ourzion.com/passionplay/history.html; Dorothy S. Wilson, "The Passion Play"; and Peter Wynne, "The Passion Play of Union City, N.J." For a study of outdoor passion plays in the United States, see Charlene Faye Monk, "Passion Plays in the United States."

82. Wright, "Development of the Black Hills Passion Play," 177, based on information in letters from Spearfish and Lake Wales clergymen.

83. Hayden White, *Tropics of Discourse*.

84. Brochure, "The Black Hills Passion Play," 1939, in my collection.

85. See the websites for both plays: http://www.passionplayusa.org and http://www.american passionplay.org.

86. Brochure, "The Black Hills Passion Play," in my collection. The brochure is undated, but can be dated to the early 1950s by internal references claiming that Meier has performed in the play for the past fifteen years; since it makes no mention of the Lake Wales performances, which started in 1953, it might predate them.

87. Pierre Bourdieu, *The Logic of Practice,* 56. In the quoted lines, Bourdieu is offering a definition of the *habitus.*

88. Brochure, "Black Hills Passion Play," in my collection. The brochure is undated, but its original owner penciled in "1973" on it and included the program from the 1973 Lake Wales performance, which she or he presumably attended.

89. William Bygrave, "Obituary of Josef Meier."

90. See http://www.blackhills.com/bhpp/pp=_theplay3.htm.

91. See http://www.blackhills.com/bhpp/pp=_theplay3.htm.

6. Medieval Plays and Medievalist Players

1. Peter Stallybrass, "'Drunk with the Cup of Liberty,'" 69. The duke's letter is reproduced in S. A. Strong, ed., *A Catalogue of the Letters and other Historical Documents in the Library at Welbeck,* 226–27.

2. John Marshall, "Modern Productions of Medieval English Plays," 290–92.

3. For a detailed account of the performance, see Robert Speaight, *William Poel and the Elizabethan Revival,* especially 161–66.

4. *St. James's Gazette,* 15 July 1901, 6; quoted in Robert A. Potter, *The English Morality Play,* 3.

5. For a summary of early productions see Peter Meredith, "Original-Staging Production of English Medieval Plays," especially 65–66. For a list of early productions see John R. Elliott, Jr., "A Checklist of Modern Productions of the Medieval Mystery Cycles in England."

6. Meredith, "Original-Staging," 65.

7. See the discussion of the 1951 York plays in John R. Elliott, Jr., *Playing God,* especially 72–82. It is worth noting that the 1951 festival coincided with parliamentary debates in 1949 about the appropriateness of a National Theatre, expressing what Loren Kruger describes as a desire for a homogeneous national tradition to be displayed through theater. Kruger sees the 1951 festival as summing up a postwar era of "decaying national self-confidence" (130); see *The National Stage,* 127–30.

8. Elliott, *Playing God,* 79–82.

9. See the description of the early work of PLS in Joel H. Kaplan and George Shand, "The *Poculi Ludique Societas,*" and Milla C. Riggio, "Have Play, Will Travel," 161.

10. Marshall, "Modern Productions," 290.

11. This point has been made by Eckehard Simon in the preface to his collection of essays mapping the state of medieval drama studies; see his preface to *The Theatre of Medieval Europe,* xvi.

12. Peter F. McDonald, "Drama Criticism and the Value of Productions," 13. This remark also helps explain why cultural materialist, feminist, and new historicist interpretations, so vital in renaissance drama studies since the early 1980s, have until quite recently been neglected in medieval drama.

13. John McKinnell, "Staging the Digby *Mary Magdalen,*" 127.

14. Harold Gardiner, *Mysteries End.*

15. For an argument against the notion of a systematic official and ecclesiastical campaign to shut them down, see Lawrence M. Clopper, *Drama, Play, and Game,* 268–93; Richard K. Emmerson, "Eliding the 'Medieval,'" has also shown that medieval plays persisted longer than has generally been thought.

16. The expenses associated with putting on the plays had by the end of the fifteenth century led the oligarchies in some cities to impose taxes on nonparticipants to help defray the cost of the plays, an unpopular move that Clopper, *Drama, Play, and Game,* 286, sees as laying the groundwork for ecclesiastical and royal intervention.

17. Peter Womack, "Imagining Communities," 107.

18. Eamon Duffy, *The Stripping of the Altars,* offers a detailed account both of the structures and activities of traditional religion and its dismantling starting in 1530.

19. The decree can be found in *Records of Early English Drama: York,* 2:649–50.

20. See Steven Mullaney, *The Place of the Stage,* for an analysis of the ideological meanings of the locations of the first English playhouses.

21. Kathleen M. Ashley, "Cultural Approaches to Medieval Drama," 65.

22. Huston Diehl, *Staging Reform, Reforming the Stage.*

23. Robert Weimann, *Shakespeare and the Popular Tradition in the Theater.*

24. Cited in Elliott, *Playing God,* 7.

25. Shakespeare's Autolycus, for instance, says that he has "compassed a motion [i.e., devised a puppet show] of the Prodigal Son" (*Winter's Tale,* IV.iii.102); records offer evidence of puppet shows on such topics as the Creation, the Flood, and Dives and Lazarus, during the reign of Queen Anne; and in 1709 the *Tatler* reported on a puppet show in Bath in which Punch and his wife danced in the Ark. See Elliott, *Playing God,* 12–13, for these and other examples of the survival of medieval plays.

26. Frank Fowell and Frank Palmer, *Censorship in England,* 26–27.

27. Elliott, *Playing God,* 8.

28. From the 1680s on, the Lord Chamberlain took over the censorship duties of the Master of Revels; his powers were confirmed by an Act of Parliament in 1737 and lasted until 1968 when

the censorship system was finally abolished. The activities of the eighteenth-century censors are detailed in the Huntington Library's Larpent Collection, which contains copies of every play submitted for licensing in England from 1737 to 1824; see Douglas McMillan, *Catalogue of the Larpent Plays in the Huntington Library,* and L. W. Connolly, *The Censorship of English Drama.*

29. See Elliott, *Playing God,* 17–19.

30. For a discussion of Poel's career, see ibid., 42–44.

31. For a thorough discussion of the revival of *Everyman,* see Potter, *The English Morality Play,* 231–32.

32. David Mills provides an extensive account of Monck's plan and of the reactions of the Chester Council of the Historic Society, which eventually decided not to assume responsibility for the production, thus squelching what would have been the first revival of a complete cycle; see his "Reviving the Chester Plays," 39–51.

33. Quoted in ibid., 41, from the *Chester Courant* reprint of the *Guardian* article.

34. See Elliott, *Playing God,* 22–4.

35. Quoted in Isaac F. Marcosson and Daniel Frohman, *Charles Frohman: Manager and Man,* 226.

36. See Winifred F. E. C. Isaac, *Ben Greet and the Old Vic,* 77.

37. Ibid., 78.

38. *New York World,* October 14, 1902; quoted in Potter, *Morality Play,* 223.

39. Isaac, *Ben Greet,* 82, quoting from a copy of the program supplied (with a photograph of the stage set) by Helen D. Willard, curator of the Harvard College Library Theatre collection.

40. Sybil Thorndike, for example, played Everyman at the Old Vic in 1916.

41. Isaac, *Ben Greet,* 89.

42. Ibid., 95.

43. Ibid., 112.

44. Marcosson and Frohman, *Charles Frohman,* 175–78.

45. Publicity brochure, Redpath Chautauqua Collection, Special Collections, University of Iowa Libraries, Iowa City.

46. Ibid.

47. James Russell Lowell, "The Old English Dramatists," 75–84.

48. "A Middle English Nativity."

49. See Mills, "Reviving the Chester Plays," especially 47.

50. Isaac, *Ben Greet,* 80.

51. See Potter, *English Morality Play,* 237–38.

52. Elliott, *Playing God,* 59. For the era's religious drama, see Gerald C. Weales, *Religion in Modern English Drama,* and George Ralph, "Medievalism and Twentieth-Century Religious Drama."

53. Elliott, *Playing God,* 59–60.

54. Sarah Beckwith, *Signifying God,* 12.

55. For photographs of the Festival Church performance, see photographs nos. 4 and 12, Art File E93, nos. 1–12, Folger Shakespeare Library, Washington, D.C.

56. This information comes from a note on the back of photograph no. 1 in the Folger Shakespeare Library, Art File E93, nos. 1–12.

57. Elliott, *Playing God,* 72–101, offers detailed accounts of these productions, up through 1980.

58. Edward Burns, "Seeing Is Believing," 2, 8.

59. Publicity flyer, Ben Greet's *Everyman,* Brooklyn Academy of Music, January 31, 1930, Redpath Chautauqua Collection, Special Collections, University of Iowa Libraries, Iowa City.

60. Publicity flyer, Redpath Chautauqua Collection, Special Collections, University of Iowa Libraries, Iowa City.

61. Playbill, Redpath Chautauqua Collection, Special Collections, University of Iowa Libraries, Iowa City.

62. See the discussion of folklore's roots by Timothy H. Evans, "Folklore as Utopia," 245–68.

63. See Lee Patterson, *Negotiating the Past,* especially 3–39, and "On the Margin," 87–108; and Anne Middleton, "Medieval Studies."

64. C. Clifford Flanigan, "Comparative Literature and the Study of Medieval Drama."

65. Potter, *English Morality Play*, 192–210.

66. Robert Dodsley, ed., *A Select Collection of Old English Plays;* the quotation is from 1:2. In the first volumes of Dodsley's *Old Plays* in 1744, no medieval plays whatsoever were included.

67. Thomas Hawkins, *The Origin of the English Drama.*

68. Flanigan, "Study of Medieval Drama," 58.

69. Theresa M. Coletti, "Reading REED"; the quotation is from 257.

70. Ibid., 256.

71. Samuel Schoenbaum, *Shakespeare's Lives*, vii, x; quoted in Coletti, "Reading REED," 260. For a discussion of Halliwell-Phillips' work, see J. A. B. Somerset, "James Orchard Halliwell-Phillips and his Scrapbooks."

72. Halliwell-Phillips, "Proposals for issuing, by subscription, amongst a very small number of subscribers . . . entire facsimiles in small quarto volumes, of all the editions of Shakespeare's dramas and poems printed before 1623" (n.d.), 4; quoted in Coletti, "Reading REED," 260.

73. See the description of this performance by Alexandra F. Johnston, the executive director of REED, under whose auspices the cycle was produced, in her "The York Cycle: 1977."

74. See Kaplan and Shand, "*Poculi Ludique Societas*," 141–42.

75. See the discussion of the redemptive mission of the salvage operation of medieval literary studies in my "Medieval Ethnography: Fieldwork in the European Past," especially 7–9.

76. Louise Fradenburg, "Voice Memorial"; the quotation is from 173.

77. An exception is the Cathedral Players, an acting company founded in 1978 by Michael Tabelak; its performance space is the Gothic Cathedral of St. John the Divine in New York City. The company, inspired by Tabelak's communal vision, has often performed for religious festivals, conferences, and prayer meetings; see the review of its 1986 performance of *Everyman* (which was performed under the title, *Everybody*) by Patricia S. White, "Everybody: On Stage in New York."

78. See the review by Martin Stevens of the second production in the fall of 1986, "The Nativity Cycle at Irvine."

79. The Trinity production was reviewed by Theresa Coletti and Pamela Sheingorn, "Playing Wisdom at Trinity College."

80. See the review of this festival by Riggio in "Have Play, Will Travel," 161–75.

81. Middleton, "Medieval Studies," 21–22.

82. For the "does-it work-approach," see Meredith, "Original-Staging," 66. For the mock-jousting scene, see Peter Meredith, "'Farte pryke in cule' and Cock-fighting," complete with photographs and diagrams. For the Towneley "proof," see Martin Stevens, "*Processus Torontoniensis,*" 189–90.

83. See the comments by Stanley J. Kahrl, "The Staging of Medieval English Plays," 132, and Alexandra F. Johnston, "Four York Pageants," 104.

84. A claim made by Kahrl, "Staging," 140.

85. See the report by Michelle M. Butler in "Census of Medieval Drama Productions," 206.

86. See the comments on metonymy's appeal for historians by Nancy Partner, "Making Up Lost Time," especially 105–7.

87. John Ganim observes that the use of scientific models by the humanities in America has always been linked with attempts at legitimization and acceptance; see his "The Literary Uses of the New Historicism," 210.

88. Report by Steve Urkowitz in "Census of Medieval Drama Productions," 259.

89. A notable exception to these amateur performances is *The Mysteries*, produced in England by the National Theatre, 1977–85, which was also filmed for Channel Four.

90. See the discussion of the 1960 and 1963 performances in Elliott, *Playing God*, 87–92. The quotation comes from a press release from the festival manager's office, *Daily Telegraph*, 28 January 1969; *London Times*, 6 February 1969; quoted in Elliott, *Playing God*, 94.

91. Michael D. Bristol, *Shakespeare's America, America's Shakespeare*, 35.

92. Stevens, "*Processus Torontoniensis*," 189–90.

93. Quoted in Ronald Grimes, *Ritual Criticism*, 92. At the invitation of medieval scholars involved in the production, Grimes attended the 1985 performance of the Towneley cycle and

analyzed it from an anthropologist's perspective, noting among other things the desire for a transformative experience.

94. Joanne Gates, "The Digby *Mary Magdalene.*"

95. See the description in Elliott, *Playing God,* 88–89.

96. Both moments happened at the Toronto Chester cycle in 1983.

97. For a discussion of the construction of a naturalistic Middle Ages grounded on appropriation of the genres of bourgeois realism such as the fabliau, see R. Howard Bloch, "Naturalism, Nationalism, Medievalism."

98. See Sheila Lindenbaum, "Ceremony and Oligarchy," 171–73.

99. Gail McMurray Gibson, "The York Cycle at Toronto," 116.

100. Peter F. McDonald, "The Towneley Cycle at Toronto," 58.

101. Riggio, "Have Play Will Travel," 161–62.

102. These are the words of the directors of *The Four Daughters of God* performed at Duquesne University in 1999; see "Census of Medieval Drama Productions," 244.

103. McDonald, "Towneley," 59.

104. *The Massacre of the Innocents* pageant was first staged at York in William Gaskill's unpopular 1963 production; see Elliott, *Playing God,* 91. The Crucifixion was first shown openly in performances of the cycles in 1969. Margaret Birkett, who directed the *Ludus Coventriae* in 1966 in Grantham, Lincolnshire, omitted a direct representation of the Crucifixion, saying "a modern audience could not take anything so cruel on stage"; quoted in Kahrl, "Staging," 35. In 1968, the Lord Chamberlain deleted the phrase "kiss my arse" (Cain's insult to Abel in *The Killing of Abel*) from an acting version of the Wakefield plays; see Elliott, *Playing God,* 108.

105. Burns, "Seeing Is Believing," 1.

106. Darryll Grantley, "The National Theatre's Production of *The Mysteries.*"

107. Stevens, "*Processus,*" 198.

108. Bristol, *Shakespeare's America,* 10–11.

Epilogue

1. Fredric Jameson, "Postmodernism, or the Cultural Logic of Late Capitalism," 71.

2. See Brian Stock, "The Middle Ages as Subject and Object," especially 537–39.

3. Patrick Wright, *On Living in an Old Country,* 217–21.

4. Jody Enders has cogently drawn attention to the connections among memory, history, and performance; see her *The Medieval Theater of Cruelty,* especially 152–59.

5. See Raphael Samuel, *Theaters of Memory,* x.

6. Stuart Hall, "Notes on Deconstructing 'the Popular,'" especially 227.

7. Ibid., 235.

Bibliography

1. Manuscripts and Primary Sources

"Albany Fifty Years Ago." *Harper's New Monthly Magazine* 14 (March 1857): 451–63.

American Indian Myths and Legends. Edited by Richard Erdoes and Alfonso Ortiz. New York: Pantheon, 1984.

Beauvallet, Leon. *Rachel and the New World.* New York, 1856.

Bierce, Ambrose. *The Enlarged Devil's Dictionary.* Edited by Ernest J. Hopkins. Garden City, N.Y.: Doubleday, 1967.

"Black Hills Passion Play." Various Brochures. Author's collection.

Black Hills Passion Play website. http://www.blackhills.com/bhpp/pp=_theplay3.html.

Blackburn, Henry. *Art in the Mountains: Story of the Passion Play.* London, 1870.

Bourcard, Francesco de. *Usi e costumi di Napoli e contorni.* Naples, 1853–55. 2:8–11. Quoted in Avella, *Annali della festa dei gigli (1500–1950),* 1:40.

Breck, Samuel. *The Recollections of Samuel Breck, with Passages from his Note-Books (1771–1862).* Edited by H. E. Scudder. Philadelphia, 1877.

Bremer, Frederika. *The Homes of the New World: Impressions of America.* Translated by Mary Howitt. 2 vols. New York, 1854.

Bull, Henry. "Memoir of Rhode Island." *Rhode Island Republican* (19 August 1837): 1.

Burton, Richard F. *A Glance at the "Passion-play".* London, 1861.

Bushby, Anna S. "The Passion Play at Oberammergau in Bavaria." *Colburn's New Monthly Magazine* 147 (1870): 288–98.

Bygrave, William. "Obituary of Josef Meier." *Lake Wales Ledger* (Lake Wales, Florida), February 2, 1999.

Carr, John Foster. *Guide for Immigrant Italians in the United States of America.* New York: Doubleday, 1911. Reprint, New York: Arno, 1975.

Conway, M. D. "A Passion-Play Pilgrimage." *Harper's New Monthly Magazine* 43 (November 1871): 919–29.

Cooper, James Fenimore. *Satanstoe, or the Littlepage Manuscripts: A Tale of the Colony.* Edited by Kay Seymour House and Constance Ayers Denne. Albany: State University of New York Press, 1990.

Coventry, Alexander. *Recollections and Diary, July 1783–August 1789.* Manuscripts Collection. New York State Library, Albany, New York.

Croxton Play of the Sacrament. In *Non-Cycle Plays and Fragments,* edited by Norman Davis, 58–89. EETS ss 1 (Oxford: EETS, 1970).

Day, F. Holland. "Sacred Art and the Camera." *Photogram* 6(February 1899): 97–99.

Díaz del Castillo, Bernal. *Historia verdadera de la conquista de la Nueva España.* Edited by Joaquín R. Cabañas. 3 vols. Mexico City: Robredo, 1939.

Dodsley, Robert, ed. *A Select Collection of Old English Plays.* 10 vols. London, 1744–45.

"The Drama." *Tribune,* October 18, 1880. Quoted in Winter, *Life of Belasco,* 116–17.

Dunlap, William. "Diary of William Dunlap." *New York Historical Society Collections* 62 (1929): 161.

Durán, Diego. *Historia de las Indias de Nueve España e islas de la Tierra Firme.* Edited by A. M. Garibay. 2 vols. Mexico: Editorial Porrúa, 1967.

Earle, Alice Morse. *Colonial Days in Old New York.* New York: Scribner's, 1896.

Egan, Maurice F. "A Day in the Ma'sh." *Scribner's Monthly* 22(July 1881): 343–53.

Eights, James S. "Pinkster Festivities in Albany Sixty Years Ago." In *Collections on the History of Albany, from its Discovery to the Present Time,* edited by Joel Munsell, 2:323–27. 4 vols. Albany, 1865–71.

Eliot, Ada. "Two Italian Festivals." *Charities* 7 (October 19, 1901): 321–22.

"Everyman." 1951 Festival Church Performance. Photographs nos. 4 and 12, Art File E93. Folger Shakespeare Library, Washington, D.C.

La Festa Antica: Quaderno fotografico. Compiled by G. Antonio Napolitano. Nola: Edizione "La Contea Nolana," 1996.

Fountain, Lucy. "Passion Play at Ober-Ammergau." *Putnam's Monthly Magazine* 16 (October 1870): 436–40.

Fray Alonso de Benavides' Revised Memorial of 1634. Edited and translated by Frederick W. Hodge, George P. Hammond, and Agapito Rey. Albuquerque: University of New Mexico Press, 1945.

Furman, Gabriel. *Antiquities of Long Island.* New York, 1874.

Gebhard, Elizabeth L. *The Parsonage between Two Manors: Annals of Clover-Reach.* Hudson: Bryan Printing, 1909.

Gigli in Cartolina: Quaderno fotografico. Compiled by G. Antonio Napolitano. Nola: Edizione "La Contea Nolana," 1997.

"The Giglio Festa." *Household Words* 14 (August 16, 1856): 115–18.

Gilbert, Olive. *Narrative of Sojourner Truth.* Edited by Nell Irvin Painter. New York: Penguin Books, 1998.

Giusti, Giuseppe. "Omaggio a S. Paolino 1997." In *Tifiosissimo della Città di Nola.* Nola: Tribunale di Nola, 1997.

"A Glimpse of an Old Dutch Town," *Harper's New Monthly Magazine* 62 (1881): 524–39.

Gonzalez, David. "Celebration of an Ancient Italian Feast Yields Lessons for Modern Brooklyn," *New York Times,* July 14, 1994.

Grant, Rev. Percy Stickney. "The Passion Play on the American Stage." *Theatre* 2 (May 1902): 10–12.

Great Passion Play website. http://www.greatpassionplay.com.

Gregory I, Pope. *Dialogues.* 3 vols. Paris: Editions du Cerf, 1978–80.

Hakluyt, Richard. *The Principal Navigations, Voyages, Traffiques and Discoveries of the English Nation.* 2d ed. 12 vols. 1598–1600. Reprint, Glasgow: MacLehose, 1903–5.

"Harper's Magazine Advertiser." *Harper's New Monthly Magazine* 83 (November 1891): B017–C001.

Hawkins, Thomas. *The Origin of the English Drama.* London, 1773.

Hinds, Michael deCourcy. "Philadelphia Journal: The Frivolous Reign at this Parade." *New York Times,* December 31, 1991.

Historical Society of Pennsylvania. *Collections*. Philadelphia, 1853.

Hudson-Fulton Celebration Commission, New York. *The Fourth Annual Report of the Hudson-Fulton Celebration Commission to the Legislature of the State of New York*. Prepared by Edward H. Hall. 2 vols. Albany: J. B. Lyon, 1910.

"The Hull-House Labor Museum." *Chautauquan* 38 (September 1903): 60–61.

Humphreys, Mary Gay. *Catherine Schuyler*. New York: Scribner's, 1897.

"The Italian Problem," *Extension Magazine* 12 (September 1917): 3–4.

The Jesuit Relations and Allied Documents: Travels and Explorations of the Jesuit Missionaries in New France, 1610–1791. 73 vols. Edited by Rueben Gold Thwaites. Cleveland: Burrows Brothers, 1896–1901.

Johnson, William. *The Autobiography of Dr. William Henry Johnson*. 1900. Reprint, New York: Haskell House, 1970.

"Judge Allows Two Bands to Join New Year Parade." *New York Times*, November 8, 1981.

Kalm, Pehr. *The American of 1750: Peter Kalm's Travels in North America, the English Version of 1770*. Edited by Adolph B. Benson. New York: Dover, 1964.

"The Last Representation of the Ober-Ammergau Play—in the Summer of 1880." *New Englander and Yale Review* 39 (1880): 794–802.

Leone, Ambrogio. *Nola: la terra natìa*. Venezia, 1514. Quoted in Avella, *Annali della festa dei gigli (1500–1950)*, 1:29–30.

"Letter." *Albany Centinel* (June 1803). Reprint, *New York Daily Advertiser*, June 29, 1803.

"Letter from Salmi Morse, to the Public of San Francisco." *Illustrated Wasp*, May 15, 1880. Quoted in Nielsen, *Great Victorian Sacrilege*, 52.

"London—Plantagenet: III. The People." *Harper's New Monthly Magazine* 83 (October 1891): 784.

Lowell, James Russell. "The Old English Dramatists." *Harper's New Monthly Magazine* 85 (June 1892): 75–84.

Lubin, Sigmund. "The Passion Play," J-127. In *Motion Picture Catalogs by American Producers and Distributors, 1894–1908: A Microfilm Edition*, edited by Charles Musser, Thomas E. Jeffrey, and Reese V. Jenkins. Frederick, Md.: University Presses of America, 1984.

MacColl, Malcolm. *The Ober-Ammergau Passion Play*. 4th ed. London, 1871.

Machyn, Henry. *The Diary of Henry Machyn, Citizen and Merchant-Taylor of London, from A.D. 1550 to A.D. 1563*. Edited by John G. Nichols. London, 1848.

Mangano, Antonio. "Italian Tent Work in Brooklyn." *Baptist Home Mission Monthly* 28 (October 1906): 370–71.

Mason, George C. *Re-Union of the Sons and Daughters of Newport, Rhode Island*. Newport, 1859.

Memorials of London and London Life. Edited by Henry Thomas Riley. London, 1868.

"A Middle English Nativity." *Harper's New Monthly Magazine* 94 (December 1896): 5–7.

Moses, Montrose J., trans. *The Passion Play at Oberammergau*. New York: Duffield, 1909.

Motolinía, Toribio de. *Historia de los indios de la Nueva España*. Edited by Georges Baudot. Madrid: Castalia, 1985.

———. *History of the Indians of New Spain*. Translated by Francis B. Steck. Washington: Academy of American Franciscan History, 1951.

"Mr. Abbey's Decision." *New York Times,* November 28, 1880.

Newell, W. W. "Christmas Maskings in Boston." *Journal of American Folklore* 9 (1896): 178.

Nicholson, Arnold. "America's Passion Play." *Saturday Evening Post,* April 24, 1943, 16–17, 42–44.

Nineteenth Century Programmes Scrapbook. Billy Rose Theatre Collection, New York Public Library at the Lincoln Center.

"The Original Passion Play of the Black Hills." Playbill. Redpath Chautauqua Collection, Special Collections, University of Iowa Libraries, Iowa City.

The Passion. Produced by Tom Maguire, San Francisco, 1879. Programme. San Francisco Archives. San Francisco Room, San Francisco Public Library, San Francisco.

The Passion Play. Produced by Richard G. Hollaman and Albert Eaves. Photographed by William Paley. 22 min. B & W. Silent. 1898. George Eastman House Film Archive, Museum of Modern Art Film Study Center, New York City, New York.

"The Passion Play." *San Francisco Chronicle,* March 7, 1879.

"Passion Play (Cinema 1898)." Clipping Files. Billy Rose Theatre Collection, New York Public Library at the Lincoln Center, New York.

"The Passion Play at Oberammergau." *Century* 25, no. 6 (April 1883): 913–21.

The Passion Play at Oberammergau, 1900: Being a Lecture Designed to Accompany a Set of 50 Photographic Stereoptican Views. n.p., 1900.

"The Passion Play in Oberammergau, 1870." *Harper's New Monthly Magazine* 42 (January 1871): 174–87.

"The Passion Play Read." *New York Times,* December 4, 1880.

Passion Play website. http://www.passionplayusa.org.

Patterson, Ada. "James O'Neill—the Actor and the Man," *Theatre Magazine* (April 1908): 101–4, ix.

Phillips, James D. *Salem in the Eighteenth Century.* Boston: Houghton Mifflin, 1937.

Pierre-Pierre, Garry. "Museum of the Giglio: In Celebration of an Age-Old Rite." *New York Times,* June 12, 1994.

"A Pinkster Ode for the Year 1803: Most Respectfully Dedicated to Carolus Africanus Rex . . . by His Majesty's Obedient Servant Absalom Aimwell." Albany, 1803. Clipping Files. New York Historical Society, Albany, New York.

Porter, Jeff. *The Men Who Dance the Giglio.* VHS, 30 min. Iowa City, Iowa: Daedalus Productions, 1997.

Posen, I. Sheldon, and Joseph Sciorra. "Brooklyn's Dancing Tower." *Natural History* 92 (1983): 30–37,

———. "The *Giglio:* Brooklyn's Dancing Tower." Brochure. Brooklyn Historical Society Exhibit. Brooklyn, N.Y., 1989–90.

Program for the 108th Annual Feast of Saint Paulinus (July 5–16, 1995). Brooklyn, N.Y.: Printed by Our Lady of Mount Carmel Church, 1995.

Programme for *The Passion.* San Francisco, 1879.

Rainolds, John. *The Overthrow of Stage Plays.* Middleburg, 1599.

Records of Early English Drama: Chester. Edited by Lawrence M. Clopper. Toronto: University of Toronto Press, 1979.

Records of Early English Drama: York. Edited by Alexandra F. Johnston and Margaret Rogerson. 2 vols. Toronto: University of Toronto Press, 1979.

Reiss, Winold. "Oberammergau Players." *Century Magazine* 104 (1922): 727–42.

"Religious Relics in London." *Harper's New Monthly Magazine* 42 (1871): 894–903.

Remondini, Gianstefano. *Della Nolana Ecclesiastica Storia.* Naples, 1747. Quoted in Avella, *Annali della festa dei gigli (1500–1950)*, 1:32.

Review of *Art in the Mountains: Story of the Passion Play,* by Henry Blackburn. *Atlantic Monthly* 27 (March 1871): 397–98.

Ricart, Robert. *The Maire of Bristow Is Kalendar.* Edited by Lucy Toulmin Smith. London: Camden Society, 1872.

Robbins, William. "For Philadelphia, a Day of Spectacle." *New York Times,* January 1, 1984.

Roselli, Bruno. "An Arkansas Epic." *Century* 89 (January 1920): 377–86.

Ross, Edward A. "Racial Consequences of Immigration." *Century Magazine* 87 (February 1914): 617.

Sahagún, Bernardino de. *Florentine Codex: General History of the Things of New Spain.* Translated by Arthur J. O. Anderson and Charles E. Dibble. Santa Fe: School of American Research, 1954.

Sellar, Alexander Craig. "The Passion-Play in the Highlands of Bavaria." *Blackwood's Magazine* 107 (1870): 381–96.

Shelton, Jane De Forest. "The New England Negro: A Remnant," *Harper's New Monthly Magazine* 88 (1894): 536–37.

Simms, Jeptha R. *History of Schoharie County.* Albany, 1845.

Skwa Village Passion Play. Photograph. The Albert Henry Barnes Collection, no. 542, University of Washington Libraries, Seattle, Washington.

Spayd, Liz. "A Foray into Days of Yore." *The Washington Post,* October 5, 1992.

"The Stage." *San Francisco Examiner,* December 12, 1880. Quoted in Nielsen, *Great Victorian Sacrilege,* 158.

Stanley, Arthur Penrhyn. "The Ammergau Mystery; or Sacred Drama of 1860." *Macmillan's Magazine* 2 (1860): 463–77.

Strong, Sandford A., ed. *A Catalogue of the Letters and other Historical Documents in the Library at Welbeck.* London: J. Murray, 1903.

"The Supervisors Discuss It." *San Francisco Chronicle,* March 4, 1879.

Sutliffe, Albert. "Amusement Notes." *San Francisco Chronicle,* April 22, 1879.

"To Keep Out Southern Italians." *World's Work* 28 (August 1914): 378–79.

Trebay, Guy. "The Giglio," *New Yorker* 66 (1990): 78–89.

Trumbull, J. Hammond, ed. *The Memorial History of Hartford County Connecticut.* 2 vols. Boston, 1886.

Tyler, Royall. *Four Plays by Royall Tyler.* Edited by Arthur W. Peach and George F. Newbrough. Princeton: Princeton University Press, 1941.

Usk, Adam of. *The Chronicle of Adam Usk, 1377–1421.* Edited and translated by Chris Given-Wilson. Oxford: Oxford University Press, 1997.

"View of Saint Mary's Church, 1797, showing Pinkster Hill." Prints 1732+. Manuscript Collection of the New York State Library. Albany, New York.

Villagrá, Gaspar Pérez de. *Historia de la Nueva México, 1610.* Edited and translated by Miguel Encinias, Alfred Rodríguez, and Joseph P. Sánchez. Albuquerque: University of New Mexico Press, 1992.

Weed, Thurlow. *Letters from Europe and the West Indies* (Albany, 1866). In *After Africa: Extracts from British Travel Accounts and Journals of the Seventeenth, Eighteenth, and Nineteenth Centuries concerning the Slaves, their Manners, and Customs in the British West Indies,* edited by Roger D. Abrahams and John F. Szwed. New Haven: Yale University Press, 1983.

Wilson, Dorothy S. "The Passion Play." *Buffalo Tales*, Buffalo County Historical Society 10, no. 6 (June 1987): 1–2.

Winter, William. *The Life of David Belasco*, 2 vols. New York: Moffat, Yard, 1918.

Wurdemann, J. G. *Notes on Cuba*. Boston, 1844.

Zárate Salmerón, Gerónimo de. *Relaciones: An Account of Things Seen and Learned by Father Jerónimo de Zárate Salmerón from the year 1538 to year 1626*. Translated by Alicia R. Milich. Albuquerque, N.M.: Horn and Wallace, 1966.

Zarrilli, John. "A Suggestion for the Solution of the Italian Problem," *Ecclesiastical Review* 70 (January 1924): 70–77.

Zion (Illinois) Passion Play website. http://www.ourzion.com/passionplay/history.html.

2. Newspapers

Call-Philadelphia
New York Times
Pennsylvania Inquirer
Philadelphia Evening Bulletin
Philadelphia Evening Star
Philadelphia Public-Ledger
Philadelphia Record
Philadelphia Times
San Francisco Chronicle
San Francisco Daily Morning Call

3. Secondary Sources

Abrahams, Roger D. " 'Pull Out Your Purse and Pay': A St. George Mumming from the British West Indies." *Folklore* 79 (1968): 176–201.

Aimes, Hubert H. S. "African Institutions in America." *Journal of American Folklore* 18 (1905): 15–32.

Alba, Richard D. "The Twilight of Ethnicity among Americans of European Descent: The Case of the Italians." *Ethnic and Racial Studies* 8 (1985): 134–58.

Alexander, Doris. *The Tempering of Eugene O'Neill*. New York: Harcourt, Brace, and World, 1962.

Arróniz, Othón. *Teatro de evangelización en Nueva España*. Mexico: Universidad Nacional Autónoma de México, 1979.

Ashley, Kathleen M. "Cultural Approaches to Medieval Drama." In *Approaches to Teaching Medieval Drama*, edited by Richard K. Emmerson, 57–66. New York: The Modern Language Association of America, 1990.

Ashley, Kathleen M., and Véronique Plesch. "The Cultural Processes of 'Appropriation.' " Special issue of *Journal of Medieval and Early Modern Studies* 32 (2002): 1–15.

Austin, Mary. "Folk Plays of the Southwest." *Theater Arts Monthly* 17 (1933): 599–610.

Avella, Leonardo. *Annali della festa dei gigli (1500–1950)*. 2 vols. Naples: Istituto Grafico Editoriale Italiano, 1989.

Balmer, Randall H. *A Perfect Babel of Confusion: Dutch Religion and English Culture in the Middle Colonies.* Oxford: Oxford University Press, 1989.

Baring-Gould, Sabine, Rev. *The Lives of the Saints.* Rev. ed. 16 vols. Edinburgh: John Grant, 1914.

Baskervill, Charles Read. "Dramatic Aspects of Medieval Folk Festivals in England." *Studies in Philology* 17 (1920): 19–87.

Bastide, Roger. *African Civilisations in the New World.* Translated by Peter Green. New York: Harper and Row, 1971.

Baudrillard, Jean. *America.* Translated by Chris Turner. London: Verso, 1988.

Bauman, Richard. "Belsnickling in a Nova Scotia Island Community." *Western Folklore* 31 (1972): 229–43.

Beckwith, Sarah. *Signifying God: Social Relation and Symbolic Act in the York Corpus Christi Plays.* Chicago: University of Chicago Press, 2001.

Beginnings to 1870. Vol. 1 of *The Cambridge History of American Theatre.* Edited by Christopher Bigsby and Don B. Wilmeth. Cambridge: Cambridge University Press, 1998.

Bell, Catherine. *Ritual: Perspectives and Dimensions.* Oxford: Oxford University Press, 1997.

Bergeron, David M. "Pageants, Politics, and Patrons." *Medieval and Renaissance Drama in England* 6 (1993): 139–52.

Bergmann, Rolf. *Studien zur Entstehung und Geschichte der deutschen Passionsspiele des 13. und 14. Jahrhunderts.* Munich: Fink, 1972.

Bevington, David. *Medieval Drama.* Boston: Houghton Mifflin, 1975.

Bhabha, Homi K. *The Locations of Culture.* New York: Routledge, 1994.

Biddick, Kathleen. *The Shock of Medievalism.* Durham, N.C.: Duke University Press, 1998.

Bloch, R. Howard. "Naturalism, Nationalism, Medievalism." *Romanic Review* 76 (1985): 341–60.

Bloch, R. Howard., and Stephen G. Nichols. *Medievalism and the Modernist Temper.* Baltimore: Johns Hopkins University Press, 1996.

Bloom, Lansing B. "Spain's Investment in New Mexico under the Hapsburgs." *The Americas* 1 (1944): 9–10.

Bourdieu, Pierre. *The Logic of Practice.* Translated by Richard Nice. Stanford: Stanford University Press, 1990.

Briggs, Charles L. *The Wood Carvers of Córdova, New Mexico: Social Dimensions of an Artistic "Revival."* Knoxville: University of Tennessee Press, 1980.

Bristol, Michael D. *Shakespeare's America, America's Shakespeare.* London: Routledge, 1990.

Brody, Alan. *The English Mummers and their Plays: Traces of Ancient Mystery.* Philadelphia: University of Pennsylvania Press, 1970.

Bronner, Simon. *American Folklore Studies: An Intellectual History.* Lawrence: University of Kansas Press, 1986.

Brooklyn in Transition. New York: Municipal Research Institute, 1985.

Buckley, Peter G. "Paratheatricals and Popular Stage Entertainment." In *Beginnings to 1870,* 424–81.

Burns, Edward. "Seeing Is Believing: The Chester Play of the Nativity at Chester Cathedral, Summer 1987." *Cahiers Elisabethains* 34 (1988): 1–9.

Campbell, Marie. "Survivals of Old Folk Drama in the Kentucky Mountains." *Journal of American Folklore* 51 (1938): 10–24.

Candeloro, Dominic. "Italian-Americans." In *Multiculturalism in the United States: A Comparative Guide to Acculturation and Ethnicity,* edited by John D. Buenker and Lorman A. Ratner, 173–92. New York: Greenwood, 1992.

Cantú, Norma E. "*Los Matachines* de la Santa Cruz de la Ladrillera: Notes toward a Socio-Literary Analysis." In *Feasts and Celebrations,* 57–67.

"Census of Medieval Drama Productions." Compiled by Peter Greenfield. *Research Opportunities in Renaissance Drama* 39 (2000): 237–59.

Cervantes, Fernando. *The Devil in the New World: The Impact of Diabolism in New Spain.* New Haven: Yale University Press, 1994.

Chambers, E. K. *The English Folk-Play.* Oxford: Clarendon, 1933.

Champe, Flavia W. *The Matachines Dance of the Upper Rio Grande.* Lincoln: University of Nebraska Press, 1983.

Christian, William A., Jr. *Local Religion in Sixteenth-Century Spain.* Princeton: Princeton University Press, 1981.

Christmas Mumming in Newfoundland: Essays in Anthropology, Folklore, and History, edited by Herbert Halpert and G. M. Story. Toronto: University of Toronto Press, 1969.

City and Spectacle in Medieval Europe. Edited by Barbara A. Hanawalt and Kathryn L. Reyerson. Minneapolis: University of Minnesota Press, 1994.

Clarke, John, and Stuart Hall, Tony Jefferson, and B. Roberts. "Subcultures, Cultures and Class." In *Resistance Through Rituals: Youth Subcultures in Post-War Britain,* edited by Stuart Hall and Tony Jefferson, 9–79. London: Hutchinson, 1976.

Clendinnen, Inga. *Ambivalent Conquests: Maya and Spaniard in Yucatán, 1517–1570.* Cambridge: Cambridge University Press, 1987.

Clifford, James. "Identity in Mashpee." In *The Predicament of Culture: Twentieth-Century Ethnography, Literature, and Art,* 277–346. Cambridge: Harvard University Press, 1988.

Clopper, Lawrence M. *Drama, Play, and Game: English Festive Culture in the Medieval and Early Modern Period.* Chicago: University of Chicago Press, 2001.

Cockrell, Dale. "Callithumpians, Mummers, Maskers, and Minstrels: Blackface in the Streets of Jacksonian America." *Theatre Annual* 49 (1996): 15–34.

Cohen, David Steven. *The Dutch-American Farm.* New York: New York University Press, 1992.

———. "In Search of Carolus Africanus Rex: Afro-Dutch Folklore in New York and New Jersey." *Journal of the Afro-American Historical and Genealogical Society* 5 (1984): 149–62.

Cohen, Jeffrey H. "*Danza de la Pluma:* Symbols of Submission and Separation in a Mexican Fiesta." *Anthropological Quarterly* 66 (1993): 149–58.

Coletti, Theresa M. "Reading REED: History and the Records of Early English Drama." In *Literary Practice and Social Change in Britain, 1380–1530,* edited by Lee Patterson, 248–84. Berkeley: University of California Press, 1990.

Coletti, Theresa M., and Pamela Sheingorn. "Playing Wisdom at Trinity College." *Research Opportunities in Renaissance Drama* 27 (1984): 179–84.

Connolly, L. W. *The Censorship of English Drama, 1737–1824.* San Marino, Calif.: Huntington Library, 1976.

Conteh-Morgan, John. "African Traditional Drama and Issues in Theater and Performance Criticism." *Comparative Drama* 28 (1994): 3–18.

Cypress, Sandra Messenger. *La Malinche in Mexican Literature: From History to Myth*. Austin: University of Texas Press, 1991.

Davidson, David M. "Negro Slave Control and Resistance in Colonial Mexico, 1519–1650." *Hispanic American Historical Review* 46 (1966): 235–53.

Davis, Allen F. *Spearheads for Reform: The Social Settlements and the Progressive Movement, 1890–1914*. New York: Oxford University Press, 1967.

Davis, Natalie Zemon. "The Rites of Violence: Religious Riot in Sixteenth-Century France." *Past and Present* 59 (1973): 51–91.

Davis, Susan G. " 'Making Night Hideous': Christmas Revelry and Public Order in Nineteenth-Century Philadelphia." *American Quarterly* 34 (1982): 185–99.

——. *Parades and Power: Street Theatre in Nineteenth-Century Philadelphia*. Philadelphia: Temple University Press, 1986.

DeJong, Gerald F. *The Dutch Reformed Church in the American Colonies*. Grand Rapids, Mich.: Eerdmans, 1978.

Díaz Roig, Mercedes. "La Danza de la Conquista." *Nueva Revista de Filología Hispanica* 32 (1983): 176–95.

DiCarlo, Denise Mangieri. "The Interplay of Ritual for Italians in Multicultural Society." In *Italian-Americans in a Multicultural Society*, edited by Jerome Krase and Judith N. DeSena, 107–13. Stony Brook, N.Y.: Forum Italicum, 1994.

Diehl, Huston. *Staging Reform, Reforming the Stage: Protestantism and Popular Theater in Early Modern England*. Ithaca: Cornell University Press, 1997.

Diemer, Hermine von Hillern. *Oberammergau and Its Passion Play: A Survey of the History of Oberammergau and Its Passion Play*. Munich: C. A. Seyfried, 1900.

Dirks, Robert. "Slaves' Holiday." *Natural History* 84 (1975): 82–90.

Don Juan de Oñate: Colonizer of New Mexico, 1595–1628. Edited and Translated George P. Hammond and Agapito Rey. Albuquerque: University of New Mexico Press, 1953.

Dozier, Edward P. *The Pueblo Indians of North America*. New York: Holt, Rinehart, and Winston, 1970.

Duffy, Eamon. *The Stripping of the Altars: Traditional Religion in England, c.1400–c.1580*. New Haven: Yale University Press, 1992.

Dussel, Enrique D. *A History of the Church in Latin America: Colonialism to Liberation (1492–1979)*. Grand Rapids, Mich.: Eerdmans, 1981.

Eaton, Allen. *Immigrant Gifts to American Life*. New York: Russell Sage Foundation, 1932.

Eco, Umberto. "Dreaming of the Middle Ages." In *Travels in Hyperreality: Essays*, translated by William Weaver, 61–72. New York: Harcourt Brace Jovanovich, 1986.

Elliott, John H. *Spain and Its World, 1500–1700: Selected Essays*. New Haven: Yale University Press, 1989.

Elliott, John R., Jr., "A Checklist of Modern Productions of the Medieval Mystery Cycles in England." *Research Opportunities in Renaissance Drama* 13–14 (1970–71): 259–66.

——, *Playing God: Medieval Mysteries on the Modern Stage*. Toronto: University of Toronto Press, 1989.

Emmerson, Richard K. "Eliding the 'Medieval': Renaissance 'New Historicism' and

Sixteenth-Century Drama." In *The Performance of Middle English Culture: Essays on Chaucer and the Drama in Honor of Martin Stevens,* edited by James J. Paxson, Lawrence M. Clopper, and Sylvia Tomasch, 25–41. Cambridge: D. S. Brewer, 1998.

Enders, Jody. *The Medieval Theater of Cruelty: Rhetoric, Memory, and Violence.* Ithaca: Cornell University Press, 1999.

Englekirk, John E. "The Source and Dating of New Mexican Spanish Folk Plays." *Western Folklore* 16 (1957): 232–55.

Evans, Timothy H. "Folklore as Utopia: English Medievalists and the Ideology of Revivalism." *Western Folklore* 47 (1988): 245–68.

Fabre, Geneviève. "Pinkster Festival, 1776–1811: An African-American Celebration." In *Feasts and Celebrations,* 13–28.

Falvey, Kathleen C. "The Italian Saint Play: The Example of Perugia." In *The Saint Play in Medieval Europe,* edited by Clifford Davidson, 181–204. Kalamazoo: Western Michigan University Press, 1986.

Farriss, Nancy M. *Maya Society under Colonial Rule: The Collective Enterprise of Survival.* Princeton: Princeton University Press, 1984.

Feasts and Celebrations in North American Ethnic Communities. Edited by Ramón Gutiérrez and Geneviève Fabre. Albuquerque: University of New Mexico Press, 1995.

Feldberg, Michael. "The Crowd in Philadelphia History." *Labor History* 15 (1974): 323–36.

Flanigan, C. Clifford. "Comparative Literature and the Study of Medieval Drama." *Yearbook of Comparative and General Literature* 35 (1986): 56–104.

———. "Medieval Latin Music-Drama." In *Theatre of Medieval Europe,* 21–41.

Foner, Philip S. *History of the Labor Movement in the United States.* 4 vols. New York: International Publishers, 1947–65.

Forrest, John. *Morris and Matachin: A Study in Comparative Choreography.* London: English Folk Dance and Song Society, 1984.

Forster, Arnold, and Benjamin Epstein. *The New Anti-Semitism.* New York: McGraw-Hill, 1974.

Foster, George M. *Culture and Conquest: America's Spanish Heritage.* New York: Wenner-Gren Foundation for Anthropological Research, 1960.

Fowell, Frank, and Frank Palmer. *Censorship in England.* New York: B. Franklin, 1970.

Fradenburg, Louise. "Voice Memorial: Loss and Reparation in Chaucer's Poetry." *Exemplaria* 2 (1990): 169–202.

Frantzen, Allen. *Desire for Origins: New Language, Old English, and Teaching the Tradition.* New Brunswick, N.J.: Rutgers University Press, 1990.

Freise, Dorothea. *Geistliche Spiele in der Stadt des ausgehenden Mittelalters.* Göttingen: Vandenhoeck and Ruprecht, 2002.

Friedman, Saul S. *The Oberammergau Passion Play: A Lance Against Civilization.* Carbondale: Southern Illinois University Press, 1984.

Fuchs, Barbara. *Mimesis and Empire: The New World, Islam, and European Identities.* Cambridge: Cambridge University Press, 2001.

Gagey, Edmond M. *The San Francisco Stage: A History.* New York: Columbia University Press, 1950.

Ganim, John. "The Literary Uses of the New Historicism." In *The Idea of Medieval Literature: New Essays on Chaucer and Medieval Culture in Honor of Donald R.*

Howard, edited by James M. Dean and Christian Z. Zacher, 209–26. Newark: University of Delaware Press, 1992.

———. "Native Studies: Orientalism and Medievalism." In *The Postcolonial Middle Ages,* edited by Jeffrey J. Cohen, 123–34. New York: St. Martin's, 2000.

Garber, William Allen. *The Passion Play Graft: Or, Oberammergau With the Lid Off.* Dayton, Va.: W. A. Garber, 1911.

Gardiner, Harold C. *Mysteries' End: An Investigation into the Last Days of the Medieval Religious Stage.* New Haven: Yale University Press, 1946.

Gates, Joanne. "The Digby *Mary Magdalene.*" *Research Opportunities in Renaissance Drama* 26 (1983): 120–21.

Geffen, Elizabeth. "Violence in Philadelphia in the 1840s and 1850s." *Pennsylvania History* 36 (1969): 381–410.

Gellner, Ernest. *Nations and Nationalism.* Oxford: Basil Blackwell, 1983.

Gibson, Charles. *The Aztecs under Spanish Rule: A History of the Indians of the Valley of Mexico, 1519–1810.* Stanford: Stanford University Press, 1964

———. *Tlaxcala in the Sixteenth Century.* New Haven: Yale University Press, 1952.

Gibson, Gail McMurray. "The York Cycle at Toronto: October 1 and 2, 1977." *Research Opportunities in Renaissance Drama* 20 (1977): 114–17.

Gilroy, Paul. *The Black Atlantic: Modernity and Double Consciousness.* Harvard: Harvard University Press, 1993.

Glassberg, David. *American Historical Pageantry:The Uses of Tradition in the Early Twentieth Century.* Chapel Hill:University of North Carolina Press,1990.

Glassie, Henry H. *All Silver and No Brass: An Irish Christmas Mumming.* Bloomington: Indiana University Press, 1975.

Golab, Caroline. "The Immigrant and the City: Poles, Italians, and Jews in Philadelphia, 1870–1920." In *The Peoples of Philadelphia: A History of Ethnic Groups and Lower-Class Life, 1790–1940,* edited by Allen F. Davis and Mark H. Haller, 203–30. Philadelphia: Temple University Press, 1973.

Goodfriend, Joyce D. "Burghers and Blacks: The Evolution of a Slave Society in New Amsterdam." *New York History* 59 (1978): 125–44.

Goody, Jack. "Against 'Ritual': Loosely Structured Thoughts on a Loosely Defined Topic." In *Secular Ritual,* edited by Sally F. Moore and Barbara G. Myerhoff, 25–35. Assen: Van Gorcum, 1977.

Grantley, Darryll. "The National Theatre's Production of *The Mysteries:* Some Observations." *Theatre Notebook* 40 (1986): 70–73.

The Greater Passion Play from Carmina Burana. Singers and Instrumentalists of the Early Music Institute. Thomas Binkley. Focus 831.

Greenblatt, Stephen. *Marvelous Possessions: The Wonder of the New World.* Oxford: Clarendon, 1991.

Greene, Lorenzo J. *The Negro in Colonial New England, 1620–1776.* New York: Columbia University Press, 1942.

Greenleaf, Richard E. *Zumarrága and the Mexican Inquisition, 1536–1543.* Washington, D.C.: Academy of American Franciscan History, 1961.

Grimes, Ronald L. *Beginnings in Ritual Studies.* Rev. ed. Columbia: University of South Carolina Press, 1995.

———. *Ritual Criticism: Case Studies in Its Practices, Essays on Its Theory.* Columbia: University of South Carolina Press, 1990.

Gutiérrez, Ramón. *When Jesus Came, the Corn Mothers Went Away: Marriage, Sexuality, and Power in New Mexico, 1500–1846.* Stanford: Stanford University Press, 1991.

Hackett, David. *The Rude Hand of Innovation: Religion and Social Order in Albany, New York, 1652–1839.* Oxford: Oxford University Press, 1991.

Haines, Aubrey B. "A Passion Play Comes to America," *Pen* 43 *(1968):* 4–9.

Hall, Stuart. "New Ethnicities." In *Black Film/British Cinema,* edited by Kobena Mercer, 27–31. London: Institute of Contemporary Arts, 1988.

———. "Notes on Deconstructing 'the Popular.'" In *People's History and Socialist Theory,* edited by Raphael Samuel, 227–40. Boston: Routledge and Kegan Paul, 1981.

Halpert, Herbert. "A Typology of Mumming." In *Christmas Mumming in Newfoundland,* 34–61.

Harris, Max. "The Arrival of the Europeans: Folk Dramatizations of Conquest and Conversion in New Mexico." *Comparative Drama* 28 (1994): 141–65.

———. *The Dialogical Theatre: Dramatizations of the Conquest of Mexico and Questions of the Other.* New York: St. Martin's, 1993.

———. "Disguised Reconciliations: Indigenous Voices in Early Franciscan Missionary Drama in Mexico." *Radical History Review* 53 (1992): 13–25.

———. "Moctezuma's Daughter: The Role of La Malinche in Mesoamerican Dance." *Journal of American Folklore* 109 (1996): 149–77.

———. "Muhammed and the Virgin: Folk Dramatizations of Battles between Moors and Christians in Modern Spain." *Drama Review* 38 (1994): 45–61.

Herrera-Sobek, María. "The Mexican/Chicano *Pastorela:* Toward a Theory of the Evolution of a Folk Play." In *Feasts and Celebrations,* 47–56.

Herskovits, Melville J. *The Myth of the Negro Past.* New York: Harper and Brothers, 1941.

Hobsbawm, Eric. "Introduction: Inventing Traditions." In *The Invention of Tradition,* edited by Eric Hobsbawm and Terence Ranger, 1–14. Cambridge: Cambridge University Press, 1982.

Horcasitas, Fernando. *El teatro náhuatl.* Mexico: Universidad Nacional Autónomo de México, 1974.

Horn, Rebecca. *Postconquest Coyoacan: Nahua-Spanish Relations in Central Mexico, 1519–1650.* Stanford: Stanford University Press, 1997.

Howell, George, and Jonathan Tenney. "Slavery in Albany." In *Bicentennial History of Albany, New York from 1609 to 1886,* 300–3. New York: Munsell, 1886.

Hummelen, Wim M. H. "Illustrations of Stage Performances in the Work of Crispijn Passe the Elder." In *Essays on Drama and Theatre: Liber Amicorum Benjamin Hunningher,* 67–84. Amsterdam: Baarn, Moussault, 1973.

Hutton, Ronald. *The Rise and Fall of Merry England: The Ritual Year, 1400–1700.* Oxford: Oxford University Press, 1994.

Isaac, Winifred F. E. C. *Ben Greet and the Old Vic: A Biography of Sir Philip Ben Greet.* London: Published by the author, 1964.

Jameson, Fredric. "Postmodernism, or the Cultural Logic of Late Capitalism." *New Left Review* 146 (1984): 53–92.

Johnston, Alexandra F. "Four York Pageants." *Research Opportunities in Renaissance Drama* 31 (1988): 101–4.

———. "The York Cycle: 1977." *University of Toronto Quarterly* 48 (1978): 1–9.

Kahrl, Stanley J. "The Staging of Medieval English Plays." In *The Theatre of Medieval Europe*, 130–48.

Kaplan, Joel H., and George Shand. "The *Poculi Ludique Societas:* Medieval Drama at the University of Toronto." *Research Opportunities in Renaissance Drama* 11 (1968): 141–61.

Kinser, Sam. *Carnival, American Style: Mardi Gras at New Orleans and Mobile.* Chicago: University of Chicago Press, 1990.

Knight, Alan E. "France." In *Theatre of Medieval Europe*, 151–68.

Kruger, Loren. *The National Stage: Theatre and Cultural Legitimation in England, France, and America.* Chicago: University of Chicago Press, 1992.

Kurath, Gertrude P. "The Origin of the Pueblo Indian Matachines." *El Palacio* 64 (1957): 9–10.

Laurie, Bruce. *Working People of Philadelphia, 1800–1850.* Philadelphia: Temple University Press, 1980.

Lindenbaum, Sheila. "Ceremony and Oligarchy: The London Midsummer Watch." In *City and Spectacle in Medieval Europe*, 171–88.

Lindstrom, Diane. *Economic Development in the Philadelphia Region, 1810–1850.* New York: Columbia University Press, 1978.

Marcosson, Isaac F., and Daniel Frohman. *Charles Frohman: Manager and Man.* New York: Harper and Brothers, 1916.

Marshall, John. "Modern Productions of Medieval English Plays." In *The Cambridge Companion to Medieval English Theatre,* edited by Richard Beadle, 290–311. Cambridge: Cambridge University Press, 1994.

Mason, Jeffrey D., and J. Ellen Gainor, eds. *Performing America: Cultural Nationalism in American Theatre.* Ann Arbor: University of Michigan Press, 1999.

McBride, Kevin. "The Source and Mother of the Fur Trade: Native-Dutch Relations in Eastern New Netherland." In *Enduring Traditions: The Native Peoples of New England,* edited by Laurie Weinstein, 31–51. Westport, Conn.: Bergin and Garvey, 1994.

McDonald, Peter F. "Drama Criticism and the Value of Productions." *Fifteenth-Century Studies* 13 (1987): 13–21.

———. "The Towneley Cycle at Toronto." *Medieval English Theatre* 8 (1986): 51–60.

McKinnell, John. "Staging the Digby *Mary Magdalen.*" *Medieval English Theatre* 6 (1984): 127–52.

McManus, Edgar. *A History of Negro Slavery in New York.* Syracuse, N.Y.: Syracuse University Press, 1966.

McMillan, Douglas. *Catalogue of the Larpent Plays in the Huntington Library.* San Marino, Calif.: Huntington Library, 1939.

Medievalism in American Culture: Papers of the Eighteenth Annual Conference of the Center for Medieval and Early Renaissance Studies. Edited by Bernard Rosenthal and Paul Szarmach. Binghamton, N.Y.: CEMERS, 1989.

Meredith, Peter. " 'Farte pryke in cule' and Cock-fighting." *Medieval English Theatre* 6 (1984): 30–39.

———. "Original-Staging Production of English Medieval Plays—Ideals, Evidence and Practice." In *Popular Drama in Northern Europe in the Later Middle Ages: A Symposium,* edited by Flemming G. Andersen, 65–100. Odense: Odense University Press, 1988.

Merwick, Donna. *Possessing Albany, 1630–1710: The Dutch and English Experiences.* Cambridge: Cambridge University Press, 1990.

Middleton, Anne. "Medieval Studies." In *Redrawing The Boundaries: The Transformation of English and American Literary Studies,* edited by Stephen Greenblatt and Giles Gunn, 12–41. New York: Modern Language Association of America, 1992.

Mills, David. "Reviving the Chester Plays." *Medieval English Theatre* 13, nos. 1–2 (1991): 39–51.

Mondello, Salvatore. *The Italian Immigrant in Urban America, 1880–1920, As Reported in the Contemporary Periodical Press.* New York: Arno Press, 1980.

Monk, Charlene Faye. "Passion Plays in the United States: The Contemporary Outdoor Tradition." Ph.D. diss., Louisiana State University, 1998.

Mullaney, Steven. *The Place of the Stage: License, Play, and Power in Renaissance England.* Chicago: University of Chicago Press, 1988.

Musser, Charles. "The Eden Musée in 1898: Exhibitor as Co-Creator." *Film and History* 11 (1981): 73–86.

———. *The Emergence of Cinema: The American Screen to 1907.* New York: Scribner, 1990.

———. *High-Class Moving Pictures: Lyman H. Howe and the Forgotten Era of Traveling Exhibition, 1880–1920.* Princeton: Princeton University Press, 1991.

Nielsen, Alan. *The Great Victorian Sacrilege: Preachers, Politics, and the Passion, 1879–1884.* Jefferson, N.C.: McFarland, 1991.

Orsi, Robert A. *The Madonna of 115th Street: Faith and Community in Italian Harlem, 1880–1950.* New Haven: Yale University Press, 1985.

Ortiz, Alfonso. "Ritual Drama and the Pueblo World View." In *New Perspectives on the Pueblos,* edited by Alfonso Ortiz, 135–61. Albuquerque: University of New Mexico Press, 1972.

Orvell, Miles. *The Real Thing: Imitation and Authenticity in American Culture, 1880–1940.* Chapel Hill: University of North Carolina Press, 1989.

Pagden, Anthony. *Lords of All the World: Ideologies of Empire in Spain, Britain, and France, c. 1500–c. 1800.* New Haven: Yale University Press, 1995.

Palmer, Colin A. *Slaves of the White God: Blacks in Mexico, 1570–1650.* Cambridge: Harvard University Press, 1976.

Parmentier, Richard J. "The Pueblo Mythological Triangle: Poseyemu, Montezuma, and Jesus in the Pueblos." In *Southwest,* 609–22.

Partner, Nancy. "Making Up Lost Time: Writing on the Writing of History." *Speculum* 61 (1986): 90–117.

Patterson, Lee. *Negotiating the Past: The Historical Understanding of Medieval Literature.* Madison: University of Wisconsin Press, 1987.

———. "On the Margin: Postmodernism, Ironic History, and Medieval Studies." *Speculum* 65 (1990): 87–108.

Pearce, T. M. "The New Mexican 'Shepherds Play.'" *Western Folklore* 15 (1956): 77–88.

Pettitt, Thomas. "English Folk Drama and the Early German Fastnachtspiele." *Renaissance Drama* 13 (1982): 1–34.

———. "English Folk Drama in the Eighteenth Century: A Defense of the *Revesby Sword Play.*" *Comparative Drama* 15 (1981): 3–29.

———. "'Here Comes I, Jack Straw': English Folk Drama and Social Revolt." *Folklore* 95 (1984): 3–20.

———. "Tudor Interludes and the Winter Revels." *Medieval English Theatre* 6 (1984): 16–27.

Phelan, John L. *The Millennial Kingdom of the Franciscans in the New World.* Berkeley: University of California Press, 1970.

Pickering, James H. "Fenimore Cooper and Pinkster." *New York Folklore Quarterly* 22 (March 1966): 15–19.

Piersen, William. *Black Yankees: The Development of an Afro-American Subculture in Eighteenth-Century New England.* Amherst: University of Massachusetts Press, 1988.

Pleat, Geraldine R., and Agnes N. Underwood. "Pinkster Ode, Albany, 1803." *New York Folklore Quarterly* 8 (1952): 31–45.

Posen, I. Sheldon, and Joseph Sciorra. "Brooklyn's Dancing Tower." *Natural History* 92 (1983): 30–37.

Posen, I. Sheldon, and Daniel Franklin Ward. "Watts Towers and the Giglio Tradition." *Folklife Annual* (1985): 143–57, 144.

Potter, Robert A. "Abraham and Human Sacrifice: The Exfoliation of Medieval Drama in Aztec Mexico." *Fifteenth-Century Studies* 13 (1988): 543–53.

———. *The English Morality Play: Origins, History, and Influence of a Dramatic Tradition.* Boston: Routledge and Kegan Paul, 1975.

———. "The Illegal Immigration of Medieval Drama to California." *Comparative Drama* 27 (1993): 142–44.

Pratt, Mary Louise. *Imperial Eyes: Travel Writing and Transculturation.* New York: Routledge, 1992.

Rael, Juan B. "New Light on the Origins of Los Pastores." *New Mexico Folklore Record* 6 (1951–52): 1–6.

Ralph, George. "Medievalism and Twentieth-Century Religious Drama." In "Twentieth-Century Medievalism," edited by Jane Chance. Special issue of *Studies in Medievalism* 2, no. 1 (1982): 35–57.

Ramsaye, Terry. *A Million and One Nights: A History of the Motion Picture through 1925.* 1926. Reprint, New York: Touchstone Books, 1986.

Ravicz, Marilyn Ekdahl. *Early Colonial Religious Drama in Mexico.* Washington, D.C.: Catholic University Press, 1970.

Read, Karen. "The Symondsbury Mumming Play, and the People Who Uphold It." *English Dance and Song* 46 (1984): 11–14; and 47 (1985): 12–14.

Reidy, Joseph P. " 'Negro Election Day' and Black Community Life in New England, 1750–1860." *Marxist Perspectives* 3 (1978): 102–117.

Riggio, Milla C. "Have Play, Will Travel: The Poculi Ludique Societas Twenty-Five Plus Festival of Early Drama." *Research Opportunities in Renaissance Drama* 32 (1993), 161–75.

Roach, Joseph. *Cities of the Dead: Circum-atlantic Performance.* New York: Columbia University Press, 1996.

Robe, Stanley L. "The Relationship of Los Pastores to Other Spanish-American Folk Drama," *Western Folklore* 16 (1957): 281–89.

Rodríguez, Sylvia. "Defended Boundaries, Precarious Elites: The Arroyo Seco Matachines Dance." *Journal of American Folklore* 107 (1994): 248–67.

———. *The Matachines Dance: Ritual Symbolism and Interethnic Relations in the Upper Río Grande Valley.* Albuquerque: University of New Mexico Press, 1996.

Rosenwaike, Ira. *Population History of New York City.* Syracuse, N.Y.: Syracuse University Press, 1972.

Rothberg, Andrea Ignatoff. "Philadelphia Mummery: Individual Rewards and Social Interaction." Ph.D. diss., University of Wisconsin, 1980.

Ruíz, Teofilo F. "Elite and Popular Culture in Late Fifteenth-Century Castilian Festivals." In *City and Spectacle in Medieval Europe*, 296–318.

Ryan, Joseph, ed., *White Ethnics: Their Life in Working-Class America*. Englewood Cliffs, N.J.: Prentice-Hall, 1973.

Samuel, Raphael. *Theatres of Memory*. London: Verso, 1994.

Sando, Joe S. *Nee Hemish: A History of Jemez Pueblo*. Albuquerque: University of New Mexico Press, 1982.

———. *Pueblo Indians*. San Francisco: Indian Historian Press, 1976.

Schechner, Richard. *Between Theater and Anthropology*. Philadelphia: University of Pennsylvania Press, 1985.

Schoenbaum, Samuel. *Shakespeare's Lives*. Oxford: Clarendon, 1970.

Scholes, Frances V. *Troublous Times in New Mexico, 1659–1670*. New York: AMS Press, 1977.

Sciorra, Joseph. "Religious Processions in Italian Williamsburg." *The Drama Review* 29, no. 3 (1985): 65–81.

———. " 'O' Giglio e Paradiso': Celebration and Identity in an Urban Ethnic Community." *Urban Resources* 5, no. 3 (1989): 15–20, 44–46.

Scott, James C. *Domination and the Arts of Resistance: Hidden Transcripts*. New Haven: Yale University Press, 1990.

Shapiro, James S. *Oberammergau: The Troubling Story of the World's Most Famous Passion Play*. New York: Pantheon Books, 2000.

Shergold, N. D. *A History of the Spanish Stage from Medieval Times until the End of the Seventeenth Century*. Oxford: Clarendon, 1967.

Shoemaker, Alfred. *Christmas in Pennsylvania: A Folk-Cultural Study*. Kutztown, Pa.: Pennsylvania Folklife Society, 1959.

Simmons, Marc. "History of Pueblo-Spanish Relations to 1821." In *Southwest*, 178–93.

Simms, Norman. "Ned Ludd's Mummers Play." *Folklore* 89 (1978): 166–78.

Simon, Eckehard. "Preface" to *Theatre of Medieval Europe*, x–xx.

Smith, George L. *Religion and Trade in New Netherland*. Ithaca: Cornell University Press, 1973.

Somerset, J. A. B. "James Orchard Halliwell-Phillips and his Scrapbooks." *REED Newsletter* 4, no. 2 (1979): 13–14.

Southwest. Edited by Alfonso Ortiz. Vol. 9 of *Handbook of North American Indians*, edited by William C. Sturtevant. Washington, D.C.: Smithsonian Institution Press, 1979.

Speaight, Robert. *William Poel and the Elizabethan Revival*. Cambridge: Harvard University Press, 1983.

Sponsler, Claire. "Medieval America: Drama and Community in the English Colonies, 1580–1610." *Journal of Medieval and Early Modern Studies* 28 (1998): 457–82.

———. "Medieval Ethnography: Fieldwork in the European Past." *Assays: Critical Approaches to Medieval and Renaissance Texts* 7 (1992): 1–30.

Sprogel, Howard O. *The Philadelphia Police, Past and Present*. Philadelphia, 1887.

Stallybrass, Peter. " 'Drunk with the Cup of Liberty': Robin Hood, the Carnivalesque, and the Rhetoric of Violence in Early Modern England." In *The Violence of Repre-*

sentation: Literature and the History of Violence, edited by Nancy Armstrong and Leonard Tennenhouse, 45–76. New York: Routledge, 1989.

Steckey, John. "The Warrior and the Lineage: Jesuit Use of Iroquoian Images to Communicate Christianity." *Ethnohistory* 39 (1992): 478–509.

Steinbach, Rolf. *Die deutschen Oster- und Passionspiele.* Cologne: Böhlau, 1970.

Sten, Maria. *Vida y muerte del teatro Náhuatl.* Mexico City: Sep/Setentas, 1974.

Stern, Charlotte. *The Medieval Theater in Castile.* Binghamton, N.Y.: Medieval and Renaissance Texts and Studies, 1996.

———. "Reassessing the Nahua Autos: A Propos of Jerry M. Williams's El Teatro del México Colonial: Epoca Misionera." *Bulletin of the Comediantes* 52 (2000): 113–65.

Stevens, Martin. "The Nativity Cycle at Irvine." *Research Opportunities in Renaissance Drama* 29 (1986–87): 95–97.

———. "*Processus Torontoniensis:* A Performance of the Wakefield Cycle." *Research Opportunities in Renaissance Drama* 28 (1985): 189–99.

Sticca, Sandro. *The Latin Passion Play: Its Origins and Development.* Albany: State University of New York Press, 1970.

Stock, Brian. "The Middle Ages as Subject and Object: Romantic Attitudes and Academic Medievalism." *New Literary History* 5 (1973–74): 527–47.

Story, G. M. "Mummers in Newfoundland History: A Survey of the Printed Record." In *Christmas Mumming in Newfoundland,* 165–85.

Strietman, Elsa. "The Low Countries." In *Theatre of Medieval Europe,* 225–52.

Stuckey, Sterling. *Slave Culture: Nationalist Theory and the Foundation of Black America.* New York: Oxford University Press, 1987.

Surtz, Ronald E. "The 'Franciscan Connection' in the Early Castilian Theater." *Bulletin of the Comediantes* 35 (1983): 141–52.

Swift, Janet H. M. *The Passion Play of Oberammergau: Its History and Significance.* New York: Fleming H. Revell, 1930.

The Theatre of Medieval Europe: New Research in Early Drama. Edited by Eckehard Simon. Cambridge: Cambridge University Press, 1991.

Thompson, E. P. " 'Rough Music': le charivari anglais." *Annales, E.S.C.* 27 (1972): 285–312.

Thompson, Roger. *Mobility and Migration: East Anglian Founders of New England, 1629–1640.* Amherst: University of Massachusetts Press, 1994.

Tiddy, Reginald J. E. *The Mummers' Play.* Oxford: Clarendon, 1923.

Todorov, Tzvetan. *The Conquest of America: The Question of the Other.* Translated by Richard Howard. New York: Harper and Row, 1984.

Tomasi, Silvano M. *Piety and Power: The Role of the Italian Parishes in the New York Metropolitan Area, 1880–1930.* New York: Center for Migration Studies, 1975.

Toppin, Edgar A. *A Biographical History of Blacks in America since 1528.* New York: David McKay, 1969.

Travers, Len, *Celebrating the Fourth: Independence Day and the Rites of Nationalism in the Early Republic.* Amherst: University of Massachusetts Press, 1997.

Trextler, Richard C. "We Think, They Act: Clerical Readings of Missionary Theater in Sixteenth-Century New Spain." In *Understanding Popular Culture: Europe from the Middle Ages to the Nineteenth Century,* edited by Steven L. Kaplan, 189–227. Berlin: Mouton, 1984.

Turner, Kay F. "The Virgin of Sorrows Procession: A Brooklyn Inversion." *Folklore Papers of the University Folklore Association* 9 (1980): 1–26.

Turner, Victor. *The Ritual Process: Structure and Anti-Structure.* Chicago: Aldine, 1969.

Twycross, Meg. "The Flemish Ommegang and Its Pageant Cars." *Medieval Theatre* 2 (1980): 15–41, 80–98.

Vance, Eugene. "The Modernity of the Middle Ages in the Future: Remarks on a Recent Book." *Romanic Review* 64 (1973): 140–51.

Vecsey, Christopher. *On the Padres' Trail.* Notre Dame: University of Notre Dame Press, 1996.

Vedder, Ann. "History of the Spanish Colonial Arts Society, Inc." In *Hispanic Arts and Ethnohistory in the Southwest: New Papers Inspired by the Work of E. Boyd,* edited by Marta Weigle, 205–17. Santa Fe: Ancient City Press, 1983.

Versényi, Adam. "Getting Under the Aztec Skin: Evangelical Theatre in the New World." *New Theatre Quarterly* 15 (1989): 217–26.

Wade, Melvin. " 'Shining in Borrowed Plumage': Affirmation of Community in the Black Coronation Festivals of New England (c. 1750–c. 1850)." *Western Folklore* 40 (1981): 211–31.

Waldstreicher, David. *In the Midst of Perpetual Fetes: The Making of American Nationalism, 1776–1820.* Chapel Hill: University of North Carolina Press, 1997.

Walsh, Martin W. "Christmastide Performance in Native New France." Paper delivered at the International Society for Medieval Theatre (SITM), Toronto, August 1995.

Warner, Sam. *The Private City: Philadelphia in Three Periods of its Growth.* Philadelphia, University of Pennsylvania Press, 1968.

Warning, Rainer. "On the Alterity of Medieval Religious Drama." *New Literary History* 10 (1979): 265–92.

Weales, Gerald C. *Religion in Modern English Drama.* Philadelphia: University of Pennsylvania Press, 1961.

Weber, David J. *The Spanish Frontier in North America.* New Haven: Yale University Press, 1992.

Weigle, Marta. *Brothers of Light, Brothers of Blood: The Penitentes of the Southwest.* Albuquerque: University of New Mexico Press, 1976.

———. "From Desert to Disney World: The Santa Fe Railway and the Fred Harvey Company Display the Indian Southwest." *Journal of Anthropological Research* 45 (1989): 115–37.

Weimann, Robert. *Shakespeare and the Popular Tradition in the Theater: Studies in the Social Dimension of Dramatic Form and Function.* Translated by Robert Schwartz. Baltimore: Johns Hopkins University Press, 1978.

Welch, Charles E., Jr., " 'Common Nuisances': The Evolution of the Philadelphia Mummers Parade." *Keystone Folklore Quarterly* (1963): 95–106.

———*Oh! Dem Golden Slippers.* New York: Thomas Nelson, 1970.

Whisnant, David E. *All That Is Native and Fine: The Politics of Culture in an American Region.* Chapel Hill: University of North Carolina Press, 1983.

White, Hayden. *Tropics of Discourse: Essays in Cultural Criticism.* Baltimore: Johns Hopkins University, 1978.

White, Max E. "Sernatin': A Traditional Christmas Custom in Northeast Georgia." *Southern Folklore Quarterly* 45 (1981): 89–99.

White, Patricia S. "Everybody: On Stage in New York." *Research Opportunities in*

Renaissance Drama 29 (1986–87): 105–107.

White, Shane. " 'It Was a Proud Day': African Americans, Festivals, and Parades in the North, 1741–1834." *Journal of American History* 81 (1994): 13–50.

———. "Pinkster: Afro-Dutch Syncretism in New York City and the Hudson Valley." *Journal of American Folklore* 102 (1989): 68–75.

———. "Pinkster in Albany, 1803: A Contemporary Description." *New York History* 70 (1989): 191–99.

Williams, Raymond. *Marxism and Literature.* Oxford: Oxford University Press, 1977.

———. *Problems in Materialism and Culture.* London: Verso, 1980.

Williams Myers, A. J. "Pinkster Carnival: Africanisms in the Hudson River Valley." *Afro-Americans in New York Life and History* 9 (1985): 7–18.

Womack, Peter. "Imagining Communities: Theatres and the English Nation in the Sixteenth Century." In *Culture and History 1350–1600: Essays on English Communities, Identities and Writing,* edited by David Aers, 91–145. Detroit: Wayne State University Press, 1992.

Wright, James Camp. "Development of the Black Hills Passion Play in Spearfish, South Dakota and Lake Wales, Florida." M.A. thesis, Ohio State University, 1974.

Wright, Patrick. *On Living in an Old Country: The National Past in Britain.* London: Verso, 1985.

Wynne, Peter. "The Passion Play of Union City, N.J.: Its History, Sources and Performances." M.A. thesis, New York University, 1979.

Young, Karl. *The Drama of the Medieval Church,* 2 vols. Oxford: Clarendon, 1933.

Index